D0891808

QUALITY
FINANCIAL
REPORTING

QUALITY FINANCIAL REPORTING

PAUL B. W. MILLER

PAUL R. BAHNSON

McGraw-Hill

New York   Chicago   San Francisco   Lisbon   London   Madrid
Mexico City   Milan   New Delhi   San Juan   Seoul   Singapore
Sydney   Toronto

Library of Congress Cataloging-in-Publication Data

Miller, Paul B. W.
   Quality financial reporting / by Paul B. W. Miller and Paul R. Bahnson.
      p. cm.
   ISBN 0-07-138742-0 (hardcover: alk. paper)
   1. Financial statements.   2. Corporations—Accounting.   I. Bahnson, Paul R.
II. Title.

   HF5681.B2 M475 2002
   657'.3—dc21   2002005272

McGraw-Hill

A Division of The McGraw·Hill Companies

Copyright © 2002 by Paul B. W. Miller. All rights reserved. Printed in the United States of America. Except as permitted under the United States Copyright Act of 1976, no part of this publication may be reproduced or distributed in any form or by any means, or stored in a data base or retrieval system, without the prior written permission of the publisher.

1 2 3 4 5 6 7 8 9 0   AGM /AGM   0 9 8 7 6 5 4 3 2

ISBN 0-07-138742-0

This publication is designed to provide accurate and authoritative information in regard to the subject matter covered. It is sold with the understanding that the publisher is not engaged in rendering legal, accounting, or other professional service. If legal advice or other expert assistance is required, the services of a competent professional person should be sought.

> —*From a declaration of principles jointly adopted by a committee of the American Bar Association and a committee of publishers.*

 This book is printed on recycled, acid-free paper containing a minimum of 50% recycled, de-inked fiber.

McGraw-Hill books are available at special quantity discounts to use as premiums and sales promotions, or for use in corporate training programs. For more information, please write to the Director of Special Sales, Professional Publishing, McGraw-Hill, Two Penn Plaza, New York, NY 10121-2298. Or contact your local bookstore.

To the many mentors, colleagues, students, and others who have helped us along the way to understand and articulate these ideas and encouraged us to share them with you.

CONTENTS

Answer each of the following 10 questions about financial reporting strategies and practices as if you are the top manager of a large company that must distribute its financial statements to its thousands of public stockholders.

Question	Answer
1. Would you prefer the company's annual reported earnings to be biased upward or to approximate the truth?	
2. Would you prefer all of the company's liabilities to be reported on the balance sheet, or would you like some to be left off the balance sheet to produce a lower debt-to-equity ratio?	
3. Would you prefer compensation expense from stock options to be reported on the income statement as a deduction from earnings or described in a footnote that presents pro forma earnings?	
4. Would you prefer that the company's independent auditors be easy to get along with or tough and thorough?	
5. Would you prefer that the company's independent auditing firm provide substantial amounts of nonaudit services or none at all?	
6. Would you prefer that the amounts paid to the auditors for audit and nonaudit services be disclosed plainly?	
7. Would you prefer the company's financial statements to be published more often or less often?	
8. Would you prefer the company's assets to be described in the financial statements at their depreciated historical cost or at their approximate market value?	
9. Would you prefer that the company's reported earnings be biased to be smooth or that they be designed to reflect real volatility?	
10. Would you prefer that the company's financial statements report its business combinations as poolings of interest or outright purchases?	

Now, answer each of the following 10 questions about financial reporting strategies and practices as if you are a financial analyst trying to assess the value of a large company's stock or one of its thousands of public stockholders trying to assess the top management's performance.

Question	Answer
1. Would you prefer the company's annual reported earnings to be biased upward or to approximate the truth?	
2. Would you prefer all of the company's liabilities to be reported on the balance sheet, or would you like some to be left off the balance sheet to produce a lower debt-to-equity ratio?	
3. Would you prefer compensation expense from stock options to be reported on the income statement as a deduction from earnings or described in a footnote that presents pro forma earnings?	
4. Would you prefer that the company's independent auditors be easy to get along with or tough and thorough?	
5. Would you prefer that the company's independent auditing firm provide substantial amounts of nonaudit services or none at all?	
6. Would you prefer that the amounts paid to the auditors for audit and nonaudit services be disclosed plainly?	
7. Would you prefer the company's financial statements to be published more often or less often?	
8. Would you prefer the company's assets to be described in the financial statements at their depreciated historical cost or at their approximate market value?	
9. Would you prefer that the company's reported earnings be biased to be smooth or that they be designed to reflect real volatility?	
10. Would you prefer that the company's financial statements report its business combinations as poolings of interest or outright purchases?	

We don't know for sure, but we venture to guess that most, if not all, of your answers on the second table differ from those on the first one.

Based on our experience prior to the spectacular bankruptcy of Enron, we expected your answers to be like these:

Topic	Answers for Managers (*Based on Supply*)	Answers for Analysts and Investors (*Based on Demand*)
1. Reported earnings	Biased upward	Approximate truth
2. Liabilities	Off the balance sheet	On the balance sheet
3. Options expense	In a footnote	On the income statement
4. Auditors	Easy	Tough and thorough
5. Nonaudit services	Substantial	None
6. Nonaudit fees	Not disclosed	Disclosed plainly
7. Reporting frequency	Less frequent	More frequent
8. Assets on the balance sheet	At historical cost	At market value
9. Earnings volatility	Smoothed	Unsmoothed
10. Business combinations	Pooling	Purchase

The point of this exercise is to lead you by surprise into contrasting the perspectives of managers and financial statement users, with the ultimate goal of demonstrating the huge disconnect between the desires of those who supply financial reporting information and the desires of those who demand it. We suspect, even hope, that some of your answers in the managers column changed because of the exposure given to the scandalous acts at Enron. If they did, you may be especially eager to learn more about how to improve your financial reporting practices. If your answers in that column are unaffected by Enron, we know with confidence that you are in a position to benefit greatly from what the rest of this book has to say to you.

One of our central themes is that financial reporting descended over several decades into the condition where its practitioners (managers and accountants alike) learned to forget about users' needs, with disastrous effects. Enron is important because those effects for that company were made painfully obvious to the public. Before Enron, there was a chasm between the two sets of answers. After Enron, that gap may be starting to close. We want this book to close it even more, maybe even all the way.

We invite you to join us on a journey that could greatly change the way managers accomplish public financial reporting.

A BOARDROOM, SOMETIME IN THE 1970s

The personnel vice president of a major business is talking to the executive committee about the need to seriously address a number of problems involving the employees. The VP proposes developing and implementing an "HRM" (Human Resource Management) system that will identify good candidates for employment, train them, provide them with attractive benefits, nurture them during their careers, and otherwise build a solid relationship with the workforce. The other executives, used to facing down unions by putting up with strikes every three or four years and accustomed to advancing family friends and graduates of their alma maters, chuckle while they somehow manage to stifle any incredulous comments, ask no questions, and turn their attention to the next item on the agenda with no action taken.

ANOTHER BOARDROOM, SOMETIME IN THE 1980s

The marketing vice president of an auto manufacturing company has just presented a report to the executive committee that suggests that American drivers are dissatisfied with domestic cars' features, size, quality, gas consumption, and price. The report speculates that Japanese carmakers' giant strides in production efficiency and product design will allow them to take over a large share of the U.S. market. The VP goes on to recommend that the whole company, from top to bottom, develop an attitude of "customer orientation" to ensure that its products are attractive, priced right, and otherwise highly marketable. A key part of this shift would be adopting a new philosophy called "TQM" (Total Quality Management) that would streamline the entire production system while increasing quality and cutting costs at the same time. The executives give a polite word of thanks, roll their eyes, and turn their attention to the next item on the agenda with no action taken.

STILL ANOTHER BOARDROOM, SOMETIME IN THE 1990s

The production vice president of a large manufacturing company is presenting a report from a consultant that recommends that the company begin to implement a new inventory management system, called "JIT" (Just-in-Time) that will require the company to have close working relationships with vendors to coordinate their activities and quality standards with the company's needs. The executives, who know from their own experience that vendors must be kept off balance and in line by making them compete with each other, murmur politely while exchanging furtive looks, and turn their attention to the next item on the agenda with no action taken.

YET ANOTHER BOARDROOM, SOMETIME IN THE 2000s

The finance vice president of a widely held public company has just made a presentation to the executive committee that recommends a new policy of reporting as much useful financial information as possible to the capital markets, including the public, the stockholders, and the company's creditors. The VP urges that the company go well beyond the minimum standards created by the Financial Accounting Standards Board and the Securities and Exchange Commission by voluntarily providing market value–based and other information that the capital markets consider to be useful for assessing the value of the company's securities. This practice, called "QFR" (Quality Financial Reporting), is intended to reduce the cost of capital by stimulating demand for the company's stock, by reducing the capital markets' efforts in generating and analyzing their own alternative information, by otherwise decreasing uncertainty about the company's future, and by building a new trust-based relationship with the stockholders and creditors. The executives sitting around the table have never understood very much about financial statements, but they do know that the capital markets automatically react to reported earnings per share, especially if they come out lower than expected. They sit quietly, hoping against hope that the VP won't propose an action item. . . .

CONNECTING WITH THE FOUR MARKETS

These four scenarios reflect this key fact of economic activity in a free enterprise economy: in order to be successful, management must learn to deal productively with the participants in four different markets: workers in the labor market, customers in the product or service market, suppliers and vendors in the supply chain, and investors and creditors in the capital markets. Figure P-1 represents the situation graphically.

Although success in dealing with these four markets involves managing both supply and demand, in times past (and still today), many managers have tried to succeed in each of them by focusing on supply without paying much attention to demand.

FIGURE P-1

The Firm with Its Markets in High Orbits

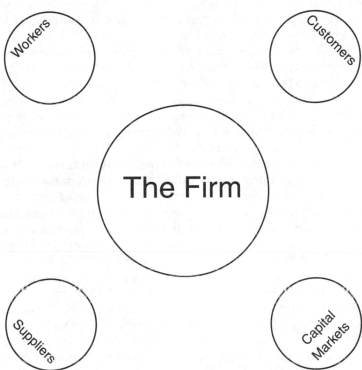

In the labor market, for example, many managers used to consider workers nothing more than inanimate objects to be exploited. In effect, they viewed their firms as suppliers of jobs, such that all they had to do was offer positions on their own terms and the workers would show up and go to work. The thinking behind Human Resource Management changed that picture dramatically by seeing employees as partners who will achieve the greatest productivity only when they are satisfied, nurtured, respected, and fully informed.

In markets for products and services, the old thinking focused on supplying what the firm could make cheaply and then selling it to customers for the highest possible price. This attitude can be called "supply-push" because management takes whatever the company can make and tries to push it out into the market place. The new concepts of customer orientation and Total Quality Management raised managers' awareness of the advantages of being aligned with the needs and wants of the customers. Instead of supply-push, "demand-pull" thinking has gained favor. Under this concept, management first determines what customers need or want and then sets out to provide it in a way that outdoes the competition. By building in quality and paying attention to service and value, for example, management creates a strong and mutually beneficial relationship with customers, who are no longer held in a high orbit but are joined together with the firm and kept fully informed.

Following the lead of successful managers in other countries, many U.S. managers have embraced the idea that the members of their supply chain should also be catered to. In the past, virtually all managers acted as if they were in charge of the supply chain in the sense that they expected to be provided with whatever they demanded without regard for the needs of the vendors. This attitude led to browbeating and tough negotiations in which vendors who didn't meet the company's requirements were abandoned. However, when the quest to achieve the advantages of Just-In-Time inventory management made it apparent that dependable quality and delivery are just as important as low purchase costs, some forward-looking managers began to look after their supply chain more carefully. This new attitude led again to building mutually beneficial relationships characterized by open and complete communications. The consequence has been a stunning revolution in supply chain management.

With these developments, today's progressively managed companies look more like the picture in Figure P-2, which shows the workers, customers, and suppliers being brought into mutually beneficial relationships with the firm, while the capital markets remain in high orbit.

In talking about how the future will be affected by communication and information sharing, Michael Dell of Dell Computer Corporation expressed these thoughts that agree with our brief history of these recent management revolutions:

> A manufacturer will no longer be able to afford to treat a supplier like a vendor from whom every last ounce of cost-saving must be wrung. Nor can a customer be treated simply as a market for products and services at the best possible price. Instead, both suppliers and customers will come to be treated as information partners, jointly looking for ways to improve efficiency across the entire spectrum of the value chain, not just in their respective businesses.[1]

The anomaly is that virtually all managers, including Dell, have not yet made the same sorts of discoveries about the capital markets and have never even considered bringing them into the inner circle. We gained a special insight into this situation one day when one of our former students (now a manager with a high-tech firm) described his attitude toward the capital markets by saying that he considered them to be nothing more than a "necessary evil." In fact, the capital markets are essential to any company for providing the capital that it needs at a rea-

FIGURE P-2

The Firm with One Remaining High-Orbiting Marketplace

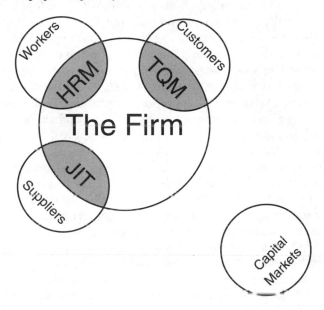

sonable price. The markets also provide liquidity and valuation information for the company's stockholders, thus greatly increasing the demand for and the market value of its shares. In addition, well-functioning capital markets are essential to the entire economy because they provide the mechanism for raising and allocating capital among those who want it and compete for it. If these markets aren't working, an economy grinds to a halt (as the world saw in the 1930s) or never gets started (as we have seen in some former collectivist countries that have tried to convert to capitalism without capital).

Despite this truth about the centrality of capital markets for sustaining, growing, and stabilizing a firm and an economy, we think most managers agree with our student that they are nothing more than necessary evils. We have reached this conclusion because we have watched corporate managers treat the capital markets just like they used to treat the other three markets. Specifically, we see that they still approach the capital markets from the supply-push perspective because they keep putting out financial information that they want to publish instead of the information that capital market participants say they want or that careful analysis suggests that they need or would benefit from having. Just as some blinkered managers continue to manage the supply of jobs and products without paying attention to demand, almost all managers still display a similarly unproductive supply-centered attitude toward these all-important markets for capital.

What evidence supports this opinion? With few exceptions, we see that virtually all managers provide the least amount of required public information. We also see them choosing to do such things as engaging in off-balance-sheet financing, publishing obscure footnotes, reporting mergers as poolings of interest, presenting complex and otherwise indecipherable cash flow statements, and leaving significant expenses off their income statements. What is especially puzzling to us is that they are doing these things despite pleas from sophisticated financial statement users for more useful information. We're also puzzled when we see spectacular business collapses that are based in part on accounting schemes devised by managers trying to prop up an overvalued stock. Enron's 2001 plunge from an apparent market capitalization of $60+ billion to essentially zero was precipitated by the unraveling of financial reporting schemes that would never have gotten started if the management had set out from the beginning to tell the truth about the company's activities and conditions.

What created this seemingly universal condition of disdain for the capital markets, and, perhaps more importantly, what sustains it today? We think that the main origin is the poor training in financial reporting that managers typically receive. As a result, they behave as if they believe very naive theories about the ability of the capital markets to process public information and gather private information. It's clear to us that they think they can fool the markets by merely managing the reported information instead of revealing what is really happening. We understand their confusion; in fact, we have to admit we used to be caught up in similar mistaken beliefs.

In addition, we also think this dysfunctional behavior has been promoted by executive incentive programs that are tied to financial statement numbers. As a result, many managers direct their attention to manipulating the *reported* results instead of managing the *real* results. In turn, this manipulation is enabled and facilitated by financial accounting standards and principles that are highly flexible and subject to a great deal of discretion. All of this activity significantly compromises the quality of the information provided to capital markets as well.

To our still-unfolding astonishment, we caught a vision for a different financial reporting system once we stepped outside our old paradigm. Instead of leaving the capital markets out there in a distant orbit, we believe that the time has come for managers to join with them in collaborative and mutually beneficial relationships by applying what we call *Quality Financial Reporting*.

The essence of QFR is that managers will be able to raise capital at a lower cost and enjoy many other advantages when they reach out to the capital markets and pull them into the inner circle, as suggested by the diagram in Figure P-3.

Just like the other market revolutions led to replacing aloofness and exploitation with partnership and cooperation in dealing with workers, customers, and suppliers, we envision QFR as the revolution that replaces old attitudes toward investors and creditors with new relationships characterized by frequent, open, truthful, and otherwise trustworthy communication.

So, how will this revolution come about? The answer is revealed and developed in the rest of the book. Section I describes why the capital markets will respond positively to information that is better than the highly deficient reports that managers now prepare. Section II explains the huge flaws in the conventional wisdom that generally accepted accounting principles (GAAP) are sufficient for putting high-quality information into public financial reports. Section III backs up our observations and conclusions with thoughts from financial analysts, investors, and accountants; it also includes a summary of relevant empirical research. Section IV leads managers and their accountants to confront their own practices and attitudes by causing them to assess the quality of the information they prepare for public distribution. Section V then presents our suggestions for ways that managers can build the bridges that will draw capital market participants into a QFR relationship. Finally, Section VI discusses how QFR can affect the financial reporting standard-setting process and shows how the management at Enron produced a perfect example of how not to do QFR.

FIGURE P-3

The Firm with Its Low-Orbiting Markets

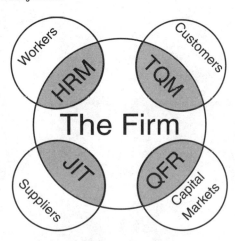

All in all, we think we have a challenging yet very valuable message to get out. We know from experience that some will resist it because it demands a massive change in attitudes and actions. However, we also know that a great many more managers will grasp the QFR vision and will want to know how to put it into practice. So, let's get on with it!

NOTES

1. *Economist, The World in 1999* (annual edition), p. 96.

Four Axioms and
Seven Deadly Sins

When we talk about Quality Financial Reporting in this book, we are really talking about a major change in attitude from the status quo. In effect, we conceive of the switch to QFR as a paradigm shift away from thinking of financial reporting issues in terms of how they affect information providers to analyzing and resolving those issues from the point of view of the information's consumers. In effect, we think a great deal of progress can be made by shifting from the supply perspective to the demand side.

In order for a shift of this magnitude to occur, practitioners have to go through two experiences. First, they have to grow dissatisfied with the present paradigm. Second, they have to be attracted to a new paradigm with sufficient strength to take the risk of leaving the old one behind. It isn't enough for merely one or the other of these things to happen. It doesn't matter how much dissatisfaction is generated, no one will shift unless there is something better to shift to. And it doesn't matter how good the alternative might be, no one will shift unless there is deep and widespread dissatisfaction with the old ways.

This section includes two chapters that will get you started down both paths by showing you what it is about generally accepted accounting principles that is unsatisfactory and what it is about QFR that offers advantages over GAAP.

CHAPTER 1

Foundation for a Revolution

We are unabashed in calling for a financial reporting revolution. Based on our observations over a couple of decades, and as made evident to a great many people by Enron's collapse in 2001, we know that the time has come for old habitual thought processes and practices to be put aside and replaced with something else that is quite different. Although the old way may have served the world well for a time, we are now frankly hard-pressed to understand how it ever worked at all.

Our task of stimulating this kind of change is even more challenging because we're proposing more than a revolution in what people *do*. We go beyond that point to persuade those same people of the advantages in changing what they *think* about what they're doing before they go out and do it.

Despite this drastic change, we are convinced that this revolution will not be violent or even disruptive because we are not advocating throwing out generally accepted accounting principles or doing away with capital market regulation and familiar reporting procedures. The Quality Financial Reporting revolution will not displace these things; rather, it will make them better by adding to them. Of course, when the revolution is firmly entrenched, we think managers, auditors, regulators, financial statement users, and even accounting and finance professors will all have a whole new outlook on GAAP and financial reporting. They will think differently about what is going on, in terms of both the content of the financial statements and the processes that shape that content.

We are especially intrigued by the prospect that the QFR revolution will not come about by coercion or compulsion. Rather, we believe that a new paradigm will inspire managers and accountants to think in new ways and do new things that will make essentially everyone better off.

The only ones who might be hurt fall into two categories. First, there are the very few managers (like Enron's) who have somehow used misleading financial reporting to successfully fool the capital markets into paying too much for their stock. Second, there are others who have gained illicit access to useful insider information before it is made public. It seems clear to us that there is no point in shedding any tears over the losses incurred by those who fall into these categories, even without considering the huge gains that will be created for everyone else.

As described in the prologue, this revolution involves reaching out to the capital markets to establish new relationships that are open and honest. These relationships will be mutually beneficial and long-lasting if they are built along the lines that we describe.

THE QUALITY FINANCIAL REPORTING REVOLUTION

Basically, the management of a company[1] has only two things to offer investors and creditors:

1. Opportunities to receive future cash flows
2. Information about those opportunities

Figure 1-1 represents this situation. As we see it, managers need to focus their attention on enhancing both the real opportunities and the quality of the information instead of working only on one while neglecting or short-changing the other. By looking after both future cash flows *and* users' needs for information about future cash flows, managers will find themselves competing more effectively in the capital markets for the money they need. They will also create shareholder value by increasing security prices.

Let's look more closely at these two factors and how they can be managed:

- If your firm has good cash flow potential, you won't be able to raise funds at a fair price if all you do is provide the capital markets with information about them that is nondescriptive, unreliable, evasive, misleading, or otherwise of low quality.

- If your firm does not have good cash flow potential and you candidly and honestly reveal that fact in your financial statements and other reports, you won't be able to raise many funds, although your cost of capital will reflect only the risk associated with your cash flows. At least you will be rewarded for the quality of your reported information.

- What if your firm doesn't have good cash flow potential and you decide to fabricate false financial reports that make it look like it

FIGURE 1-1

The Firm with Its Twin Offerings

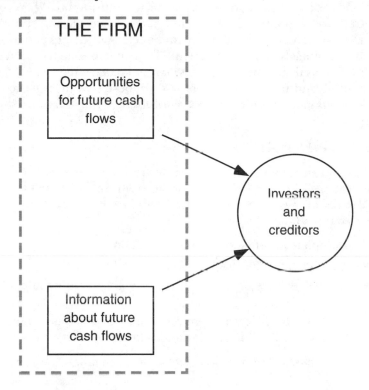

does? While you might be able to raise some money at first, you will run afoul of the law in some circumstances and otherwise find yourself in deep water. Even beyond that regulatory consequence, your demonstrated propensity to mislead will make it very hard to gain access to any capital at any price in the future.

- The best situation occurs if your firm has good cash flow opportunities and you provide up-front, trustworthy, and complete information that describes that potential with sufficient detail and clarity. Under these circumstances, you will be able raise all the funds you need at the right price for the risk associated with your company.

This last case is the one that offers the greatest potential benefits to the management, the employees, the investors, the creditors, and indeed the economy. We think that the many firms that have good cash flow potential can tap into those benefits by adopting Quality Financial Reporting with the clear goal of meeting the capital markets' demand for useful information.

The next discussion uses four simple economic axioms to show why QFR promises to be both revolutionary and widespread. Trust us—we're not talking rocket science or other academic mumbo jumbo. When you get down to it, you will find that our main points are simple and straightforward. Despite that fact, a great many managers and their expert accountants have completely overlooked them. The same mistake has been made by many financial statement users and capital market regulators, as well as accounting and finance educators. We propose that these basic truths provide the foundations for the QFR revolution.

THE FOUR AXIOMS

By definition, an axiom is an unassailably true statement that also serves as a logical basis in a system of reasoning. With regard to the following four QFR axioms, we have not yet found any flaw that makes them assailable, much less a fatal flaw:

- Incomplete information creates uncertainty.
- Uncertainty creates risk for investors and creditors.
- Risk makes investors and creditors demand a higher rate of return.
- A higher rate of return for investors and creditors is a higher cost of capital for the firm and produces lower security prices.

See what you think as we describe them in more detail.

Incomplete Information Creates Uncertainty

Without knowledge, we humans are hopelessly adrift—we don't know where we are, we don't know what's going on, we may not even know what has happened, and we certainly don't have a clue about what will happen. The same situation exists in financial reporting when poor-quality reports cause capital market participants to not know what is happening, what has happened, or what might happen. Incomplete information can be caused by omissions, misrepresentations, or simply lack of trustworthiness. Even if the managers are actually telling the truth, no one will act on it if they don't trust the reports.

Uncertainty Creates Risk
for Investors and Creditors

In addition to universal uncertainty about the future, more uncertainty about the past and present means that capital market participants simply cannot anticipate future cash flows with any comfort or assurance of success. In effect, the uncertainty about the past and present compounds the uncertainty about the future, and leads to a lack of confidence in predictions about what is going to happen. This state of mind constitutes risk for investors and creditors. But, what does that mean?

Risk Makes Investors and Creditors Demand a Higher Rate of Return

If two investment opportunities seem to provide equivalent expected future cash flows but one has more uncertainty and risk associated with it, investors and creditors will demand a higher rate of return to compensate for the uncertain outcome. For them to act otherwise would be totally irrational. As a consequence, managers are mistaken if they think investors will pay a premium price to face more risk, especially if that risk comes from a lack of confidence in the reported information and those who prepared it.

A Higher Rate of Return for Investors and Creditors is a Higher Cost of Capital for the Firm and Produces Lower Security Prices

Of course, if investors and creditors demand a higher expected rate of return from a firm, the managers on the other side of the transaction inevitably face a higher cost of capital. For example, interest income for a recipient is interest expense for the payer. According to economic theory (most of which is nothing more than common sense), the market value of a debt or equity security is a consensus present value of the expected future cash flows from that security discounted at the investors' and creditors' expected rate of return. Thus, the higher the expected rate of return (and the higher the cost of capital), the lower the present value of the prospective cash flows. It follows that the market values of a company's securities are diminished when investors and creditors demand a higher rate of return.[2]

A DIFFERENT SLANT

Because the world has both pessimists and optimists, this analysis can also be approached more positively. For positive thinkers, the four QFR axioms can also be stated in these different terms:

- More complete information reduces uncertainty.
- Less uncertainty reduces risk for investors and creditors.

FIGURE 1-2

The Links Between Information and Security Prices

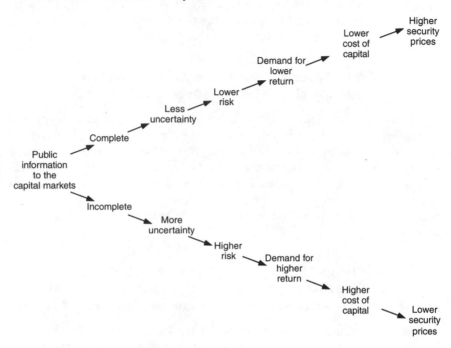

- Reduced risk makes investors and creditors satisfied with a lower rate of return.
- A lower rate of return for investors and creditors is a lower cost of capital for the firm and produces higher stock prices.

Figure 1-2 summarizes the axioms and the chain reactions between the information provided to the public and the company's security prices.[3]

No matter how anyone describes this relationship between information completeness and security prices, it seems to us totally self-evident and unarguable. However, our experience proves that nearly everyone acts like it has neither of these qualities. Let's look at how awareness of these axioms could—and probably will—change the way managers construct their reporting strategies.

USING THE AXIOMS TO DEFINE FINANCIAL REPORTING STRATEGIES

As far as we're concerned, the implication of the four axioms is totally clear: if you want to reduce your company's cost of capital and raise its security prices, you have to choose appropriate strategies for both operations and financial reporting.

First of all, you must choose between two alternative general strategies for operating your business:

1. You can manage the company in such a way that you will increase the potential cash flows to be realized in the future. In other words, you try to do something to turn the company's securities into better investments by boosting the probability of providing more cash to their owners.

2. You can manage the company however you would like, paying little attention to present and future cash flows. In other words, you can merely respond on a day-to-day basis without much concern for building the company's value or otherwise benefiting the owners for the long term.

In addition, you must choose between two alternative general strategies for reporting information about your business:

3. You can provide financial statements that are so complete, timely, trustworthy, and thoroughly informative that they reduce the uncertainty faced by the investors and creditors and cause them to give you their money while fully understanding the operating and financial risks that they face by dealing with you.

4. You can try to use GAAP and financial reporting policy choices to present financial statements that make your company look more attractive than it really is so that you can tease, cajole, entice, and otherwise trick investors and creditors into giving you their money on an impulse, hoping for the best.

It seems obvious that the best overall plan combines strategies 1 and 3. Under this plan, managers work to actually improve the cash flow potential *and* tell the world exactly what they have done.

However, our experience shows that many corporate managers are somehow seduced into choosing operating strategy 2 instead of 1 and choosing reporting strategy 4 instead of 3. By doing so, they hope to manage their GAAP financial statements to present false pictures that cover up their poor operating results and weak financial position. To put it another way, they mistakenly think it is sufficient for them to merely *look* good in the statements instead of actually *being* good. In order to act this way, the managers must believe that the capital markets are incapable of understanding the financial reports and that the investors and creditors have no other place to put their money.

This behavior involves what psychologists call *denial*, because the managers refuse to acknowledge the realities that the capital market participants have access to other investment opportunities and that they have other sources of information that allow them to penetrate the smog in the financial statements and fully understand what is going on inside the company.

The augmented diagram in Figure 1-3 shows that managers are clearly not in control of all the choices available to investors and creditors. The next paragraphs explain the implications of this more complete reality.

First, investors and creditors have plenty of choices among other firms that have come to the markets seeking equity and debt capital. Many of these firms actually offer better opportunities for future cash flows; if a particular company looks weak compared to its competitors, it will face a smaller demand for its securities and their prices will be discounted. Managers cannot go to the markets assuming that they have top-drawer access, even if they are in charge of the leading companies in an industry. Because no economic force of gravity can keep investors from investing in other industries, essentially all managers are in competition with all other managers in the capital markets.

Second, investors and creditors have access to other sources of information about a particular firm. They don't have to rely simply on the pub-

FIGURE 1-3

The Firm Is Not in Control of Investors and Creditors

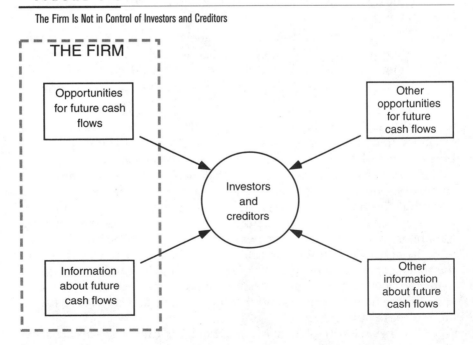

lic self-representations offered up by managers who think they have something to gain by presenting favorable financial pictures of themselves. If this other information is inconsistent with the managers' reports, investors and creditors face additional uncertainty and risk, and again discount the company's securities.

What this analysis shows us is that it is mistake of enormous consequence for managers to assume that they can access cheap capital simply by declaring their strategies on a take-it-or-leave-it basis and by describing their situations in ways that are biased to make them look better than they really are. (Enron is surely an excellent example of applying this recipe for disaster.) There are plenty of economic incentives at work to encourage investors and creditors to look for the best combination of cash flow opportunities and information about those opportunities. Managers who fall short of the competition in one or both areas will face higher capital costs and lower stock prices. To assume otherwise flies in the face of rationality and reality.

SUMMARY

Virtually everything that follows in the rest of this book harks back to these axioms and this summary relationship—*incomplete information produces lower stock prices*. That's why we see QFR as a financial reporting strategy that will increase the market value of a company's securities and its total market value. The logic is so compelling that we are convinced that this strategy is far superior to any other. It is extremely clear to us that the decision to just try to look good with rosy financial statements does not and will not work.

In contrast, a Quality Financial Reporting strategy involves nothing more than providing more complete information to meet the markets' needs. That's really all there is to it. In fact, these ideas have been around in various forms for quite awhile. In their book, *Counting What Counts*,[4] Marc Epstein and Bill Birchard reach two centuries back into history to greet us with these very modern concepts:

> Philosopher Jeremy Bentham, John Stewart Mill's teacher, recognized 200 years ago the power of public accountability. He wrote about the "open-management principle," "all-above-board principle," and "transparent-management principle." Publicity, Bentham maintained, commits companies to do their duties. Bentham . . . foresaw as far back as the eighteenth century the powers that managers . . . exercise today: using a public commitment and accounting spurs unparalleled betterment inside the company. The combination of indisputable quantitative figures, along with public disclosure, keeps people focused on their goals. (pp. 11–12)

Our thoughts on QFR are consistent with this idea in that choosing to do a better job of reporting information about the company leads not only to providing more useful information but also to actually doing a better job of running the company. In other words, there is more to Quality Financial Reporting than just financial reporting. Epstein and Birchard describe the motivational dimension of public reporting this way:

> Rather than act as a stick to keep people in line, the principles of accountability can act as a carrot to keep them climbing to higher levels of performance. (p. 4)

This impetus to manage better is yet another benefit of QFR.

Before going further, we feel the need to convince our readers that the status quo in financial reporting is entirely different. Indeed, almost all managers seem to think they can manage security prices by managing their financial reports. In doing so, we think they commit one or more of the seven deadly sins of financial reporting that we describe in the next chapter.

NOTES

1. With the obvious exception of cash flows from donors, managers of not-for-profit organizations are subject to economic factors similar to those described here for corporate managers.

2. Although this theoretical argument may be persuasive, some may prefer to have harder evidence. In Chapter 9 we describe recent empirical research that confirms the axioms.

3. Taken from our paper, "Will You Adopt Quality Financial Reporting?", which appeared in the January 2001 issue of *Strategic Finance.*

4. Perseus Publishing, 2000.

CHAPTER 2

The Seven Deadly Sins of Financial Reporting

One thing that motivated us to produce this book is our desire to reduce the frequency of several detrimental behavior patterns that we have seen over and over again. They are so counterproductive and negative that we call them the "seven deadly sins of financial reporting."

We have observed these behaviors when managers publish their annual reports, issue press releases, and send out other forms of financial communications. We have seen them displayed in comment letters from managers to the Financial Accounting Standards Board (FASB) and the Securities and Exchange Commission (SEC) on proposed new rules. We have also seen them in managers' presentations in public hearings and in journal articles of various kinds. Alas, we have even seen them in text-books that we and other academics are supposed to use to teach our students about accounting.[1] We think that making people aware of their self-destructive behavior will encourage them to change. Thus, we are confident that the spread of QFR will make these sins far less prevalent.

Here are the sins:

1. Underestimating the capital markets
2. Obfuscating
3. Hyping and spinning
4. Smoothing
5. Minimum reporting
6. Minimum auditing
7. Preparation cost myopia

We find that the first sin lays the foundation for the others.

(*Note:* Because the story of Enron's collapse was unfolding while this book was in production, we have added appropriate comments about the non-QFR activities of its managers and auditors. In addition, we added Chapter 19 to describe more completely how they committed all seven of these sins.)

A BRIEF BACKGROUND

To help you understand why these behaviors are sins, we want to go into a little bit of financial reporting theory that some may have never had adequately explained to them or that has otherwise never quite soaked in.

Shortly after it was created in 1973, the Financial Accounting Standards Board (see sidebar) set out to define a theoretical structure that would guide its members in defining and resolving financial reporting issues. This structure was called the "Conceptual Framework," and the board started by defining the purpose to be served by financial reporting.

THE FINANCIAL ACCOUNTING STANDARDS BOARD[2]

The Financial Accounting Standards Board (FASB) is a unique private sector agency that serves the federal government and the financial reporting community. As part of this sector, it does not receive public funding; instead, it is funded by donations from its constituents and by sales of its publications.

Since the beginning, the board has had seven full-time members, with one serving as the chair. Their annual salary was $435,000 in 2002, with the chair receiving an additional $100,000. The board's work is assisted by a full-time research and technical activities staff of approximately 40. The board's offices are located in Norwalk, Connecticut, just about an hour from New York.

To add to its independence by insulating the board members from at least some political influences, the FASB has a parent organization, the Financial Accounting Foundation (FAF), which is a tax-exempt 501(c)(3) educational entity. The FAF has 16 trustees who represent the public and the primary constituencies. These trustees have the fundamental duties of appointing board members and raising the needed donations, thus keeping the members out of this sensitive activity.

The FAF and the FASB were created in 1973 through a cooperative effort by the accounting profession, financial executives, financial statement users, and others. The FASB replaced the Accounting Principles Board (APB), which was a high-level technical committee of the American Institute of Certified Public Accountants (AICPA). The political motivation for this action was a growing concern in Congress that the APB lacked sufficient independence to create tough rules.

THE FINANCIAL ACCOUNTING STANDARDS BOARD (Concluded)

After the FASB was founded, its work was endorsed by the AICPA and, more importantly, by the SEC as the authoritative source of generally accepted accounting principles (GAAP). It has operated since then under the oversight of the SEC to help ensure the quality of its standards in terms of protecting the public interest. The SEC also oversees the board in the sense that it looks after and protects its independence and the integrity of its activities.

The FASB follows a due process that involves admitting a project to the agenda, researching and framing the issues related to the project, debating the alternative positions on those issues, soliciting substantial input from constituents, and defining acceptable practices by publishing a standard (called a Statement of Financial Accounting Standards, or SFAS). As we describe in Chapter 3, this process is thoroughly and inevitably political, and that fact is reflected in virtually all forms of GAAP, including those issued by the APB and its predecessor, the Committee on Accounting Procedure. Significantly, the politics have frequently thwarted the board members' ability to produce consensus positions on the issues that advance the public's interest in useful financial statements. Instead, it has produced compromises well short of that goal.

Despite this shortcoming, there have been few serious threats to the FASB's ability to continue operating and defining GAAP. Even though its standards have created accounting practices that are much less than optimal, it remains effective in today's regulated financial reporting paradigm.

It should be noted that the board's dominant position and influence as the leading financial reporting standard setting body has been challenged by the International Accounting Standards Board (IASB), which was created in 2001 as a successor to the International Accounting Standards Committee (IASC). The IASB has adopted a structure similar to the one used by the FASB, with a board of trustees and essentially a full-time board, although it has 14 members from around the world. The IASB is potentially more powerful than the FASB but it is more ambiguously situated because it is multinational and thus does not have a clear-cut source of mandated governmental authority like the FASB enjoys. Its status also raises issues of sovereignty and jurisdiction as citizens of various countries are forced to follow the edicts of a board and process that are not controlled or even regulated by their countries' governments. Despite these limitations, the IASB's output (called International Financial Reporting Standards) and the International Accounting Standards issued by the IASC are considered to be GAAP in virtually all countries around the world except the United States, Japan, and Canada. The relationship between the FASB and the IASB was still being explored when this book was in production, so the jury is still out on the issue of whether this new board will supplant the FASB as the single source of GAAP or will complement the board's efforts. The SEC will sooner or later have to bite the bullet on the issue of whether international standards are sufficient for defining acceptable reporting practices for securities filings by domestic and foreign companies.

According to the initial component of the FASB's Framework, *Objectives of Financial Reporting for Business Enterprises,* Statement of Financial Accounting Concepts No. 1 (issued in 1978), the board members believed that the objective of financial reporting is to

> . . . provide information that is useful to present and potential investors and creditors and other users in making rational investment, credit, and similar decisions. (par. 34)

The board went on to explain that this information should

> . . . help present and potential investors and creditors and other users in assessing the amounts, timing and uncertainty of prospective cash receipts from dividends or interest and the proceeds from the sale, redemption, or maturity of securities or loans. (par. 37)

The FASB further explained this point with this very key sentence:

> Thus, financial reporting should provide information to help investors, creditors, and others assess the amounts, timing, and uncertainty of prospective net cash inflows to the related enterprise. (par. 37)

In other words, the FASB stated that the reason managers should hire accountants to do financial reporting is to transmit useful information to investors, creditors, and other financial statement users to help them anticipate future cash flows to the reporting company and then eventually to themselves so that they can make better investment and credit decisions. In contrast, if the reported information does not support this objective, its usefulness is questionable at best and nonexistent at worst. (Of course, the four axioms teach that policy choices that lead to providing useless information in turn produce higher capital costs and lower security prices.)

By setting forth this objective, the FASB created a powerful test for usefulness. However, we believe that most managers and accountants act as if they are totally unfamiliar with it, certainly in practice and possibly even in concept. It is powerful because it essentially requires managers to consider whether their reported financial information is actually useful to its recipients or merely window dressing designed to make a bad situation look better than it is. In our view, it appears that many managers are unacquainted with this idea because they seem to pursue completely different goals with their financial reports. The situation suggests that they are unaware of the powerful economic incentives that reward their pursuit of the objective of providing useful information. At the very least, managers who grasp QFR's benefits should undertake a reevaluation of their own internal incentive systems to see if they are inadvertently encouraging the opposite behavior.[3] If so, it might behoove them to amend the plans to reward efforts to achieve QFR results.

The following discussions use this objective to describe the seven deadly sins and show how they produce flawed reporting strategies.

UNDERESTIMATING THE CAPITAL MARKETS

The first sin of underestimating the capital markets is the root of all evil in financial reporting. Whenever its spell falls on managers and those who help them, they seem to display the attitude that they can mislead, even fool, the capital markets by presenting financial statements that are molded to emphasize the positive while leaving out, downplaying, or obscuring the negative. Those who commit this sin seem to assume that capital market participants are merely passive absorbers of easily obtained public reports provided by managers. The sinners also assume that the participants will not find (or even look for) other information somewhere else that corroborates or contradicts the public reports or fills in the missing holes. A third assumption behind this sin is that compliance with GAAP and all SEC regulations is sufficient for providing useful information. Even more bold is the managers' presumption that capital market participants do not have the capacity to impose any penalty for incomplete or otherwise false and misleading information, especially if the managers are in compliance with these rules. Figure 2-1 represents their faulty model.

The four axioms reveal how bogus this thinking can be. Specifically, they show that the markets respond to management's uninformative reports and condescending attitude by demanding higher rates of return while discounting security prices. The more complete diagram in Figure 2-2 shows that poor reporting causes the market participants to look elsewhere for more useful information and for other financial opportunities that are covered by more useful information. Thus the outcome of following the minimum reporting strategy has to be diminished demand and a lower price for the firm's stock.

FIGURE 2-1

An Oversimplified Model of Financial Reporting and Stock Prices

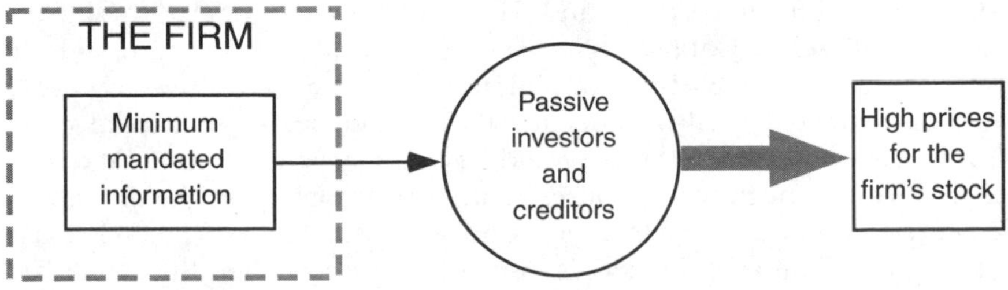

FIGURE 2-2

A More Complete Model of Financial Reporting and Stock Prices

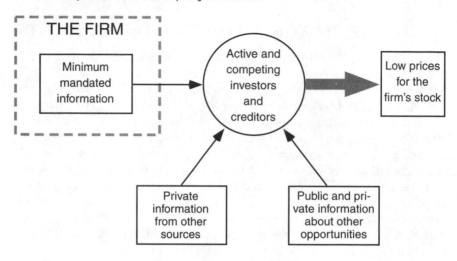

This sin can be overcome by a virtue that involves managers' learning to respect the markets' incredible abilities to evaluate public information, gather private information, and respond rationally to these
messages, all while incorporating other factors in reaching an equilibrium
stock price. If the QFR revolution can instill this attitude in managers,
there will be no limit to what they can accomplish.

OBFUSCATING

The second sin of reporting incomprehensible information is derived from
the first one. Given a choice between presenting financial information
clearly or presenting it obscurely, many managers act as if they believe
that they are better off if they choose the latter. For example, we know of
one vice president of a very large corporation who was told directly by the
CEO that the VP's job was to deliberately make the company's financial
statements difficult to understand. The four axioms show that this behavior is totally self-defeating!

By leaving out useful information or clouding the truth, an obfuscating management creates more uncertainty and raises its capital costs.
Even if the omitted messages would have conveyed bad news, the markets have two negative responses to the omissions. First, the absence of
clear reporting will cause them to assume the worst and extract what is in
all likelihood an even bigger risk penalty. Second, when the actual bad

news becomes evident, they will react to the now-proven untrustworthiness of the management by never trusting them again. Oh, they might buy the stock, but the price will be driven down. Enron's 2001 bankruptcy offers a perfect example of what happens when obfuscation is deliberately adopted as a management policy.

It isn't just us, and we're not making these ideas up. In a videotaped session before some business students from North Carolina, Warren Buffett said,

> If I pick up an annual report and I can't understand a footnote, I probably won't—no, I *won't*—invest in that company because I *know* that they don't *want* me to understand it.

It seems to us that it would be an extraordinarily dumb decision to do something that would take away Buffett's interest in your stock. The same is true for anyone who tries to put one over on the capital markets.

The cardinal virtues that offset this sin of obfuscation are clarity and candor. When management has a choice between coming clean or keeping a secret just a little longer, the four axioms reveal the right answer—do whatever reduces uncertainty, generally by decreasing the market's need to guess and otherwise anticipate the future without solid information. The resulting reduced risk will boost share prices and cut capital costs.

HYPING AND SPINNING

The sin of hyping and spinning involves deliberately trying to fool the capital markets by getting them to focus only on the good news. The sin then gets compounded by overstating the goodness of that good news. Of course, this behavior is often the objective pursued in promotional strategies for products and services. For example, when was the last time you saw a commercial for a razor that shows users cutting themselves? Or new car owners waiting a full day in the dealer's service center? Advertising serves several purposes, of course, and there are many different ways to do it. Some ads are laudable for their ability to transfer useful information to customers and bring them to buy the product. Others can get sales results by tricking customers, but they will never engender confidence, loyalty, or any other long-term positive relationship. Still other advertisements are so sleazy and obviously hyped that they will not produce sales while at the same time they create a negative image of the company that carries over to other unadvertised products.

Most managers who hype and spin in financial reporting seem to think the capital markets can be fooled by fast talk and clever choices within GAAP. Perhaps they buy into the old aphorism that "you can fool all the people some of the time." In fact, there is plenty of evidence that you can't fool the capital markets any of the time. So, why even try?

The four axioms show the futility of trying to trick the markets into paying too much and other related negative behaviors. They also point to the obvious countervailing virtue: when in doubt, tell the whole story, not just the shiny good parts. There should be no uncertainty that capital market participants are trying to discern the dark underbelly of the firm's real condition. What the four axioms reveal to managers is the economic incentives to report all the news proactively and relieve the markets' uncertainty about the true state of affairs. Those managers who adopt this kind of virtuous behavior will be handsomely rewarded by the capital markets for reducing the need to read the tea leaves on their own. However bad things really are, market participants who are less than fully informed will guess that they are worse. And, however good things really are, they will guess that they're not really that good. Therefore, being straightforward and complete will bring its market reward. We also believe that stockholders will be more than happy to reward truth-telling managers through their incentive systems.

SMOOTHING

Another behavior (or misbehavior, to be exact) commonly displayed by managers in their financial reporting strategies is trying to smooth out unanticipated variations in reported net income and its components. Managers are right when they think that volatility in their reported numbers reflects some sort of operational risk that affects the uncertainty attributed to the future cash flows that might come from the firm. The natural consequence of this risk is lower security prices. However, managers are confused if they think that they can overcome this inexorable economic force simply by eliminating the volatility from the *reported* results without doing anything to modify the underlying problem that creates the *real* volatility. This sin is the equivalent of using computer image processing to eliminate wrinkles and other undesired features in a photographic portrait. No matter how much is done to the image, the person's real appearance is unchanged.

We are not unique in considering the smoothing of financial results to be objectionable. In particular, consider this comment from a high-powered committee of financial analysts from the Association for Investment Management and Research (AIMR), the organization that grants recognition to people as Chartered Financial Analysts:

> We believe that financial analysis is best served by financial reporting that reports transactions as and when they occur. If there is smoothing to be done, it is the province of analysts to do it. If there are financial reporting

anomalies that are attributable to seasonality, it is far better to report and explain them than to conceal them with undocumented smoothing.[4]

Regrettably, a lot of smoothing is preengineered into reports by the political compromises imbedded in GAAP. In fact, much of the pressure on standard-setters has focused on the issue of the volatility of income measures resulting from applying a new method. As a result of the politicized process described in Chapter 4, we observe that smoothing is widely prevalent in GAAP.

For example, consider cost-based depreciation, which basically takes what could be highly variable fluctuations in asset values and averages them over some anticipated future period. GAAP also allow managers to postpone reporting gains and losses on most investments in marketable securities until they are sold; in fact, this approach causes income to not be reported when it occurs and to be reported when it does not. GAAP also require sellers to defer some of their revenue when they still have outstanding commitments to the buyers; although the idea was to help prevent eager managers from overstating revenue, software companies turned this provision into a loophole for smoothing out the highly cyclical revenue they receive from bringing out new versions of their products every few years. Pension accounting under GAAP is a monument to smoothing; although SFAS 87 is much too complex to go into here, you can trust us when we say that it created never-before-seen ways to smooth the effects of actuarial gains and losses, market value changes in pension assets, retroactive benefit increases, and transitioning to SFAS 87 from its predecessor. (These details are briefly described in Chapter 17.)

The four axioms reveal that smoothing is equivalent to static in a radio message because it does nothing but make the real facts harder to ascertain. And, if those facts are harder to get, smoothing inevitably leads to lower stock prices instead of higher ones.

The corresponding virtue is simple. As the AIMR committee suggested, managers should simply describe the results of every relevant event that happens as soon as it happens and without glossing over its impact. Of course, another virtue would be to develop operating strategies that tend to smooth out the actual volatility. Combining that real action with QFR will surely produce higher stock prices and lower capital costs.

MINIMUM REPORTING

The fifth cardinal sin of reporting as little as possible is subtle and very common, but nonetheless devastating in terms of its effect on capital costs. In light of the political processes that define rules for financial reporting, compromises often create certain minimum requirements while permitting or recommending more complete disclosures. Given what we've covered about the four axioms, it should be clear that managers are mistaken when they report only the minimum because the outcome is certain to be incomplete information in the financial statements. By now, everyone reading this book surely understands how incomplete information leads to higher capital costs and lower stock prices.

Management's accomplices in this unwise practice may be the company's attorneys. Members of that profession have a much different slant on disclosure because they are trained to keep all the information they know to themselves until they are forced to reveal it or until they see a clear legal advantage in revealing it publicly. Thus, they tend to advise their clients to do nothing more than the minimum. One can hardly expect lawyers to have a strong background in finance, so perhaps we can excuse their poor advice in this case. However, knowledge of the four axioms should help them and managers see the disadvantage of this strategy.

A stunning fact that emerges from this behavior is that the managers are actually relying on regulators to design their financial reports. By analogy, think what consumer products would be like if they were to be designed only to meet the barest minimum government standards. For example, what if car designers were content to build vehicles that merely comply with minimum safety, mileage, and pollution standards? No car would have such things as comfortable seats, cruise control, power steering, CD players, or any of the other features that would increase its marketability. These options are provided on cars because the designers have determined that they can sell more units if they go beyond the minimum requirements. Thus, it strikes us as highly ironic, even indefensible, that managers are totally content to publish financial statements that barely meet the minimum standards inherent in GAAP. Isn't it certain that they could reap lower capital costs and higher stock prices by going beyond the minimum required disclosures? We think it is.

With regard to the offsetting virtue, it seems clear that huge advantages will flow to managers who engage in careful and full disclosure of useful information beyond the minimum. But, it isn't enough to just dump tons of data on the markets. It's essential for it to be organized and otherwise accessible.

Timeliness is also incredibly important, especially when the legal minimum reporting frequency is only four times per year. The four axioms reveal that management's decision to wait the allowed 90 days to provide the next round of information does nothing but cause users' uncertainty to grow greater and greater during the three months. The inevitable consequence is that the cost of capital goes higher and higher during the quarter. Just think how much uncertainty could be relieved if managers reported once each month or even more frequently.[5]

MINIMUM AUDITING

The sixth sin of financial reporting occurs when the significance of the independent audit is underrated. While this sin might be somewhat excusable for managers, it is unfortunately and unforgivably prevalent among auditors themselves. In general, managers who commit this sin see audits only as value-consuming activities that are needed merely to achieve minimum compliance with legal requirements.

At the end of the audit, the only question anyone (including the auditor) asks is, "Do these financial statements comply with GAAP?" As a result, managers look for auditors who can answer this question affirmatively for the lowest price. They also look for auditors who will not merely tolerate their reporting sins but actually help commit them.

Many auditors have responded to this situation shortsightedly by cutting back on their procedures to the barest legal minimums so that they can be the low bidder. Also, they have turned audits into loss leaders that open up opportunities for them to be engaged by their audit clients to perform nonaudit services. Of course, even if auditors and managers deny it, increasing amounts of fees from these services cause the auditors to lose their independence, certainly in appearance if not in fact. Surely, the apparent loss of auditor independence increases uncertainty and depresses security prices. We present some empirical proof of this effect in Chapter 13. In addition, we point out the widespread incredulous responses to claims by Enron's auditors that they were independent of their client despite collecting audit and nonaudit fees in excess of $50 million in one year.

At the heart of the minimum auditing sin is managers' failure to comprehend that audits are supposed to *create* value by reducing investors' uncertainty. More than a little of that uncertainty is caused by the fact that the statements are management's representations about some complex activities and conditions. Absent an audit, the markets' trust in the financial statements would be low and uncertainty would be extremely high, with the consequence that the company's cost of capital would be elevated.

With an effective audit, some uncertainty still exists, but the overall level ought to be alleviated, with the consequence of lower capital costs. However, the opposite result can occur if the managers and auditors negotiate lower audit fees or cut back on their auditing procedures because they are actually colluding (perhaps unwittingly) to diminish the audit's ability to alleviate uncertainty.

In opposition to this sin, management can adopt the virtue of using the auditors as independent third parties to greatly enhance the value of the financial statements. Under QFR, these two questions would be asked at the end of the audit: "Are these financial statements useful for decision making?" and "What can we do to make them more useful?" What a different world it would be if managers pursued sincere and complete answers to these questions instead of merely stopping as soon as the company achieves minimum compliance with GAAP!

In addition, managers who really want lower capital costs and higher stock prices should do everything they can to protect their auditors' real and apparent independence. Once the audit is complete, they could even advertise the fact that their financial statements survived the scrutiny of these tough auditors.

With regard to auditors themselves, the sin of minimum auditing is manifested in their doing the least work possible while remaining in compliance with minimum generally accepted auditing standards (GAAS).[6] In contrast, QFR thinking should show auditors that they are uniquely positioned to add value to the financial statements by creating more credibility than exists without their third-party attestation. In turn, this realization could lead them to maximize the value they add by doing all that they can to guard their independence and not fritter it away by various compromises with their clients. Instead of the often present practice of aiding and abetting their clients' minimal compliance with GAAP for illusory advantages, they can do a great deal more to add real value to the statements. We offer further analysis and discussion of QFR and audits in Chapter 13.

PREPARATION COST MYOPIA

Underlying many financial reporting shortcomings is an unproductive management focus on the costs of providing public information. Just so we're not misunderstood, we know that these costs are important and need to be managed. What we find objectionable is that so many managers seem to focus only on the cost of preparing the financial statements and fail to comprehend or even notice the benefits that the statements could and do provide for them. They also seem to be oblivious to the costs incurred by the users of financial statements.

We see two origins for this phenomenon. First, we venture a guess that the financial reporting function in every company is managed as a "cost center." Under this arrangement, the performance of the CFO or other financial reporting manager is evaluated solely on the costs incurred in producing the minimum required external reports. The intended consequence is that the manager will look after the preparation costs and not let them run out of control. However, the unintended consequence is a hyperfocus on minimizing those costs to the exclusion of considering the impact of that minimization on the usefulness of the financial statements. Given a choice between generally acceptable reporting method A that costs less than generally acceptable reporting method B but produces less useful information for financial statement readers, the cost center manager will always prefer A in the quest for personal advancement and bonuses.

But, let's stop and consider what would happen if the total costs used to evaluate the CFO were to include the firm's cost of capital. Under this structure, the financial reporting managers would be motivated to consider whether an alternate accounting principle with a higher preparation cost would reduce uncertainty by a greater amount and thereby reduce the cost of capital. Doing so would allow them to achieve their bonuses by behaving in a fashion that is more congruent with the goals of the organization and its stockholders.

The second origin of this sin is, of course, the distinct possibility that most managers do not actually understand that they can obtain benefits from adding more value to the financial statements. Thus, the fact that the CFO's operation is run as a cost center may not be just a matter of convenience. Rather, it is possible that no one in the firm has ever had enough vision to see any benefit to compare to the preparation costs. This lack of knowledge may be promoted by the attitude that preparing the financial statements is nothing more than a burdensome cost of complying with government standards.

An opposite (but still negative) phenomenon occurs when management decides to incur additional preparation costs and even extra transaction costs for the purpose of trying to look better. In particular, they engage in certain activities with the sole purpose of producing financial statements that do such things as increase the amount of *reported* earnings or reduce the debt-to-equity ratio based on the *reported* balance sheet numbers. For example, prior to the issuance of SFAS 141 in July 2001, managers had to incur substantial costs to qualify a business combination for a pooling. In the same way, managers often choose to incur additional costs to design a lease that evades the capitalization criteria in SFAS 13 and thus produces off-balance-sheet financing. The managers just don't seem to mind the additional preparation costs in these circumstances because they think they will reap benefits by keeping the capital markets from learning what is really going on. As we describe in more detail in Chapter 19, Enron's managers fell prey to this version of the sin when they engaged what one commentator described as "legions of lawyers and accountants to help it meet the letter of federal securities laws while trampling on the intent of those laws."

The four axioms certainly create a different perspective on these questionable behaviors. Specifically, they reveal that the offsetting virtue is a simple awareness that cutting the quality of reported information negatively impacts capital costs and stock prices. Once this awareness is in place, managers should be willing to incur additional preparation costs to produce useful information that reduces uncertainty, risk, and the cost of capital. If, for example, GAAP allow two different methods, management's choice between them should be based on an analysis that includes their impact on financial statement users' uncertainty, not merely what they cost to implement. The fact that these benefits are difficult to quantify is an obstacle but not an excuse for failing to consider them when establishing financial reporting policies.

SUMMARY OF THE SINS

So, what does all this talk about the sevens sins of financial reporting mean? By now, we hope you will understand that you may have been operating under some significant misconceptions about financial reporting.

In a sense, we are writing this book to turn the financial reporting world upside down. Ever since we got our own tight grip on the handle of the four axioms and conceived the idea of Quality Financial Reporting, we cannot look at practice the same way that we used to. Every place we look, we see defects, limitations, and shortsightedness. We think we're right, and we want you to come to see the world as we now do and grasp the need for improvement. Of course, acting to satisfy this need is also acting to claim tremendous financial advantages.

IT ISN'T THE ETHICS AS MUCH AS THE ECONOMICS

We also think it is important for us to acknowledge that the four axioms make a cogent economic argument for telling the truth without ever raising the question of whether managers are unethical to engage in minimum reporting. In fact, we are not really making an ethical argument in favor of telling more of the truth more openly. Although we used to approach the sins from that perspective, we have now come to understand that managers actually have huge economic incentives that encourage them to tell the truth without even considering whether doing so will help them sleep better at night.

This point seems important to us because it shows that managers—even those with unethical proclivities—are in the position to enjoy the benefits of QFR without taking the risk of being caught in the middle of a scheme to leave the capital markets misinformed or merely uninformed. The clear consequence of that kind of scheme is higher capital costs and lower stock prices.

With this perspective in place, the next section explains more about public financial reporting, with a particular emphasis on its shortcomings. The objective is to convince you that mere compliance with GAAP is sure to fall short of achieving Quality Financial Reporting.

NOTES

1. One particularly egregious example came across our desks in an advertisement for a book to be used in a self-study professional education course. Astonishingly, the ad read: "Learn how to manipulate financial statements to control the perceptions of investors and creditors." We don't think that book is worth buying. (Or writing, for that matter.)

2. For more information about the FASB, see our book *The FASB: The People, the Process, and the Politics* (4th ed.), McGraw-Hill, 1998.

3. A great deal of empirical research has been completed on issues surrounding internal incentives and financial reporting policy choices; in general, it confirms the commonsense idea that managers manage their accounting policies to produce measures of income that give them higher bonuses or to otherwise enrich themselves personally.

4. AIMR, *Financial Reporting in the 1990s and Beyond*, 1993, p. 58. More information about this book is presented in Chapter 7.

5. We think this relatively infrequent reporting has put a disproportionate premium on analysts' expectations for future earnings results. What would these predictions be worth if reports were due out every few weeks instead of only four times a year? Next to nothing, we think.

6. Like GAAP, GAAS are created in a political process that produces compromises that tend to diminish the impact of the standards. One should also realize that the auditing standards are produced by auditors, with the consequence that it can only be true that the standards are more likely to advance auditors' interests than the interests of any other parties.

GAAP Aren't Good Enough

The three chapters in this section are aimed at showing why all participants in financial reporting (managers, financial statement users, regulators, auditors, and academics) should be experiencing ever increasing dissatisfaction with the status quo paradigm.

Despite decades of history and countless hours of human effort, the political process for establishing generally accepted accounting principles continues to fall short of addressing the issues from the users' perspective. Instead, the concerns of auditors and managers still take precedence and attention is given to the supply side of financial reporting instead of the demand side.

This section describes that political process with more candor than is usually found in other more official commentaries. That candor reflects our own willingness to confront the shortcomings; it is also intended to promote general dissatisfaction with the way the system has been working and will continue to work unless a new paradigm gains dominance.

Be warned, these chapters include numerous examples of areas where the politics of the system have significantly limited the ability of GAAP financial statements to convey useful information to the capital markets. Some time-honored and closely held beliefs will be challenged as never before.

CHAPTER 3

Financial Reporting in the U.S. and Elsewhere

Without a doubt, public financial reporting is a central and highly visible form of communication between managers and the capital markets. Thus, managers should understand this process if they want to reach out and bring capital market participants into a Quality Financial Reporting relationship. This chapter describes more about how the whole financial reporting system is thought to work and how it actually works. In this chapter, we also explain the procedures for creating GAAP, with an emphasis on the political conflicts that dominate the process and severely limit the usefulness of its output for fully informing the capital markets.

A BRIEF HISTORY

Despite its importance to modern economies, mandatory public financial reporting is relatively new in the sweep of history. Although it is now well settled in U.S. law that public companies must register with the Securities and Exchange Commission, this legislation was issued only as recently as 1934. While public financial reporting was required before that date by stock exchanges and by contracts with individual investors and creditors, it was not ubiquitous until the federal securities legislation was passed in the 1930s. (Of course, regulated public financial reporting is even newer in most other countries.)

The ideas for this legislation and the SEC emerged from a need for ways of escaping the throes of the depression that came out of the 1929 market crash, which in turn came out of a high-flying investing decade without regulated reporting. The uncertainty caused by the lack of information produced risk and wild actual returns, both positive and negative. Then, a different psychology seemed to click in, just as it has in other situ-

THE SOCIAL SIGNIFICANCE OF FINANCIAL REPORTING

In general, people tend to think that financial reporting is performed in order to ensure that a corporation's stockholders are informed of the company's activities and its management's achievements. While there is a basis for this stewardship dimension of public reporting, a much more significant social purpose justifies regulating this activity.

As shown in Figure 3-1, public reporting is intended to provide at least some of the financial information needed to make rational investment and credit decisions. In turn, these decisions are concentrated in the capital markets, including large public stock exchanges, venture capital situations, and the banking and leasing industries. Indeed, the capital markets encompass all activities in which investors and creditors turn their cash over to someone else in exchange for potential future cash flows.

But the capital markets serve a much broader purpose than helping investors and creditors earn a return. Specifically, they are one of the engines that make an economy function efficiently. They fulfill this role by creating competition among those who have cash to invest and among those who have future cash flow opportunities to exchange for that cash. Thus, capital providers compete with each other to obtain the highest returns for their risk level while capital seekers compete with each other to obtain the lowest capital cost for their risk level. These competitions work best when all participants have access to an abundance of relevant and reliable financial information.

The more efficient the capital markets are, the more productive the overall economy becomes. If capital resources are available at appropriate prices that match risk and return, managers can use them to create more wealth, which in turn enriches the society as a whole. The greater a society's prosperity (which involves not only wealth creation but wealth distribution), the better off are its members.

When all of these links are put together, we can see that financial reporting is a socially significant activity and that the quest for greater social prosperity is the public policy purpose served by regulating public financial reporting.

ations over history. When the crash finally came, there was very little public confidence in the capital markets, including not just the stock exchanges but also the banking system. The result was a huge economic stagnation that spread rapidly all over the world.[1]

Out of this desperate situation, the SEC was eventually created with the mandate to raise public confidence in the capital markets so that they could start creating and allocating capital more efficiently. This restoration

FIGURE 3-1

Decision-Making Chain of Information Provided by Public Financial Reporting

would, in turn, allow the economy to generate more wealth and distribute it among the population through investment returns, jobs, and commercial activity. Toward this goal, Congress originally endowed the SEC with the power to establish reporting regulations, including accounting principles to be followed in preparing financial statements. (The sidebar on page 32 describes the often overlooked relationship between a society's well-being and the capital markets.)

The initial step toward regulating financial reporting was the provision in the Securities Act of 1933 that requires managers to register their companies' securities before initially offering them to the public.[2] Part of a firm's registration document is a set of its financial statements. This first law was followed quickly by the Securities and Exchange Act of 1934, which required managers of companies with registered securities to go beyond the initial registration report to conduct regular and ongoing public financial reporting. Based on the customs and technology of the time, the choice was made to require abbreviated quarterly reporting, with more complete reports filed annually and in conjunction with proxy solicitations.

After substantial discussion, the designers of the legislation also determined that the public would have more confidence in the capital markets if the reports were perceived to have high quality. Two features were created to promote this higher quality. First, the SEC was granted authority to establish accounting rules to be followed by all registrants. The idea was that uniformity would promote usefulness for comparisons and help end abuse. Second, it was determined that the financial statements would have to be audited by independent public auditors. This requirement was supposed to help boost confidence by eliminating (or at least moderating) the fear that the statements would be management's fabrications instead of legitimate reports about actual events and conditions.

After several years passed, the SEC (which was created by the 1934 Act) decided to abandon its own efforts to define suitable accounting practices and called in the auditing profession. The idea was that these professional accountants were in a better position than the SEC staff lawyers to define rules that would help provide useful information to absentee owners. Although the SEC's decision in 1938 to delegate this authority had its own wisdom, it eventually led to much of the quality problem that we face today in financial reporting.

Once the auditors were given the rule-making authority, they responded as anyone does when they are empowered to make choices. Specifically, they began to use this power to advance and protect what they considered to be their own interests. Perhaps subconsciously, the auditors produced biased reporting principles that did (and still do) reflect their concerns about having defensible practices that allow them to avoid recrimination from disgruntled or otherwise unhappy investors. Unfortunately for the public, the auditors' pursuit of their own interests often caused them to overlook the point that the main purpose for the rules is to provide capital market participants with the information they need to understand what's going on.

Instead of aiding the public by encouraging market efficiency, auditors have produced generally accepted accounting principles (GAAP) and generally accepted auditing standards (GAAS) in a way that tends to make life safer for themselves. To our way of thinking, this auditor-centric mentality has unproductively prevailed into the modern era.[3] For example, the 1980s saw auditors growing concerned over an expanding "expectations gap" between what the public expected and what auditors were able to deliver. In our view, the profession's response was to close that gap by trying to lower those expectations to match up with what the auditors were willing to do instead of raising the quality of what auditors do to match up with the users' expectations. By failing to see the economic advantages of meeting the markets' needs for useful information, the behavior in this case demonstrates our general observation that accountants have displayed monopolists' supply-push thinking instead of demand-pull competitive entrepreneurship.

WHERE DOES THE INFORMATION GO, AND HOW IS IT USED?

Against this backdrop, we can now address another major shortcoming in the political process for establishing financial reporting standards. In particular, we attribute many of the shortcomings in GAAP (and in the application of GAAP) to a deficient concept of who the financial statement users are and what they do with the reported information.

Ostensibly, GAAP and other reporting requirements have been created to protect the interests of individual investors by ensuring that they are fully informed. The underlying assumption behind the regulation is that individual investors ought to receive information directly from management through public communication channels, as shown in Figure 3-2.

While it is true that individual investors often bear the brunt of bad investments and frauds and are thus deserving of full disclosure and protection, we believe that the real linkage between management disclosures and these investors is much more complex. Nonetheless, this simple model is the one most often put forward by the SEC to justify its regulatory powers and activities. For example, one of the timeworn phrases used by the commission to defend regulation is the need for "creating a level playing field" that allows all investors to compete on even terms. In contemplating this image, we have come to question whether it matters that

FIGURE 3-2

An Oversimplified Model of Financial Reporting to Investors

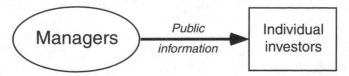

the playing field is level if a single unpadded tennis player is trying to play football against the fully decked-out starting defensive lineup of the Denver Broncos. In the same way, it makes little sense to expect individual investors to be able to compete in the capital markets against the panoply of expert investors and analysts who are in much better positions to make fully informed investment decisions.

Another manifestation of this grossly oversimplified paradigm is found in the practices used to distribute business news through popular media. The information disseminated in these media can only be considered to be news by those who have no other sources of information. In fact, by the time it is broadcast over television, published in a newspaper or magazine, or even posted on a website, it is certainly too old to be used by any investor (sophisticated or otherwise) to earn a return or avoid a loss.

In contrast to the conventional simple worldview, we think actual practice reflects a much different process. Instead of going directly to individuals who then use it to make decisions, relevant information actually passes through various intermediaries, including (1) company specialists, (2) industry analysts, (3) institutional analysts (also called buy-side analysts), (4) financial advisers, and then (5) individuals. Further, it comes through both public and private communication channels. This flow of information is symbolized in Figure 3-3 and discussed in the following paragraphs.

The diagram represents the flow of financial information to and through the capital markets as being much more complicated than the simple level playing field idea contemplated by Congress and defended by the SEC. Instead of that oversimplified situation, we believe that some powerful economic incentives have combined with sufficiently vast and rich capital markets to create the need for various levels of specialists.

At the highest level are financial analysts who specialize in one or at most a few companies. As suggested by the wide arrows flowing into their box in Figure 3-3, these highly competent people are the most likely group to consume the largest amounts of information in public reports. They have this competence because they have studied the company so much that they know nearly as much about it as management does. We also believe it's very important to see that they also have the greatest access to the most effective back channels of private information about particular companies. Their network of sources is sufficiently rich to give them a leg up on other capital market participants who are not as specialized. For what it's worth, we think these individuals are likely to actually know more than management because their objectivity makes them less inclined to believe the company's public information as much as the managers might; they are also less likely than managers to pathologically deny the

FIGURE 3-3

A More Complete Model of Financial Reporting to Investors

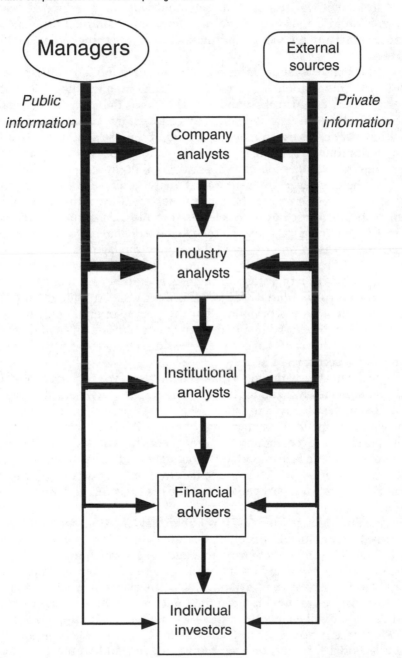

validity of negative information that reflects poorly on management performance. Prior to the SEC's issuance of Regulation FD (for Fair Disclosure) in 2000, it was true that management was also a source of private information for sophisticated analysts. The regulation requires managers to ensure that any releases of information are made at the same time to all parties.[4]

At the next level down in specialization are industry analysts who work with information about a group of similar companies. While they may not know as much about individual firms as the company specialists know, they have an advantage over other investors and analysts because they have better access to reports prepared by those specialists. In addition, these industry specialists can also tap into extensive private information sources that some company specialists cannot reach.

At the next stage are institutional analysts who advise professional investors, most commonly the money managers for mutual funds and pension funds. These buy-side analysts compile the information received from the public reports, the more specialized analysts, and still other external sources in order to help the money managers work their way through their investment strategies and decisions. In effect, these analysts consume a lot of predigested information from other sources that probably turns out to be more useful to them than formal public reports filed with the SEC. It is worth noting that the people operating at this level move more money into different investment products than any others and are thus most likely to have the greatest direct effect on actual market prices of the securities.

At the next level down are financial advisers who serve as individuals' primary gateways into the capital market. These advisers may include commission-based advisers (such as brokers) or fee-based investment advisers and financial planners who help individual investors manage their portfolios. Even though they may be somewhat acquainted with some of the public facts reported by managers and potentially connected with some external private sources, they rely mainly on the information compiled by institutional analysts to make their recommendations to their clients.

Finally, we reach the level of individual investors who are, as we described, championed by regulators. However, we believe that the public information sent to them from management is much too complex and much too old to be of any use in helping them reach optimum or timely decisions. If there is even a modicum of market efficiency, individual investors can never hope to open the mail and read an annual report to find facts that will enable them to anticipate a major future move in the stock's market price. The various specialists would have been aware of those facts days, weeks, or even months earlier and would have made their investment decisions long before the report was printed, much less received by investors through the mail. As we have said, the same is true for so-called business "news" disseminated by television, radio, magazines, or newspapers—by the time it is made public, it is unlikely to have any investment value. Although the Internet speeds up public distribution, it does little or nothing to accelerate the initial market impact of the news. Thus, even online investors are virtually certain to fall behind the extensive and expensive intelligence-gathering efforts of the specialists.

At this point, it is fitting to ask whether this more complex model diminishes the significance of information that is distributed to individual investors. We have to answer that it obviously does. In fact, this model shows that there is little investment value in public information by the time it gets to individual investors in whatever form it arrives.

But, what does this model say in answer to the question of whether *any* value is generated by the process of distributing public information? We just as firmly say that this value does exist. In fact, we think this more complete view elevates the importance of public distribution of timely reports by management because it reduces possible friction in the capital markets by decreasing all of the participants' dependence on secondary and tertiary sources of speculative and otherwise less reliable information. Further, the release of the public information allows users of private information (principally the specialists) to confirm the quality of their sources.

WHAT DOES THIS MODEL MEAN FOR QFR?

We believe that this more complete model contains a key point for Quality Financial Reporting. Specifically, we think it shows that managers are in a position to enjoy significant benefits from reducing some of the inefficiencies created in the capital markets by (1) the virtually total dependence of sophisticated analysts on private information and (2) the delays caused by passing potentially useful information through as many as four filters. By issuing more complete and more consumable reports more often, managers can more quickly and thoroughly reduce capital market uncertainty, as well as reduce the time period in which specialists can use proprietary private information to extract their extra returns. In effect, it is in this time frame that the specialists can trade on their information and bleed off abnormal returns to themselves that would otherwise show up in a lower cost of capital for the corporation. Therefore, managers can enrich themselves and their stockholders by improving the content of their public reports and by preparing and disseminating them as quickly as possible instead of once every three months.

In addition, this model should guide managers in developing their financial reporting strategies. As described in Chapter 2, the seven deadly sins of financial reporting cause managers to report as infrequently, cheaply, obscurely, and minimally as they can. They even use the politically compromised regulatory requirements to justify their own suboptimal activities. Instead, QFR shows that managers would be better off if they would focus their financial reporting strategy on ensuring that the company and industry specialists receive consumable and complete public information as quickly as it can be produced with as much reliability as possible. Because these participants have the greatest financial clout and the best access to timely private information, they are the actors that actually make the markets efficient. In effect, they are the real consumers of the public information, not the unskilled investors who buy and sell in blind obedience to their financial advisers, who are themselves dependent on the specialists. If managers really want to connect with the capital markets to discover and then service their needs, they must start by addressing the needs of these specialists. This strategy is entirely different from managers' being satisfied that the markets are informed simply because their quarterly public reports comply with minimum federal standards and GAAP. It is only by actually identifying and then serving these users' needs with timeliness that managers can draw the capital market participants into close and mutually beneficial relationships like they have with their employees, customers, and suppliers. Again we see the difference between supply-push and demand-pull behavior.

Here, then, is the essence of the QFR revolution: it is not enough for managers to merely comply with regulations created by a political process that appeals to a rationale based on a simplified capital market model. Rather, their financial communications must be sufficient to meet the needs of all levels, not to the exclusion of anyone but certainly not dumbed down to the level of the least sophisticated. All of this means that management must develop and maintain the confidence and trust of the specialists while keeping them well informed. Further, the same useful information must be made available to everyone else at the same time in order to reduce uncertainty and perceived risk. As we mentioned, SEC Regulation FD requires this practice, and we applaud its existence and its potential for increasing the overall quality of public financial information.

THE U.S. SYSTEM—AS GOOD AS IT GETS?

In response to those who consider the regulated financial reporting system in the U.S. to be the best in the world, we readily grant that a great deal of information does flow through the official system. We even concur with the often heard claim that the U.S. financial reporting system is the envy of the world for its transparency, although our assessment of GAAP makes us lean toward describing it as barely translucent instead of transparent. Even if some light does get through when financial statements are prepared with GAAP, the details are often blurred and otherwise indistinct.

Among other things, Total Quality Management should teach us that it is never good enough to simply be the best among an existing group of competitors. Instead, TQM calls on us to keep striving to be the best that we can be before more ambitious competitors get better and pass us by. Thus, however good the U.S. system might be compared to others, it can certainly be improved, as the next two chapters clearly show. Of course, if managers in other parts of the world comprehend the advantages of QFR before U.S. managers get the picture, many of the latter will be left behind in the global competition for capital. However, the beauty of economic incentives and their advantage over regulatory initiatives is the fact that competitive forces quickly kick in. Thus, even if other countries' managers initially outdo U.S. companies, it shouldn't be long until QFR reigns in the U.S. And, if it catches on here first, managers in other countries will be forced to try it themselves.

Therefore, the last thing the SEC and the FASB should do is rest on their laurels after hearing those oft repeated claims of greatness in financial reporting (especially the ones coming from their own lips). After all, the IASB has been created and clearly has the potential and mandate to overtake the FASB in terms of its influence on accounting practices around the world. Indeed, the U.S. stands almost as an island in the global capital markets because international standards are accepted nearly everywhere else.

With this last point being made, we are very firm in our position that the path to higher financial reporting quality doesn't run through Washington or Connecticut or London. Rather, it will start from within the private sector when a few extraordinary top managers comprehend that their financial reporting practices constitute a key value-adding policy tool that has been at best neglected and at worse misapplied with negative results. Once they realize that they can use QFR to compete successfully for lower capital costs, there is no way they will be held down to merely meeting minimum GAAP and SEC regulations. These legal requirements have to be complied with, but there is no reason for management to just stop providing information when they reach those minimums. This idea is the very heart of the QFR revolution that we're trying to spark.

NOTES

1. Some might wonder where the efficient market was when the crash came. Another good point is raised by the question of how stock prices came to be so high when public reporting was so limited. The answers are clear to us. First, market efficiency is largely a function of rapid access to useful

information. Because communications technology in the 1920s was relatively limited, we have concluded that it was unlikely to ever produce, much less sustain, a very high degree of market efficiency. As to the presence of high stock prices in the absence of information, we speculate that unsystematic but nonetheless powerful psychological factors such as avarice, impulse, and herd instinct did (and still can) drive a market into unsustainable heights and depths, notwithstanding efficiency. Of course, only fools and charlatans would claim to understand exactly how the capital markets work.

2. Hence the acronym IPO, which stands for *initial public offering*.

3. It is fair to balance out this criticism by acknowledging that caution in reporting would have been justified in the historical context of the Great Depression. However, this defense cannot rightfully be used to excuse the perpetuation of these overly cautious standards during the second half of the twentieth century and on into the twenty-first.

4. Regulation FD is consistent with the QFR paradigm because it not only promotes trust in management but also provides higher-quality information to all financial statement users. Perhaps not surprisingly, its passage has been protested by some managers who feel they have been deprived of a means of managing their stock prices, although they would never express their thoughts with those words. If pressure ever arises to revoke the regulation, we will testify against that move because we have seen that FD can act as a stimulant for analysts to express demands for higher-quality public information to replace the private information that they are no longer allowed to receive directly from managers.

CHAPTER 4

Why GAAP Aren't Good Enough

Chapter 3 pointed out the hazards of inadequate financial reporting, especially when managers and their accountants make the huge mistake of assuming that GAAP and other regulatory requirements could ever be sufficient for defining the capital markets' needs for high-quality information. This thinking is erroneous because the regulatory system is inevitably political and necessarily unimaginative. Furthermore, the system is not designed to be nimble or innovative. As a result, we can say with confidence that it is not in perfect alignment with the needs of the capital markets. Indeed, the constraints on the system mean that it is necessarily misaligned with those needs. Nonetheless, the overwhelmingly dominant attitude among managers (and their auditors) is that compliance with these minimum standards is all they need to accomplish.

The four axioms show that this attitude leads to incomplete information, uncertainty, risk, and higher capital costs. They also show that these negative consequences can be overcome by applying QFR and going beyond the regulatory minimums.

This chapter takes us into the second phase of launching this QFR revolution by helping managers, their accountants, their auditors, and even their attorneys to comprehend why GAAP aren't good enough for satisfying the markets' demands. To get started, we use this chapter to explain what the political process is, how it works (or doesn't work), and why these gross deficiencies exist. We pound that point home in the next chapter by describing some specific and serious flaws in GAAP. When we're done, we expect that our readers will be very uneasy about depending on the regulations to define the contents of their financial statements.

THE GAAP DUE PROCESS

The current procedures for setting reporting standards at both the FASB and the SEC involve a so-called "due process." Through extensive procedures, a possible new practice is carefully defined and thoroughly debated before a formal proposal is drafted. That proposal is then published to allow the potentially affected parties to explain their concerns and attempt to persuade the standard-setting body to implement, reject, or amend the proposal. The final steps are voting and then publishing the final rule.

In the U.S., at least five constituency groups participate in this due process. The FASB sits in the middle, supposedly beholden to no one, but actually acting in a way that looks (at least to us) like they're giving the most attention to those who make the most noise.

As shown in Figure 4-1, these five constituents are preparers, auditors, statement users, regulators, and academics. The following paragraphs describe each of their interests and their typical actions and impacts on the process.

FIGURE 4-1

The FASB and Its Constituents

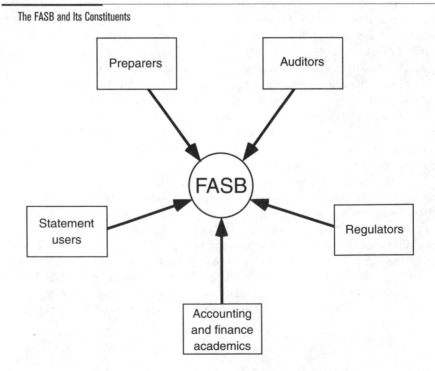

Preparers

A perhaps surprisingly significant role is played in the due process by managers, who are often called *financial statement preparers* or merely *preparers*.[1] Because of their desire to remain in control of their own situation, and perhaps because they think that the capital markets are greatly influenced by public financial statements, many of them try to use the due process to prevent change. That is, they want to protect their ability to mold the statements and accompanying disclosures to permit them to manage (or manipulate) their financial images. In a phrase, they are essentially concerned with "looking good" to the capital markets. Of course, they cannot publicly state this rationale when they participate in the FASB's process because doing so would officially uncloak their readily apparent self-serving attitude. As a result, they tend to verbally justify their positions on the issues with appeals to obsolete theoretical reporting concepts rooted in historical costs, allocations, and smoothing. They also tend to argue that their costs of complying with new reporting requirements will be too high. And, despite the widespread acknowledgement of the markets' ability to handle sophisticated and complex reports, they often insist that a new standard will only confuse investors. However, when we scratch below the surface of these weak and unsupported claims, we see that they are designed only to rationalize the status quo without seriously considering the possibility of improving.

From our point of view, the most unfortunate aspect of preparers' participation in the due process is that they much too frequently walk on its dark side by applying their substantial political power to support their view. These pressures consist of such things as mass mailings of negative comment letters, threats to withdraw their support from the FASB, and appeals to important legislators and other government officials to intimidate the board in particular and private-sector standard setting in general.

Beyond any doubt, preparers have every right to participate in the due process because the outcome affects what they do and what they look like. Where they go astray is in thinking that their own interests have a higher priority in the system than others' priorities. Their even bigger mistake is thinking that using political power to affect the contents of public financial reports will actually produce higher security prices. If anything, we think the consequence of this hardball political action is nothing other than incomplete information that increases uncertainty and reduces security prices instead of increasing them.

Auditors

Although auditors are ostensibly the first line of defense of the public interest against management abuse of the reporting system, they, too, operate within their own biases and routinely attempt to protect their own interests at least as they perceive them. Like managers, auditors tend to want to protect the status quo because they have well-established procedures for auditing current practices. They also prefer what they claim are more conservative accounting practices that are biased to reduce amounts reported for revenues, increase amounts of reported expenses, reduce amounts reported for assets, and increase amounts reported for liabilities.

In a phrase, we conclude that many of today's auditors act as if they want to work only with "safe" information that they can successfully defend when called upon in court to justify their decisions. That is, the information quality that they desire the most is *defensibility*. This tendency helps explain (at least to us) why so much of the content produced under existing GAAP is rooted in past historical costs instead of current market values.

The obvious explanation for this obsession with past numbers is that they are safe to audit because they are derived from a paper trail of signed historical documents. Of course, the auditors' defense of the status quo actually reflects their concerns for their own safety, although they are compelled by political reasons to claim that they are only looking after the safety of capital market participants who are supposedly relying on these reports.

Based on our observations in a great many settings, this caution is more easily explained by the superior defensibility of time-honored practices. After all, one of the greatest defenses in common law courts is that "everybody is doing it." This test is, of course, totally irrelevant to assessing the usefulness of the published information for helping financial statement users assess cash flow prospects. The fact that a procedure is widely used in preparing financial statements does not necessarily mean that it produces information that is useful for making decisions. As a corollary, the fact that a procedure is not being applied in practice does not mean that it would necessarily fail to provide useful information if it were to be applied.

The role played by auditors in the due process is even more ambiguous because the auditors' clients in the current environment are the same financial statement preparers that they are supposed to be checking up on. Thus, the very parties who are supposed to be reined in by auditors are the ones who pay them to perform the audits. Even though this arrangement has existed from the beginning,[2] the truth is that it takes an extraordinarily strong constitution for auditors to stand up to the managers who pay their fees. In addition to the problems that this arrangement creates concerning the trustworthiness of the statements, it also makes it very difficult for auditors to take stands in the rule-making due process that are contrary to the arguments being asserted by their clients. In this sense, the standard-setting process is potentially corrupted by close relationships between the preparers and their auditors.

Statement Users

On the surface, one might think (or at least hope) that financial statement users would be the most influential group involved in the due process for setting accounting standards. However, as we explained in the prologue, financial reporting has been and is very much supply driven instead of demand driven. It is only within the past 10 years or so that the FASB has proactively sought out users' opinions. Before then—and still continuing pretty much down through today—most users have shied away from participating in these debates. Perhaps they have done so because they trust the standard setters to act on their behalf. Alternatively, they may act this way because they doubt their ability to actually affect the standard setters' votes on the final standards by mobilizing sufficient political power to overcome the preparers' efforts.

It is also possible that users, at least sophisticated ones, prefer the status quo because they have developed secondary sources of private information that allow them to excel in predicting future cash flows. If they have, then the last thing they would want would be new rules that would turn this valuable private information into a public good available to all. Thus, it is reasonable to speculate that some strong economic motives diminish the quantity and quality of input to the due process from some users.

Although there is reason to be optimistic about the future based on the recent past, users have historically tended to have less participation and even less impact on the output of the due process than preparers and auditors. For what it's worth, they have also provided relatively few of the cash contributions that the Financial Accounting Foundation needs to maintain the FASB's budget.

Regulators

In general, the SEC keeps a low public profile when dealing with the FASB's due process, and vice versa. After all, the SEC delegated some of its rule-making authority for GAAP to the FASB, and it behooves both of them to stay out of each other's way.

However, it would be a mistake to think that representatives of these two agencies, even at the highest levels, do not communicate on the proposed changes and share their views. Regulators have indeed significantly influenced the content of GAAP, and not always for the public's benefit. For example, as we will describe later in this chapter, the SEC rejected the FASB's proposed change in accounting for oil and gas exploration costs and allowed the status quo to remain intact. Other less obvious examples also exist.

The bottom line is that the SEC's relationship with the FASB is essential for the board's existence. Without the power of the SEC behind it (expressed in the commission's *Accounting Series Release 150* in 1973, the board's first year of operations), the FASB would not be much more than an accounting debate club. Therefore, one has to assume that the board members are always conscious of the commission when they set their agenda, define the issues, debate the alternatives, and vote on a resolution.

Academics

Of the five groups participating in the due process, perhaps accounting and finance academics could have the greatest influence in advancing the public's interest in improving the quality of GAAP. After all, they have little if any direct interest in the outcome of the process. Perhaps coincidentally, they also have little if any political power to leverage against the FASB because they do not provide any of the board's funds and have little impact on the political processes for appointing and reappointing board members.

Another likely explanation for the lack of impact is academics' unfamiliarity with the sorts of issues that actually drive the political process, with the consequence that their comments and suggestions turn out to be fundamentally irrelevant to the questions being debated. Still another point is that many academicians consider their role to be scientific observers of the process instead of participants.

Whatever the reason, the fact remains that the potentially objective and creative voices of professors are seldom heard in the FASB's debates. Naturally, we think the outcome suffers as a result.

UNDERSTANDING WHAT GAAP CAN AND CANNOT DO

As we mentioned, the foundation for the due process is the idea that financial reporting quality will be improved with widespread participation in setting standards for informing the capital markets. However, because of the many conflicting interests perceived and protected by the different groups, the due process has virtually always been an adversarial struggle over what sort of incomplete information managers can be allowed to pass down to the capital markets through their financial statements. Instead of a civil debate over which practices would reduce uncertainty the most, the process almost always turns into bitter fights over who has the right to tell who what they ought to do. It isn't a pretty scene.

We cannot overemphasize the next point: the four axioms show that these due process battles are empty and otherwise pointless because they are based on the fatally flawed premise that implementing an accounting standard can affect the information that the markets actually work with.

In fact, all an accounting standard can do is affect the *content* of public financial reports. Regardless of who issues it or what the due process looks like, no accounting rule can force capital market participants to actually believe or act on that content. In fact, the users have the unrestrained ability to decide for themselves whether to rely on the information as is, use it after they modify it, or simply ignore it, all according to their own wishes. In the same way, no accounting rule can ever prevent market participants from seeking out other private information from other sources that they consider to be more useful. Further, no rule can keep them from acting on this other information exactly as they wish.[3]

Despite the clarity of this point of view, we believe that it has not actually influenced the U.S. standard-setting process throughout its nearly 70 years of life. Many of today's participants in the due process, including FASB members, still continue to act as if they are oblivious to the market participants' ability to decide what they will believe. It is incredible that so many members of the preparer constituency continue to wage huge political battles with the FASB in the process of resisting new standards that would reveal new useful information to the capital markets. As a result, we see yet again that it is imperative for managers to understand why mere minimum compliance with GAAP and SEC regulations is not sufficient for fully informing the capital markets or otherwise reducing their uncertainty.

SUMMING UP

Despite all these obvious flaws, today's standard-setting process lumbers on, not unlike a triceratops stumbling around in the post-comet cold and darkness at the end of the Late Cretaceous period, obliviously making one compromise after the other in order to temporarily defer extinction. Invariably, these compromises accommodate objections raised by managers and auditors who so clearly seem to be unaware of the enormous economic power inherent in the four axioms. These compromises show us that the FASB almost always responds politically to its critics and neglects the public's need for the capital markets to be presented with complete and useful public information (even if some sophisticated users don't want it to be made public).

As we suggested at the beginning, the main point of this chapter is that the quality of financial reporting under GAAP is severely flawed. In particular, we believe that the current standard-setting system does not really make anyone better off. Here are our thoughts on how the constituent groups are actually affected by the politicized due process that shapes GAAP.

Preparers Are Not Served

Because managers are allowed to report minimum amounts under GAAP without recrimination, they actually are disadvantaged because they are not challenged to boost the quality of the information in their reports. As a result, they do not reap the benefits of the lower capital costs and higher security prices that would follow from sending more useful information to the capital markets. Instead, their apparent political victories in shaping the standards seem to lull them into the sin of minimal reporting. Without a doubt, they are missing tremendous opportunities for growth and improvement.

Auditors Are Not Served

In today's financial reporting system, auditors have the task of attesting to management's compliance with technical GAAP. In a QFR world, they would be charged with attesting to the presence or absence of the information's truthfulness and usefulness. As harsh as it might seem, we think that essentially the only message today's auditors send to users is that they should consider the financial statements to be essentially useless because they comply with politically derived accounting principles.

In our view, auditors' intellects, training, experience, and integrity are grossly underutilized (even wasted) when all they do is perform compliance audits. As we see it, they do not add nearly as much value to management's financial reports as they could, and society is all the poorer for the waste. So are the auditors, because they could make so much more money by actually adding more value to their clients' financial statements. Unlike many, however we don't think the answer is for the auditing profession to put aside the attest function and replace it with other things.[4] In fact, one reason that we're so enthusiastic about QFR is that we believe the revolution is an important key to greatly increasing auditors' ability to add value by reducing uncertainty about the quality of the information included in management's reports.

Financial Statement Users Are Not Served

Because users know that they cannot rely on GAAP financial statements to be fully informative, they have to turn to expensive secondary and tertiary sources that produce relatively unreliable information. In addition to exerting all these redundant wasted efforts trying to discover what management already knows but refuses to report, users are forced to operate in a context that is more risky than necessary.

The Public Is Not Served

Because the current system creates so much wasted effort by management in complying with inadequate rules, by auditors in attesting to that compliance, and by users in their perpetual striving to supplement published reports with private information, public financial reporting does little if anything to promote the efficiency of the capital markets and the broader economy. Indeed, all the guessing by market participants about unreported relevant facts that could be reliably reported causes the overall cost of capital to be higher than necessary, thereby retarding economic growth and inhibiting stability.

Enough Is Enough

How can we be so confident in our unconventional conclusions? At the risk of losing our modesty, we've been through the hoops. We've been involved in the due process at various levels and on both sides, and we've been observers and commentators on the process for a great many years. We are also in the classroom every week trying (often in vain) to make sense out of GAAP for the next generation of accountants. We have grown weary of defending what now looks to us to be an indefensibly archaic and inefficient system.

PROOF IN THE PUDDING

Perhaps our description of the political process will be more credible to the incredulous if we present a few examples of the compromises it has produced. What the following situations all have in common is a shortfall in the information content of financial statements caused by compromises that arose from opposition to changes that would have provided more complete reporting. As you will see, the opposition came from managers, their auditors, or both.

Research and Development

To keep managers from reporting assets that might not exist, *Statement of Financial Accounting Standards No. 2* (SFAS 2) requires all research and development costs to be expensed, just as if all the company's efforts to find new knowledge and create new products are inevitably going to be unsuccessful with no further effects on the company's future cash flows. In this case, the FASB's concern for auditors' safety may have won out over managers' interests in looking good, while users don't get anything that helps them project future cash flows from the R&D. Although it would probably be to managers' benefit to describe their R&D efforts narratively, it appears that not very many of them try to do that.

Leases

Instead of requiring managers to capitalize all leases and thus do away with off-balance-sheet financing, the FASB stuck with the old concept that only some leases should be capitalized. The result in SFAS 13 is a set of criteria that are relatively easy for managers to elude. Indeed, skeptics like us might consider the criteria to be nothing more than guidelines for showing preparers who want to try to mislead the markets how to leave some assets and liabilities off their balance sheets. We think this compromised standard addressed the needs of auditors for clear bright-line distinctions instead of judgment calls. At the same time, it has made it possible for managers to escape the requirements for asset and liability recognition. Of course, users are left with incomplete financial statements, which, in turn, increase uncertainty and the cost of capital.

Troubled Debt

We believe that the most useful way to account for troubled debt situations is for both the debtor and creditor to write down (to smaller amounts), respectively, the liability and the receivable to market value under the new circumstances. That is, the debtors gain by debt forgiveness while creditors lose by ending up with a claim against the debtors for a smaller amount. After hearing from bankers, the FASB compromised in SFAS 15 by minimizing the size of the lender's loss for troubled debt. The gross shortcoming in this original standard was reduced but not eliminated by the new revised version (SFAS 114) that still allows bankers to avoid writing down their receivables to realistic market-based amounts. Thus, users are presented with incomplete and otherwise unreliable information, with the same negative consequences on the creditors' cost of capital and stock prices.

Oil and Gas Exploration

As part of the 1970s energy crisis, Congress charged the SEC with coming up with uniform accounting for oil and gas exploration costs. In proper

political fashion, the SEC passed the issue to the FASB, which concluded
in SFAS 19 that the costs of dry holes should be expensed. Managers of
large oil companies loved this treatment because it gave them ammuni-
tion (in the form of lower reported earnings) for showing their critics that
they weren't profiting from the crisis. Managers of small oil exploration
companies hated it because it cut their reported net incomes. Instead of
expensing, they wanted to capitalize the costs so that they could look better in the financial statements. Thus, they hoped to use GAAP to make dry
holes look like assets so that they could mislead investors into thinking
they owned something of value; at the same time, they wanted to avoid
deducting the costs on their income statements so that they could appear
to be more profitable. Responding to pressure from Congress, which had
heard from the small oil operators, the SEC rejected SFAS 19, and the FASB
went on to issue SFAS 25 that allows management to decide. This compromise still stands today, more than 20 years later, and managers of both
large and small oil and gas companies somehow think that keeping silent
and forcing capital market participants to guess important financial measures somehow leads to higher stock prices than would ensue if they
knew more of the truth. These managers are wrong, of course.

Foreign Currency

After currency exchange rates were unpegged in the 1970s, managers
found themselves subject to new real financial risks from changes in the
measures of assets and liabilities located in other countries created by
changes in currency exchange rates. The FASB acted quickly by issuing
SFAS 8 that required these exchange rate gains and losses to be reported
currently on income statements. Managers objected to revealing this real
volatility, and the FASB eventually accommodated them in SFAS 52,
which *conceals* the volatility by relegating these gains and losses to the
equity section of the balance sheet. The real economic gains and losses
still exist, of course, and are just as real as they always were. The only
difference is that they're not reported openly. Stock prices reflect the
reality of the higher underlying risk, not this false image. Indeed, the
existence of the false image can do nothing to increase security prices,
either.

Pensions and Retiree Medical Benefits

Through events that we'll describe more completely in the next chapter,
the FASB found itself in a highly controversial situation as it tried to
reform accounting for the consequences of agreeing to pay defined pension benefits and provide other types of benefits to former employees

after retirement. Under the old method established by the FASB's most immediate predecessor, the Accounting Principles Board, employers reported a pension expense essentially equal to the amount of cash that they put in special pension funds to pay these benefits. More importantly, they did not report a liability for unpaid benefits that the employees had already earned. When the FASB proposed changing to a system that would reveal more truth, the preparer constituency unloaded with a variety of threats, including curtailed donations for funding the board's budget. As before, a majority of the board members compromised in SFAS 87 and SFAS 105 by creating methods that rely heavily on the footnotes to convey the useful information while totally insulating *reported* earnings from volatility. This system actually causes the income statement to describe the expenses for pension and other benefits using numbers based on hypothetical events that were *expected* to happen instead of actual events that really *did* happen. The consequence is incomplete information, which, contrary to management's hopes, inevitably causes lower stock prices despite the prettier (but false) pictures.

Cash Flow Statements

The cash flow statement is probably the most ancient of the financial statements and surely the easiest to comprehend because all it is supposed to do is describe where cash came from and what happened to it. Despite its history, though, the statement disappeared from the customary set provided to the capital markets. When interest in it more or less spontaneously revived in the 1980s, the FASB faced the unusual situation of riding a wave of popularity in favor of producing a new standard that would satisfy the needs and wants of managers, auditors, and users. However, a kink developed when the board proposed requiring the more informative direct method of reporting operating cash flow instead of the more familiar but less informative indirect method.[5] Despite clear calls for the direct method from organizations representing financial statement users, the board heard preparers say they didn't know how to apply it and then went on in SFAS 95 to merely recommend the direct method while allowing the indirect method. In a resounding affirmation that they are still engaged in supply-push thinking, managers of more than 99 percent of public companies have ignored the recommendation and left the users' demands unfulfilled. It should also be noted that the board also appeased preparers by making the indirect method easier by including all interest payments in operating cash flows even though they clearly arise from financing activities. All income tax payments are also included in operations even when they're triggered by financing or investing events. Yet again, the board bowed to the supply-based wishes of management instead of promoting the demand-derived interests of users, as well as the public's interest.

Investments

For various reasons, managers invest their companies' funds in debt and equity securities issued by other companies to earn returns through regular cash flows (interest and dividends) and potential appreciation. In doing so, they face risks that the anticipated regular cash flows will turn irregular and that the hoped-for appreciation will actually turn out to be depreciation. As an accommodation to auditors who did not want to allow market values into the financial statements even in these circumstances, investments were accounted for at cost. In the 1970s, the FASB issued SFAS 12 that required the lower of cost or market method to be applied, with supplemental disclosure of market values that were higher than cost. Upon returning to the issues in the 1990s, the board proposed reporting all investments at market value while putting unrealized gains and losses from value changes on the income statement (whether the asset was sold or not). The preparer constituency objected, especially the banking industry (including Federal Reserve Chairman Alan Greenspan), claiming that this practice would destabilize public confidence in the banking system by creating intolerable volatility in banks' earnings. Rightly so, the board initially responded that it was only trying to reveal volatility that was being concealed under existing GAAP. Nonetheless, the bankers' unrelenting political pressure caused the board to compromise in SFAS 115 by permitting managers to identify three portfolios based on their intent (sell, maybe sell someday, hold to maturity). Depending on the category, unrealized gains and losses are reported on either the income statement, the balance sheet, or nowhere at all. Management got its wish and users were left uninformed. Oblivious to the four axioms, managers celebrated the supposed political victory that would allow them to keep their own stock prices high by withholding relevant information from the capital markets. The board gained by surviving to compromise another day. The rest of us were left holding an empty bag.

Stock Options

When the Accounting Principles Board faced the issue of whether to report an expense when management grants stock options to employees (including themselves), it punted when it issued its Opinion 25 in 1972 by saying that the employer's income statement will not show any expense unless the market value of the stock exceeds the option price on the grant date. This treatment created in many managers' minds a wonderful opportunity to pay themselves large amounts of compensation without reporting an expense. When the real but still unreported expense reached very large proportions, the FASB returned to the issue in the early 1990s and proposed that an expense be reported equal to the value of the options on the grant date. Exactly as we expected, the preparer constituency exploded and threatened the board with extinction, mainly by calling on members of Congress to bombard the board with threats. Missing a big point, the managers were hugely relieved when the board compromised in SFAS 123 by merely recommending that they report an expense on the income statement while permitting the alternative of reporting its amount in a pro forma footnote. They were completely oblivious to two ideas: (1) the information is just as available to the capital markets whether it is in the footnote or the income statement, and (2) putting it in the footnote makes it harder to find. More significantly, choosing the footnote treatment creates the clear impression that management lacks candor and trustworthiness, thus producing more uncertainty for the capital markets. Virtually all managers have acted out of this ignorance by choosing the low road of disclosure instead of recognition.[6]

Combinations and Goodwill

Accounting for business combinations and goodwill is yet another example of how managers applied political pressure to preserve their appearances despite the obvious destruction of the financial statements' ability to reduce uncertainty. The issue was the question that arises when one company acquires another or when the managers of two companies decide to merge. Specifically, the question asks how to report the assets and liabilities of the new merged entity on its balance sheet. Under one view, called *new basis*, all assets and liabilities owned by both companies are restated to their market values at the acquisition date. Under another, called *purchase*, the acquired company's assets and liabilities are restated to market value, with any excess purchase price allocated to an intangible asset called *goodwill*. Prior to 2001, this amount was then amortized systematically against the new entity's future reported earnings. The acquirer's assets and liabilities are carried forward at their GAAP book values without acknowledging their market values at the purchase date. Under a third method, called *pooling*, the assets and liabilities of both parties are left with their GAAP book values; as a result, pooling provides by far the most incomplete description of the business combination.

Being focused only on reported earnings and obsessed with looking good, managers overwhelmingly preferred pooling.[7] The APB tried to eliminate pooling in the late 1960s but could only restrict its use by putting 12 qualifying criteria in place. Never letting excessive preparation costs get in the way of looking good in the financial statements (especially when the stockholders eventually pay or otherwise bear their burden), managers hired lawyers and worked with their auditors to qualify purchases as poolings and then sat back with a smile waiting for stock prices to shoot up. They were oblivious to the effect of the four axioms and ignored the drag on stock prices created by the extra costs and the negative effect of the fact that the markets would clearly understand (1) that the reported earnings are bogus and (2) that the managers are untrustworthy. With this kind of sand in its gears, the capital market simply cannot function very efficiently.

The FASB courageously returned to the issue after nearly 30 years and proposed that pooling be eliminated. It also proposed shortening the amortization life of the goodwill recorded for purchases. As we have come to expect, the outcries from preparers were outrageous, with many managers actually threatening to just stop merging if they couldn't pool. (Obviously, they missed the point that they were declaring to the whole world that they are both ignorant of capital market efficiency and totally focused on appearances rather than economic realities.) They also rushed to complete pending pooling deals before the standard's effective date.

Again, as we have learned to anticipate, the FASB decided to pull its punch and caved in once again to preparers. Even though it did carry through by eliminating any new poolings in SFAS 141, the FASB did nothing to force restatements to eliminate the residual effects of previous poolings. The board members also retreated in SFAS 142 by doing away with systematic amortization of the so-called goodwill and trusting these same untrustworthy managers to write it off as soon as they think it has lost value below its cost. Yet again, a standard gives management a choice between complete reporting that tells more of the truth and incomplete reporting that makes them look good. As far as we're concerned, ignorance of the four axioms will cause many preparers to postpone writing off the goodwill, despite the inevitable consequence that the incomplete information and the lack of forthrightness will reduce their stock prices.

WHAT'S THE POINT?

Surely all these illustrations have made our point—managers who justify their financial reporting policies on the basis that they fully comply with GAAP are totally missing the fact that *GAAP are completely inadequate for the task of defining high quality.* Instead, virtually from the beginning, the standard-setting process has produced flawed compromises that create rather than limit management discretion. The supposed beneficiaries of the compromises are the managers because they are allowed to manipulate their images. Those managers are, of course, mistaken in thinking this freedom to look good actually works in their favor because they don't yet understand the four axioms.

To reiterate, the ultimate consequence of all this political behavior is that the quality of GAAP is insufficient for producing useful and comparable financial statements. The next chapter expands on this theme by describing many more places where GAAP produce uninformative financial statements.

NOTES

1. In displaying what we have always seen as inappropriate self-centeredness, members of the preparer group generally prefer to call themselves *the business community*, as if no one else is part of that larger constituency. Because we see the business community as all-inclusive rather than narrowly exclusive, we use the term *preparers* to refer to top managers and the accountants who work for them.

2. It's possible that it dates back to when people who were about to be beheaded would pay their executioners special fees to do their work well.

3. To be perfectly clear, we are not arguing for abolishing insider trading rules that are designed to keep investors from acting on unfairly obtained information. There are good arguments that these rules increase investors' confidence in the markets and thereby reduce perceived risk, thus bringing down the cost of capital for all firms. These rules are also good public policy from the point of view that they restrain the actions of managers who are, society maintains, fundamentally the stewards of the stockholders' property.

4. We find it difficult to swallow that some who occupy leadership positions in the accounting profession have suggested that CPAs should give up on auditing and focus on such things as developing a practice in assessing the quality of care for elderly persons. No matter how valuable that service might be, we are at a total loss to see how a CPA's training and expertise can be considered to be fully used in those nonfinancial settings, especially when there is a huge demand for more useful financial statements.

5. The direct method reports the gross cash received less the gross cash payments made for various operating items. Under the indirect method, the statement reports only the net amount of cash generated (or used) through an invariably obtuse and otherwise difficult-to-understand reconciliation of net income to this net cash flow.

6. SFAS 123 is mentioned numerous times in this book because it is typical of what happens when a misdirected political process is applied to financial reporting issues. The consequence is inevitably less informative financial statements that drive stock prices down despite making management look better.

7. Pooling also was attractive to managers because it requires the acquiring company to report the acquired company's preacquisition earnings as its own. Thus, an acquirer could buy a company just before the end of the fiscal year and boost its reported earnings on its income statement by simply adding in the reported earnings of the acquired company, despite the fact that they were earned before the merger occurred.

CHAPTER 5

PEAP, WYWAP, and POOP

In describing the limitations of the GAAP process, the previous chapter discussed some specific shortcomings of particular standards and opinions that were created because the standard-setting system produces countless political compromises. This chapter also describes shortcomings in the standards, this time with the purpose of pounding home our very important point that Quality Financial Reporting is needed because GAAP are thoroughly deficient for fully informing the capital markets.

For a little fun that helps that point get made, we present in the sidebar one of our columns from *Accounting Today* as a commentary on the general theme of inadequacy that runs throughout all GAAP.[1]

WHAT IF GOLFERS USED GAAP TO KEEP THEIR SCORE?

For several reasons, we have been thinking about golf lately, and it's occurred to us that the game would be a lot different if players kept score using GAAP. Along those lines, we've imagined that a standard setting agency for scoring might create principles for a "Generally Accepted Golf Scoring" system called GAGS.

Of course, one conspicuous difference would be that the scorecard would include ten pages of footnotes.

Included in GAGS would be the practice of allocating a predicted number of putts per round among the holes expected to be played, all without regard to the actual number. For example, it might be common to allocate 2 putts to each hole. While this practice would eliminate all fear of the three-

WHAT IF GOLFERS USED GAAP TO KEEP THEIR SCORE? (Continued)

putt, it would also do away with one-putts and chip-ins, but that would be the price of eliminating both volatility and the risk associated with reporting what really happens.

Another GAGS principle would allow off-scorecard-sand-shots when certain criteria are avoided. Even though anyone could observe that a ball landed in the trap and that the golfer took several shots to get it onto the green, the rules would allow players to leave those strokes out of the score simply because they didn't *intend* for the ball to wind up in the sand and didn't want to look bad.

Another popular feature of GAGS would be the deferral of strokes in excess of par. Under this system, players would record no score higher than par on any hole despite actually having a bogey, double bogey, or worse. The excess strokes would simply be deferred without penalty until they could be offset against birdies or eagles that might be scored in rounds to be played in the future, if ever. Again, the goal would be to eliminate volatility by destroying any connection between the carded scores and actual results.

Another standard would apply the lower-of-past-or-present-score method. Under this practice, golfers would maintain records of the lowest score ever achieved on each hole. Then, during a real round, they would enter an actual score on a given hole only if it was lower than their previous low score.

One more feature of GAGS would include pairs of alternative practices, one preferable and the other merely acceptable. For example, consider shots into water hazards. When players hit a ball into the drink, they would have the option of adding that stroke plus a penalty to their recorded score or merely disclosing them in an arcane footnote that shows the *pro forma* score computed as if the shots had actually been counted.

Now, imagine what would happen when golfers using GAGS tried to compete in tournaments with players who apply the strict rules of golf. Further, suppose that all spectators are aware of GAGS but only want to know the real number of strokes taken. Under these circumstances, isn't it true that the prize money would go to the players who have the fewest actual strokes instead of those who merely report the smallest number?

It doesn't take much imagination to see the connections between GAGS and GAAP.

- The really helpful information appears in the footnotes, not the financial statements.

- Instead of allocating putts equally among holes, accountants allocate depreciation equally among years without ever checking to see what happened to the asset's *real* value.

WHAT IF GOLFERS USED GAAP TO KEEP THEIR SCORE? (Concluded)

- Carefully crafted agreements allow lease liabilities to be left off the balance sheet.

- Lower-of-cost-or-market is still applied to inventories; even though it is no longer applied to investments, FASB requires managers to write down impaired assets but forbids writing up enhanced assets.

- The deferral method causes companies that actually pay income taxes to postpone reporting the expense until later years if and when reported pretax income is higher. Both of us personally gag over the way undesired gains and losses for defined benefit pension plans are deferred simply to avoid reporting the volatile truth.

- SFAS 123 allows managers to describe options-based compensation in *pro forma* footnotes instead of deducting it from reported earnings.

What's important to realize is that the capital market doesn't consist of ignorant or complacent spectators; instead, its sophisticated participants watch each public company carefully and develop their own scorecards based on actual events without believing the compromised, predicted, smoothed, deferred, and grossly incomplete and misleading numbers in GAAP reports. The market's prize money goes to those who create greater future cash flow potential instead of those who fabricate the highest *reported* earnings.

This analogy shows that anyone is foolish to believe that GAAP statements even approximate actual results and conditions. Just as the winner in a strict rules tournament has the lowest number of actual strokes, winners in the capital market are managers who are most likely to achieve the highest *real* future earnings and cash flows. Even if they report the occasional bad news with candor as soon as it happens, the gallery cheers them on, and they are still eligible to compete in the future. The only permanent losers are cheaters who are likely to be banished from competing at the highest level.

It's long past time for a change in outlook and practice. Because the standard setting process is so compromised by political pressure and so characterized by ducking hard issues (like goodwill), the financial statements don't reflect anything that really happens or exists. The capital market knows it and stock prices reflect it. Smart managers should stop fooling themselves because they sure aren't fooling anyone else.

In closing, let's go to the first tee for the final round of the British Open: *Fans, the championship is over. Lyon Forrest and Mel Michaelson have just compared their anticipated scores for today's rounds and Michaelson has won the tournament because his predicted score of 62 is lower than the 64 that Forrest expected to shoot. What an amazing turn of events and a great victory powered by one of the sport's greatest imaginations!*

Nonsense, but then so are most managers' GAAP earnings announcements.

So, what is the point of this slightly too long golf joke? It's really this simple—because of all the compromises and conflicting interests in the due process, there is little similarity between what management reports in GAAP financial statements and what has actually happened to a company's assets and liabilities. By staying anchored in the past and by making imaginative assumptions instead of fact-based observations, it turns out that GAAP financial statements present a great deal of nonfactual information. Even though the statements are prepared in accordance with GAAP and survive careful and meticulous audits, they are nothing but the products of applying flexible rules that are disconnected from reality. There is no way that this information can begin to fully meet the capital markets' need to predict future cash flows from firms.

WHAT SHOULD FINANCIAL REPORTING ACCOMPLISH?

Before continuing our criticism of GAAP, it makes sense for us to describe what we think financial reporting ought to accomplish. In doing so, our readers can understand more completely why we think current principles are so inadequate for reducing uncertainty, decreasing risk, producing a lower cost of capital, and generating higher security prices.

Of course, book after book and article after article have already been written on the subject of what financial reporting ought to accomplish. Out of all these, we attribute the most helpfulness to the objective devised by the FASB in its Conceptual Framework project. Even though we quoted it in Chapter 2, we think it's worth repeating here:

> Financial reporting should provide information that is useful to present and potential investors and creditors and other [financial statement] users in making rational investment, credit, and similar decisions. (SFAC 1, par. 34)

We find this objective to be helpful because it focuses on the users of the information instead of those who prepare or audit the reports. Thus, it presents a demand-driven perspective rather than the traditional supply-based perspective. We also like the idea that financial reports should reach out to the entire capital markets, not just those who have already invested in or loaned to the entity. Finally, we support the notion that the decisions must be rational. We find this point important for debunking claims that GAAP financial statements must be suitable because people use them. The need for rationality tells us that the fact that some items in financial statements are *used* to make decisions does not necessarily mean that they are *useful* for making them.

The FASB went on to interpret this definition by asserting that decisions are rational if they involve assessing the amount, timing, and uncertainty of the cash flows that the investors and creditors might receive in the future. The board then took another step by suggesting that these assessments will follow after the investors and creditors assess the amount, timing, and uncertainty of the future cash flows that the *reporting entity* might receive.

In preferring this objective, we reject others that prescribe that financial reporting should only help managers manage or help existing stockholders gauge management's stewardship. We do think, however, that useful information for investors and creditors will also serve both of these secondary purposes.

Public Policy and Accounting Standards

We resoundingly reject any suggestion that regulators should try to use financial reports to advance any public policy goal other than achieving fully informed capital markets. To pursue other policies by shaping financial statement content simply means that the policy makers are vainly hoping that they can fool the markets into believing untruthful reports so that the investors and creditors will make decisions that benefit someone else besides themselves. For example, some managers argued to the FASB that the board should encourage managers to conduct research and development programs by allowing them to capitalize those costs as assets on the balance sheet instead of expensing them on the income statement. In effect, the argument holds that it's fine to put a potentially false asset on the balance sheet to persuade investors and creditors to think the company is better off so that they will pay more for its stock. Of course, it is not advantageous for those investors and creditors to pay more than the stock is worth, and only dubious ethics would lead anyone to propose that it would be legitimate to use false information to get them to do so. Another nail in the coffin of the policy argument is that it rests on a premise that the markets are inefficient and therefore not capable of knowing when they are being lied to and lacking access to better information from other sources.

Nonetheless, opponents of change will dig up any old reason to help make their case, including this inadequate public policy rationale. In fact, it was actually used by SEC Commissioner J. Carter Beese as he went on the stump tour in the early 1990s to speak against the FASB's proposal for recording an expense for stock options.[2] He said that the board and the commission needed to protect companies in the high-tech industry in the U.S. by allowing them to avoid reporting this cost. Even if this blatant ruse would have worked (which could not happen), the consequence would have been that stockholders would pay too much for their stock and would earn an inadequate return for their risk. Frankly, we just don't see how anyone, much less one of the top securities regulators in the world, could possibly believe these vacuous and wrongheaded arguments.

To reiterate our point (which we also made in Chapter 4), financial accounting standards can only affect the content of GAAP financial statements. They cannot force investors and creditors to believe or act on that content, and they cannot keep investors and creditors from finding useful information in other places. The best use of standards is to raise the minimum level of quality for all financial statements by moving them toward providing greater amounts of information that is more useful for making rational decisions.

WHAT SHOULD FINANCIAL STATEMENTS CONTAIN?

So, what would the financial statements look like if this objective of providing useful information were to be actually pursued? With regard to the balance sheet, we envision that it would be comprehensive in the sense that it would present information about all assets that the entity owns and all liabilities that the entity owes. Further, it would not report anything as an asset or a liability when it is not. It would describe the assets and liabilities using their current market values because those amounts are the most reliable consensus estimate of the intrinsic value of the future cash flows that reflects their amount, timing, and uncertainty. Owners' equity would simply be the difference between the market values of the assets and the market values of the liabilities. Under no circumstances would we expect this amount of equity to equal the market capitalization of the firm because the latter measure would be based on capital market participants' expectations for specific cash flows that management might produce with the combined assets and liabilities and other things, including their workforce, reputation, supply chain, and distribution system. The market cap is essentially based on the equilibrium of the supply and demand for shares in the company's stock, which is an entirely different matter than the numeric sum of the equilibrium market prices for the company's reported assets and liabilities. Thus, there is every reason to expect these two amounts to be different from each other. Furthermore, the typical calculation of the market cap (total outstanding shares times the market value of one share) is likely to be different from the actual market value of the firm when it is bought in a single transaction.

The income statement would be comprehensive in the sense that it would attempt to describe all changes in owners' equity apart from investments by and distributions to owners. In doing so, it would include all revenues, expenses, gains, and losses that occurred in the reporting period and would exclude all such items that did not occur in that period. In particular, the income statement would report both realized and unrealized gains and losses.[3] Deferrals and accruals would be based only on real changes in the market values of real assets and liabilities, not on the basis of management expectations or desires for smoothing out volatility. Thus, the amount of depreciation expense would not be the result of applying often years-old predictions of the useful life and salvage value. Instead, depreciation would be reported only if the observable market value of the asset declined (and at the amount of the decline); conversely, appreciation would be reported if the asset's market value were observed to have increased. This example typifies our conviction that useful information will be produced when facts are observed and reported. This view is in contrast with many of today's generally acceptable practices that report on the basis of assumptions, averages, expectations, and predictions instead of facts. Taken as a whole, our suggested practices would cause the income statement to articulate with two successive balance sheets.

Our statement of cash flows would clearly and fully describe all types of cash flows that occurred during the reporting period. The operating section would include all operating cash flows but only operating cash flows; further, it would show gross cash receipts and gross cash disbursements for those activities. The financing cash flows would include dividend and interest payments and any income tax payments or reductions related to financing activities. The investing cash flows would include dividend and interest receipts and all income taxes paid as a result of investing activities.

Finally, we would like to see management present a *comprehensible* reconciliation of the operating cash flow to the net income number as a supplement to both the income statement and the cash flow statement, and certainly not as a substitute for the operating cash flow presentation. (We describe our suggested format in Chapter 17.)

In addition to these supplemental value-based financial statements, we suggest that management would want to provide full and complete information to ensure that the users can understand as much as possible about the company and its financial results and condition. For example, instead of making financial statement users piece together the effects of the period's events on tangible assets from several different places and making guesses to fill in the blanks, managers could provide schedules like this one:

Beginning market value	$102,500,000
Acquisitions:	
By merger	85,000,000
By direct purchase	65,000,000
Disposals	(25,400,000)
Change in market value	(28,000,000)
Effect of change in exchange rates	(3,000,000)
Ending market value	$196,100,000

Similar schedules would be provided for intangibles, investments, receivables, payables, and other major asset and liability categories.

There would be, of course, many detailed issues to resolve in executing our broad-brush designs, and we will not pretend that they would be easy to settle. However, we believe that the process for resolving them ought to focus on meeting the objective of providing useful information for decisions. This point also allows us to repeat our assertion that the most productive route to achieving these improvements would not rely on bureaucratic and political processes. Rather, they would be more likely to be produced through a competitive process as QFR-minded managers seek to outdo each other in publishing high-quality financial reports that would reduce their cost of capital.

Our suggestions for some of those details are presented at various places in this and following chapters. Our primary purpose for now is to establish these ideals as the gold standard that we can use to evaluate and otherwise identify the flaws in GAAP reporting practices.

HOW GAAP AREN'T GOOD ENOUGH

Because of all the shortcomings in generally accepted accounting principles, we are ready to suggest that the abbreviation GAAP should be replaced by one or more of these three acronyms: PEAP, WYWAP, and POOP.

PEAP–Politically Expedient Accounting Principles

Chapter 4 listed a few typical situations where accounting standard setters have based their conclusions on political pressures instead of advancing practice toward the goal of providing useful information to the capital markets. For good measure (and to eliminate vestiges of doubt in our readers' minds), the following paragraphs describe some of the most evident politically expedient compromises that rob the financial statements of their ability to describe the truth.

Inventory.   There's only one way (politics) that we could end up with alternative inventory principles that allow managers to choose among such disparate methods as FIFO and LIFO.[4] The history behind this situation involves the drive to get the tax law changed to help produce tax savings for some companies. Managers and accountants went to Congress in the 1930s to persuade the members to permit their use of LIFO in order to secure those savings. However, in the process, they caused Congress to impose the "conformity rule" that requires the taxpayer to use LIFO on the published income statement if it's used on the tax return. Over more

than 60 years, this rule has never been challenged by the accounting profession, apparently for fear of upsetting the legislators, although Congress
tolerates many other differences between the tax code and GAAP without
question and certainly without other conformity rules. Based on these
observations, we conclude that it is politically expedient to leave the rule
alone, even though the consequence is poorly informed capital markets.
Of course, more useful information about inventories would be provided
by reporting their wholesale and retail market values. Under today's
GAAP, the income statement makes it appear as if no value is added to
manufactured inventory until it is sold. As a result, using historical costs
actually reports the income attained by increasing the value of the products in the year of sale instead of the year of production, which is when the
value is actually added.[5] This misstatement can only be explained as cater-
ing to the needs of auditors for safety instead of addressing the needs of
financial statement users for knowing exactly what happened in both
years. (Of course, any managers who believe GAAP depictions of inventory and their value-adding activities are also severely misinformed and
thus likely to make poor decisions.)

Foreign Currency.   In terms of providing information useful for
decisions, there is no good reason for reporting foreign exchange gains
and losses on the balance sheet instead of the income statement. SFAS 52
was issued by the FASB to save its own skin after preparers rose up in
arms to protest SFAS 8 and the volatility it revealed. The consequence of
this expedient compromise is that the income statement is incomplete and
less than fully informative. The four axioms suggest that this approach
can do nothing to boost the value of the company's stock and may actually
decrease it by increasing the users' costs and efforts in piecing together
what happened.

Changing Prices.   Throughout the history of financial reporting,
times of significant inflation and other economic upheaval have caused
prices of assets and liabilities to change, both across the entire economy
and within certain sectors. Accountants have always watched from the
sidelines without changing their practices, usually doing little more than
having tentative discussions that address the possibility of perhaps
doing something different depending on how things turn out after several years.[6] By the time those years go by, the economic crises have usually passed and accountants lose any sense of urgency. As a result,
GAAP have remained firmly anchored in past costs and derivatives of
past costs, all measured in past dollars, thus presenting woefully incomplete information in the financial statements. This behavior pattern
was temporarily broken in the 1970s during the prolonged economic

upheaval that brought both inflation and shifts in the prices of individual assets and liabilities. Under strong urging from the SEC, the FASB finally passed SFAS 33 in 1979 to require managers to report information about assets and earnings that reflected changing prices. Being unable to decide which method would be better, the FASB required two measures to be reported—inflation-adjusted and current costs of inventory and productive assets (but not liabilities). Also being unable to muster enough political power to impose these requirements on everyone, the FASB made them mandatory for only the 1400 or so largest public companies in the U.S. Then, being unable to build sufficient courage to change the basic financial statements, the board required the information to be provided in a supplemental schedule. Next, being unable to bring auditors along as a constituency, the FASB specified that the reported information did not have to be audited. And, being unable to convince anyone, including themselves, that this long-term problem needed a long term solution, the board members bound themselves to review the "experiment" after five years. Of course, after five years, the economic crisis had passed, so the FASB rescinded SFAS 33. Being unable to feel like they had enough power to force anyone to do what was useful, the board members passed SFAS 89 that merely recommended that managers report the supplemental information instead of requiring them to report it. Because they have not previously understood the four axioms and do not fully respect the capital markets' efficiency, no managers of public companies presently abide by the recommendation. Instead, they continue reporting only cost-based information using original dollars. As a consequence, today's balance sheets and income statements fall woefully short of providing information that directly supports investor and creditor assessments of the amount, timing, and uncertainty of future cash flows.

Pensions.   Although pension accounting was mentioned in the prior chapter, it fits here perfectly as an example of PEAP. The conceptual treatment of defined benefit pensions is actually very straightforward—the employer has a liability to its employee population for deferred compensation; that liability gets bigger when benefits are increased by additional work and by interest as time passes; and the employer has an asset in the form of investments held in a trust that are earmarked for paying the liability. Furthermore, those investments are managed for their regular cash flows and their appreciation. In addition, management is inclined to occasionally increase benefits retroactively, thus causing the liability to get larger while producing nothing concrete in terms of future cash advantages that could be considered to be assets of the company. The bottom line is that management doesn't know who it's going to pay, how much it's going to pay them, or for how long it's going to pay them. History shows that a majority of FASB members working on the pensions project knew that the most useful approach involved putting the liability and the fund assets on the employer's balance sheet at their market values and reporting pension expense as the sum of the new service and interest costs net of the change in the market value of the fund assets. Adjustments in the liability from new actuarial estimates and modifications of the plan would basically flow through the income statement as gains and losses when they were made. However, such upfront truthfulness was not about to be tolerated because managers wanted to report as if this totally irrational promise was actually rational. Furthermore, they wanted to avoid revealing how much risk they had created and thought the best way would be to manage the reported numbers instead of economic reality. They then pressured the FASB to come up with a better plan that would not reveal the whole truth while producing smoother and less extreme results. A slim majority of the board (four out of seven) accommodated them wonderfully by thoroughly smoothing everything in sight. These procedures ensure that the income statement is safely buffered against the effects of the truth: (1) the expected return is deducted from the expense instead of the actual return; (2) unexpected gains and losses from actuarial adjustments to the liability are deferred indefinitely; and (3). the additional cost of retroactively increasing benefits is spread over future years as if the employees are somehow going to work harder because of the amendment. In addition, the board members prescribed putting information about all those asset and liability balances only in an abstruse footnote instead of placing them on the balance sheet. Why? The political pressure seems to have made them lose sight of the goal of providing the capital markets with useful information. Because both the balance sheet and the income statement are so grossly incomplete, no one—absolutely no one—can really believe the GAAP financial statements published by companies with defined benefit pension plans. (Chapter 17 describes our recommended disclosures for pension and other postemployment benefits.)

Income Taxes.   It would seem that nothing could be more simple than accounting for income taxes. Every year, the taxpayer figures out how much income tax must be paid and then pays it. Why can't this amount just appear on the income statement as an expense?[7] The answer involves two factors. First, the amount of taxes paid (and their size as a proportion of GAAP income) can vary substantially from year to year according to the timing of the taxpayer's deductions and credits. Reporting the actual payment as the expense could cause the reported after-tax net income to change significantly from year to year, and managers worry that just revealing this factual volatility will cause the capital markets to consider their companies to be risky. Therefore, they want to smooth the expense (remember that deadly sin?) by basing it on the GAAP pretax income reported on the income statement instead of the taxable income on the tax return. Both the APB and the FASB accommodated them beautifully by requiring deferred income taxes to be recognized in the statements. This approach has the effects of reporting amounts as tax expenses that were not actually paid and not reporting amounts as tax expenses even though they were actually paid, all for the sake of tricking an efficient capital market into thinking that everything is nice and smooth. Second, it seems likely that some managers might not want anyone, especially the press, to know how few taxes they actually pay. (Part of the public flap over Enron was created by the revelation that its management's use of overseas tax havens allowed it to avoid paying any U.S. tax for several years, despite reporting large amounts of net income.) By keeping that information "secret," managers think they can avoid adverse effects on their own public image. (This public relations concern exists completely apart from the issue of how to best inform the capital markets). Again, GAAP (or PEAP) accommodate the managers by "forcing" them to report tax expense as if they paid taxes in a year when it may be years and years before they actually pay them. (Remember what we said earlier about the lack of truthfulness in accounting?) So, once again, political expedience wins out and useful information is absent from the financial statements.

Stock Options. We have already briefly described GAAP for stock options. As we said, the FASB was hammered politically when it tried to deal with this issue by giving the capital markets a glimpse of the truth in the financial statements. The preparer constituency threatened the board's existence in all sorts of ways, and little support came from even the last lines of defense in the form of the Financial Accounting Foundation trustees and the SEC. In response, five board members voted to make the compromise of merely recommending that managers report compensation expense on the income statement while permitting pro forma disclosure in the notes. Even those five members admit that they were motivated by politics, as shown by these quotes from SFAS 123:

> The debate on accounting for stock-based compensation unfortunately became so divisive that it threatened the Board's future working relationship with some of its constituents. Eventually, the nature of the debate threatened the future of accounting standards setting in the private sector. (par. 60)

> The Board chose a disclosure-based solution for stock-based employee
> compensation to bring closure to the divisive debate on this issue—not
> because it believes that solution is the best way to improve financial
> accounting and reporting. (par. 62)

The language could not be much plainer—these FASB members could not
hold fast to what they believed was the best way to report the expense
because they feared for the board's long-term future. (The two dissenting
members were willing to face this risk by requiring managers to apply the
expense treatment.) As a result, these PEAP income statements do not provide very trustworthy representations of the compensation expense
incurred in a year.[8] Once again, political expedience won out and capital
market participants are forced to work harder to get less reliable information from outside sources even though management already has access to
it internally. The only possible result is that managers who reject the recommended method create a significant cloud of distrust over their heads
because they are known to prefer painting pretty pictures that fool no one
(except possibly themselves) instead of simply telling the truth.[9]

Investments.   The preceding chapter briefly described accounting
for investments in debt and equity securities. The FASB started out with
the good intention to get truth into the financial statements but was
unable to turn away the onslaught of opposition from managers and bank
regulators who apparently thought that truth-telling would make it
harder for them to reduce capital costs and achieve public policy goals.
The FASB caved in again, ditched the objective of providing useful information, and allowed managers of different companies holding the same
investments to report different results according to what they *intend* to do.
In effect, it is the state of management's mind, not events in the stock and
bond markets, that shapes the amounts reported in the financial statements. Of course, all this political maneuvering is in vain because the market values of investment securities just keep on changing and changing
without any regard to what the managers intend to happen. To stay with
the point of this chapter, accounting for investments has been politically
compromised and mere compliance with GAAP does not ensure that useful information reaches the capital markets. In fact, it actually guarantees
that the information won't get there at all.

Others.   Are there other politically expedient principles? Yes, including those that cover such things as leases, software development costs,
troubled debt situations, business combinations, reporting cash flows, and
derivatives. The key to recognizing them is that the financial statements
make management look good while depriving the capital markets of easy
access to useful facts.

WYWAP—Whatever You Want
Accounting Principles

At the risk of some redundancy, we can demonstrate that mere compliance with GAAP will not produce high-quality financial statements because those principles actually allow managers tremendous discretion to choose between diametrically opposite methods that produce drastically different financial statements. Furthermore, the choice is often meaningless because it doesn't have to be shaped by real differences in the situations being described. In other words, the choice isn't restricted by making managers prove that the information under the chosen method is more useful—or even useful at all. Many managers just choose the generally accepted accounting principles that make their financial statements look good instead of what does a good job of eliminating uncertainty and risk. As a result, compliance with GAAP is not a clear proclamation that managers want capital market participants to know what happened. The following paragraphs briefly describe a few situations where managers are given this kind of leeway.

Inventory.   As mentioned in the previous section, managers are basically unfettered in their choice between FIFO and LIFO despite the fact that their preference drastically affects their reported income measures. What you have to love about this choice is the ironic dilemma that it creates for managers. Because the IRS conformity rule requires LIFO to be used on the income statement if it's used on the tax return, a choice for LIFO to make the stockholders better off by reducing current tax payments is also the choice to look worse off in the financial statements because the reported income is reduced below what it would be if FIFO were used. On the other hand, if managers choose FIFO to look better, their stockholders are worse off because the future cash flows are inferior. Thus, to be better off, managers have to look worse off, and to look better off, they have to make the stockholders worse off. As a result, the fact that managers choose FIFO is pretty solid evidence that they are more concerned about their financial images than their shareholders' estates. In the meantime, the information needs of financial statement users and the capital markets are shortchanged.

Depreciation.   The extensive flexibility in GAAP is conveyed by the punch line of an old joke: "How does a CPA answer the question, 'How much is two plus two?' " The response is, "What would you like it to be?" Perhaps the biggest source of this flexibility (and pretty much the biggest black eye for the accounting profession) is the unquestioned perpetuation of the myth that useful information about income can be produced by computing ahead of time how much depreciation and amortization expense will occur in the future instead of waiting until the future comes and then reporting expense based on actually observing what really happened. Instead, GAAP call on managers to predict how long assets will be used and how much they will be sold for at the end of that useful life. Then, they select from a set of alternative methods (straight-line or accelerated) for allocating the predicted net cost of the asset over that predicted life. Absolutely nothing in this calculation is a reliable description of what happens, except possibly for the asset's original cost, but even that number is subject to error. Unfortunately (at least as we see it), there is total complacence among accountants, managers, standard setters, and even statement users where we believe there ought to be a huge controversy. At the center of the issue should be questions about the usefulness of the information produced by allocating a historical cost (measured in historical dollars) over a predicted but unobserved future period. Their absolute silence here is not proof that the old way is good. Rather, we interpret it as having two roots: (1) growing obliviously comfortable with the status quo or (2) sheer hopelessness that such an entrenched practice could ever be changed in the current political system. Regardless of the reason, the fact remains that depreciation accounting gives managers virtually unlimited leeway in producing measures of their expenses for their financial statements. (One shouldn't overlook the fact that the amount reported on the balance sheet for assets is the remaining unallocated cost, an amount that cannot have a single shred of usefulness associated with it.) Our conversion to QFR thinking has made us totally bewildered that managers would not want to report market values (which they already know) to people who are trying desperately to estimate those amounts on their own under great uncertainty. The consequence of this inertia has to be substantially higher capital costs and lower stock prices.[10]

Off-Balance-Sheet Financing.   Perhaps nothing reveals ignorance of capital market efficiency and the value of truth quite as much as the pursuit of off-balance-sheet financing (OBSF). A major portion of the outrage about Enron's financial statements was the use of literally hundreds of limited partnerships to achieve OBSF, all with the approval or even complicity of the Andersen auditors.

The basic idea behind OBSF is to allow management to take a company into debt without reporting a liability on (appropriately enough) the balance sheet. Their apparent objective is to fool financial statement users into accepting a rate of return that is lower than it should be in light of the risk associated with the additional debt, with the eventual desired consequence of higher stock prices. Of course, if the capital markets are in the least efficient, this behavior manages to accomplish two undesired results. First, engaging in OBSF provides convincing evidence that management cannot be trusted to tell the truth. Second, OBSF leads to incomplete financial statements. Both results tend to produce higher capital costs and lower stock prices. Nonetheless, managers continue to engage in this dysfunctional behavior, and accountants have been successfully enlisted to enable them to do so. In psychology, this situation is called *codependence* and its existence should lead to therapy and intervention.

Perhaps the most common method of achieving OBSF is entering into contracts that are classified as operating leases instead of capital leases. As a result, the lessee does not report an asset or a liability despite actually having one of each. The FASB set out to limit this practice in SFAS 13 and a plethora of later standards by identifying four classification criteria for telling one kind of lease from the other. However, two of these criteria are based on (of all things) the leased asset's predicted useful life and present values of predicted future cash flows. Usually with help from their auditors, managers easily escape both constraints, and, as we have suggested, these criteria have really functioned as guidelines that help managers evade capitalization instead of keeping them from producing misleading financial statements. Given that choice and the hope (vain as it may be) of being rewarded for fooling the markets, we're not surprised that managers bite the hook.

OBSF can also be accomplished in other ways. For example, a defined benefit pension plan essentially creates a large debt to the employees that isn't reported as a liability. For another example, a great many managers spent a lot of the stockholders' money to create finance subsidiaries that were not consolidated because they were in another line of business; there is no better example of this than General Motors Acceptance Corporation (GMAC). Fortunately for financial statement users, SFAS 94 now requires all majority-owned subsidiaries to be consolidated. Before this standard, the finance subsidiary would do all the parent's borrowing and use the proceeds to purchase the parent's trade receivables. The only reason for this practice was to get the debt off the parent's balance sheet. The point of this discussion is that nothing in GAAP discouraged this practice, and auditors engaged in enabling behavior for their clients who were willing to spend lots of the stockholders' money to keep the truth out of the financial statements.

The bottom line on OBSF is that it is yet another example of WYWAP that allows managers to do whatever they want to with the financial statements. Thus, compliance with GAAP does not provide any real assurance to the users that the financial statements are complete and otherwise reliable.

Business Combinations and Goodwill.
Until 2001, GAAP allowed managers some discretion in how they accounted for merging one company with another. Under the very popular pooling method, described

in Chapter 4, the whole story of the acquisition was deliberately omitted from the financial statements. Using their stockholders' money, managers aggressively sought three "advantages" of pooling: less future deprecia-tion expense, no goodwill amortization expense, and claiming as their own the acquired company's earnings that preceded the acquisition. A purchase treatment, on the other hand, provides only two real advantages: it costs less to qualify for and it reports more useful information about the merger in the financial statements. Many managers followed the siren song of higher reported earnings and did poolings that actually made the stock-holders worse off by leaving the capital markets uninformed. (For this rea-son, we have often referred to this practice as "pfooling.")

In the effort to finally restrict this discretion, the FASB issued SFAS 141 that eliminated all new poolings. Of course, the proposal to do so proved to be so controversial that the board had to compromise in some way. What happened was a major change in accounting for the price paid in excess of the net market value of the acquired company's assets and lia-bilities. This excess is called *goodwill*, and its amount had been subject to regular amortization against earnings over no more than 40 years. After first proposing to reduce the amortization period to no more than 20 years, the board members made a shift in early 2001 to bring an end to amortization. Instead, managers will be allowed to carry the goodwill amount on the balance sheet unchanged until such time as they determine that it has been impaired to a value less than cost.

We don't think we need to go any further to show how GAAP, even brand-new GAAP, create so much discretion that managers cannot count on compliance to prove to the capital markets that the financial statements are complete and otherwise fully informative. They have to do something else to gain that confidence and lower capital costs.

Just in case there are any readers who still hold fast to their faith in today's practices, we next explain yet another possible alternative acro-nym for GAAP.

POOP—Pitifully Old and Obsolete Principles

In a global economy in which something that lasts several months is a trend and anything that lasts a year or two is considered a permanent fix-ture, one might think that accountants and regulators would have been working hard to keep up with new technological capabilities in comput-ing, data management, and communications. Anyone who did think that way would be mistaken, because many of today's generally accepted accounting principles originated in the equivalent of the dark ages.

Consider this list of practices and the dates of these central principles that are still being used in today's financial statements:

- *Treasury stock:* Accounting Research Bulletin No. 1, issued in 1939[11]

- *Stock dividends and splits:* Accounting Research Bulletin No. 11, issued in 1941

- *Depreciation:* Accounting Research Bulletin No. 27, issued in 1946

- *Inventory and cost of goods sold:* Accounting Research Bulletin No. 29, issued in 1947

- *Current and noncurrent classifications of assets and liabilities:* Accounting Research Bulletin No. 30, issued in 1947

- *Long-term contracts:* Accounting Research Bulletin No. 45, issued in 1955

- *Convertible debt:* Accounting Principles Board Opinion No. 14, issued in 1969

- *Equity method of accounting for investments:* Accounting Principles Board Opinion No. 18, issued in 1971

- *Receivables and payables:* Accounting Principles Board Opinion No. 21, issued in 1971

- *Stock options:* Accounting Principles Board Opinion No. 25, issued in 1972 (de facto GAAP according to the popular implementation of SFAS 123)

- *Interim reporting:* Accounting Principles Board Opinion No. 28, issued in 1973

- *Income statement structure:* Accounting Principles Board Opinion No. 9, issued in 1966, and Accounting Principles Board Opinion No. 30, issued in 1973

- *Research and development:* Statement of Financial Accounting Standards No. 2, issued in 1974

We really don't think there is much more that we need to say about the age and applicability of ancient GAAP in our modern world, except to discuss the reporting frequency followed by all SEC registered companies and most everyone else. Specifically, the practice of reporting once a year with three supplemental quarterly reports was established for public companies by the Securities and Exchange Act of 1934. This situation begs the question of whether managers actually have more technology at their fingertips for providing interim reports more frequently than was possible with the information-processing technology of the early 1930s. (Based on what we know of the political process, we have to believe that even then this frequency was a compromise based on the capabilities of the slowest companies.) This origination date also applies to the still-standard practice of mailing printed reports to stockholders. Not long ago, one of us received a quarterly report from Berkshire Hathaway by snail mail and could hardly stop laughing at the impossibility of finding any information in that report that had not been captured in the stock price literally weeks or even months before. With all the people who watch Warren Buffett closely to pick up on his strategic and tactical moves, how could a stockholder ever hope to open the mailbox, find the quarterly report, and then read it carefully to rationally determine whether to buy, hold, or sell the stock?

ALMOST THE FINAL WORD

In light of political expedience, flexibility, and the age of GAAP, can anyone seriously hold fast to a pretense that these principles are anywhere close to good enough for informing today's highly efficient capital markets? We are, to say the least, frustrated by the lack of introspection by accountants and the total absence of a vision for doing things differently. As near as we can tell, the four QFR axioms are at work even if no one besides us admits that they are true or even if everyone acts as if they are not true.

So, what is our point? In light of all these failings in GAAP, *there is no credible defense of the current reporting system.* If managers and accountants want to defend it, much less praise it, we can only conclude that they are essentially ignorant of its limitations, somehow terribly confused and misled, or trying to perpetuate a fraud.[12] There is absolutely no way that any manager should look to GAAP to provide sufficiently useful information that will produce appropriate capital costs and adequately high stock prices. In the same vein, no investors and creditors can rest comfortably knowing that a company's financial statements were prepared using GAAP.

While GAAP may serve some useful purpose, we are no longer exactly certain as to what it might be. What we are certain about is that there is a better way, and that's what Quality Financial Reporting is all about.

AN ETHICAL INSIGHT

As we mentioned in Chapter 2, we used to think of all these weaknesses in the GAAP creation process and in implementing standards as ethical failings. While it may be true that some of them are unethical, we think that their continued existence flies in the face of good business practice. In effect, we believe that QFR stands on its own feet as smart business because the four axioms show that telling the truth, plain and unvarnished, produces results (lower capital costs and higher stock prices) that are much closer to what management wants than all the results that outright lying or clever bending of the truth can ever generate. So, if one of our readers is driven to adopt QFR by a guilty conscience, we are not going to complain; however, that motive should be unusual. What we fully expect to happen is that managers will adopt QFR in a legitimate quest to add value to their companies while enriching their stockholders.

On the other hand, we cannot keep from wondering whether it is unethical for people to hold themselves out as professional accountants, auditors, managers, regulators, or accounting and finance professors if they are ignorant of how capital markets actually respond to incomplete, misleading, outdated, and otherwise fallacious financial statements. While ignorance of these points and the four axioms might be excusable, it makes little sense to keep on acting in the same way without understanding that incomplete, unreliable, and untrustworthy information leads to higher capital costs. In fact, we have concluded that this kind of ignorance will soon be inexcusable.

NOTES

1. *Accounting Today,* July 23/August 5, 2001, pp. 14–15.

2. "Stock Option Accounting and Securities Litigation Reform," before The Association of Publicly Traded Companies, Palo Alto, CA, November 15, 1993; "Remarks before the Association for Public Corporations," Miami, FL, December 1, 1993; and "Stock Option Accounting: A Common Sense Approach," before the Western Association of Venture Capitalists and the American Entrepreneurs for Economic Growth, Menlo Park, CA, April 13, 1994. All three of Beese's speeches were published by the SEC.

3. In our reporting world, realized gains and losses would be the difference between the proceeds of selling an asset and its most recently recorded market value, not the difference between the proceeds and the asset's historical cost or other book value. This idea is discussed more completely in Chapter 15.

4. Seemingly, FIFO and LIFO are efforts to describe physical flows (first-in-first-out and last-in-first-out). In fact, they are nothing other than assumptions substituted for actual observations, and management's choice between them is motivated by reaching a desired reported result rather than describing what actually happened.

5. The same shortcoming exists for purchased inventories, where the value is added by promotion, distribution, and other marketing activities.

6. For example, Accounting Principles Board Opinion 6, issued in 1965, includes this comment: "Mr. [Sidney] Davidson agrees with the statement that at the present time 'property, plant and equipment should not be written up' to reflect current costs, but only because he feels that current measurement techniques are inadequate for such restatement. When adequate measurement methods are developed, he believes that both the reporting of operations in the income statement and the valuation of plant in

the balance sheet would be improved through the use of current rather than acquisition costs. In the meanwhile, strong efforts should be made to develop the techniques for measuring current costs." It doesn't take much to imagine the other members of the board nodding their heads and saying, "Sounds good to us," and then doing nothing to implement the recommendation. In fact, over 35 years later, the same arguments are still held dear by accountants and put forth every time someone suggests such a change. Our honest readers will admit that they felt this way upon reading our description of ideal balance sheets a few pages back. No one can accuse accountants of being glacial in their rate of change; after all, glaciers do move.

7. Indeed, there is good reason to think of taxes not as an expense at all but as an involuntary distribution of assets by the taxpayer to the government in proportion to taxable income as calculated on the tax return. Because this payment does not acquire specific assets or services for the company, it differs substantially from all other expenses. This idea has never won much support, although we wish it would.

8. With all the political attention on the primary issue of whether the option expense should be reported on the income statement, another issue was lost in the shuffle, and the FASB created a hard-to-explain answer. Specifically, the federal tax law allows the employer to take a deduction from its taxable income for the value realized by the employees for the excess of the value of their acquired stock over the option price. The board determined that the company's tax savings would not appear on the income statement as a reduction in the tax expense, thereby making the reported income number even smaller. Despite a lot of attempts to be open-minded, we just don't get this one at all.

9. The fact that omitting the expense from the income statement has not escaped anyone's attention is validated by a series of articles in the June 25, 2001 issue of *Fortune*. The writers are uniform in their disdain for the omission of the expense and their assessment of the managers that succumb to the far-too-easy route of not telling the truth.

10. Insult is added to the stockholders' injury because their hired stewards are choosing to keep this information from them and the capital markets. This lack of accountability flies in the face of literally thousands of years of customs and laws governing relationships between principals and agents.

11. In fact, the rules on treasury stock included in ARB 1 had been adopted by earlier committees of the American Institute of Accountants in 1933 and 1938.

12. Lest someone think we are being unreasonably harsh in calling compliance with GAAP fraudulent, we offer this definition of fraud: "Knowingly using false and misleading information to persuade other parties to make decisions that they would not make if they knew the truth." No matter how we slice it, we keep concluding that GAAP financial statements fall under this meaning of the term.

Building Confidence in Quality Financial Reporting

This third section, the longest of the book, represents a turning point in the sense that we now begin to explain the advantages and other attractions of the Quality Financial Reporting paradigm as a substitute for the present authoritative GAAP financial reporting system.

The discussion begins with Chapter 6, which describes a new conceptual strategy that managers can (and perhaps should) pursue in order to serve the demands in the capital markets for greater quantities of information that is more useful for making investment and credit decisions than the information provided when supply-based GAAP solutions are chosen and implemented.

Chapters 7, 8, and 9 are pivotal for understanding that QFR is truly an improvement over the status quo. The material in these chapters goes beyond our logical arguments to consider what others have written. Chapter 7 describes what sophisticated financial analysts have said that they would like to see presented in financial statements, and we think you'll find their comments quite contrary to standard supply-based thinking. Chapter 8 presents the thoughts and opinions of other expert commentators, including a large committee, investors, academics, and a member of the FASB. Chapter 9 describes recent high-level capital market research into the four axioms; although we do little more than provide a taste, there is a universal theme in the findings that information quality goes hand in hand with lower capital costs.

Chapter 10 is designed to increase confidence in QFR by dealing with numerous objections that flow from conventional thinking. We show that these complaints are misplaced and cannot justify an offhand dismissal of the new paradigm.

CHAPTER 6

The QFR Strategy for Overcoming the Old Obstacles

After the last few chapters, you may find yourself getting more than just a little down—down on accountants and managers, of course, but just plain down in terms of wondering how the financial reporting system ever got into this poor condition and whether it can ever be rescued. Discouragement isn't necessarily a bad thing, however, especially if it triggers a search for a new direction with more promise than the old one that isn't working out. The basic purpose of this book is to provide that direction by pointing out a way that the system can take that is different from the obstacle-laden, even dead-end, direction that it is now headed in.[1]

In setting forth the new vision in this chapter, we refer back to the point made earlier that those involved in financial reporting will gain by changing from their current supply-based thinking to become demand-driven. Considering only the supply of financial information leads to all sorts of unproductive behaviors and outcomes, while thinking about the information demanded by the capital markets will tend to produce different attitudes and practices. This new paradigm will produce substantial changes in the roles played by managers, auditors, financial statement users, standard setters, and regulators. Let's get into our explanation.

THE BASIC SITUATION

As we have shown, financial statement preparers have a set of information that they want, or are at least willing, to present to the public. The circle in Figure 6-1 represents that set of information.

Quite naturally, this set tends to include the kind of information that the managers believe works to their benefit. Under the current paradigm, it contains the sorts of things that make the managers and the company

FIGURE 6-1

Information Supply

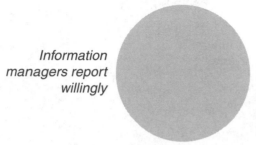

Information managers report willingly

look more attractive. Thus, it tends to involve smooth and increasing earnings and low ratios of debt to equity. Managers are willing to present this kind of information because they think it will convince participants to throw their money in the company's direction. And, as we have described, they want to produce this information cheaply.

On the other end of these transactions are investors, creditors, and their analysts, all of whom are financial statement users. They, too, have their own set of information that they want to deal with, as represented by the circle in Figure 6-2.

The information in this set consists of facts that are relevant for predicting future cash flows to investors and creditors, which, in turn, means they are relevant for predicting future cash flows to and from the firm. In addition, the information must be reliable, in the sense that it can be depended on to be an unbiased and otherwise verifiable and faithful depiction of what has happened and what presently exists. In addition, the information needs to be available on a timely basis. Of course, anyone would like to have reliable information about the future so that they

FIGURE 6-2

Information Demand

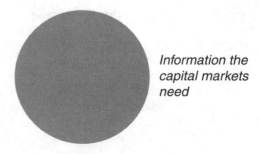

Information the capital markets need

would know exactly where to put their money. Until time travel is made practical, this information simply does not exist because information about future events cannot be verified until those events occur. As we see it, forecasting the future is what the analysts and other users do; all management needs to do is report about the past and the present, and let those users make their own predictions.

To return to the point, the first circle represents the information that managers are willing to supply, while the second one represents the information that users demand.

What happens when the two circles are placed together? We think the current situation is represented by the combined diagram in Figure 6-3.

The information subset represented by Area Ⓑ is supplied by managers and meets the users' demand. As such, it is the product of successful financial reporting. The effort of providing this information is worth making because it helps the market participants reduce their uncertainty while reducing management's capital costs. In contrast, management wastes all its efforts in supplying any information that falls in Area Ⓐ because the markets have no demand for it. Area Ⓒ represents information the markets demand that is not supplied by managers. Thus, it is the area of opportunity for those who seek a closer and more productive relationship with the capital markets.

Because the information in Area Ⓒ is useful to the markets but not available in public reports, one of three things happens:

1. The market participants have no interest in investing in that firm.
2. The market participants invest, but only under conditions of greater uncertainty.
3. The market participants invest, but only after spending a great deal of time and money gathering private information from less reliable secondary sources.

FIGURE 6-3

The Intersection Where Supply Meets Demand

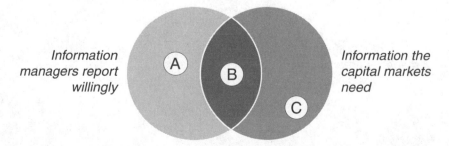

Information managers report willingly

A
B
C

Information the capital markets need

The outcome is the same in all cases—the markets' demand for the company's securities is diminished, their value goes down, and the cost of capital goes up.

This analysis makes it clear that management should pursue the financial reporting strategy of expanding Area Ⓑ while shrinking both Ⓐ and Ⓒ. But how? There are three choices. The first would involve a major public relations effort by management to get the capital markets to decide that they really want to have the information from Area Ⓐ instead of Ⓒ (in effect, the right-hand circle would move to the left to embrace more of the left-hand circle). We really don't think this possibility makes any sense because it is supply centered. The second strategy would be to keep following the status quo and hope that the market will shrug its shoulders and respond to uncertainty by bidding stock prices higher. That response seems totally unlikely. The third, and hopefully obvious, strategy is illustrated by the modified diagram in Figure 6-4.

It seems to us that the only sensible response is for management to become driven by demand and proactively try to merge its circle into the markets' circle. In less symbolic terms, the managers should find out what the markets want and need but aren't getting, and then start to provide it. Doing so will allow managers to avoid the wasted effort and costs of preparing and publishing irrelevant information. In other words, they will stop using reporting policies to construct financial images that cause the markets to view their reports with skepticism because they do not reflect reality. Importantly, this strategy will obviously address the markets' need for information and displace some of the more expensive and unreliable private information with less costly and verified public information. The ultimate results will be reduced uncertainty for the investors, lower capital costs for the firm, and higher prices for its securities.

Despite the obviousness of this kind of move, we feel like we are recommending a major innovative step in the evolution of financial reporting.

FIGURE 6-4

A Strategy for Meeting More of the Demand

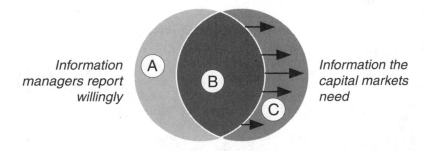

THREE PLACES TO START

To make this discussion a bit more concrete, we think managers can begin moving their circle into the market's circle by the simple step of taking the FASB at its word in three existing pronouncements that identify preferable but still optional reporting practices.

The first is SFAS 89, "Accounting for Changing Prices." This standard was issued in 1986 to rescind SFAS 33, which had required the largest U.S. companies to provide supplemental information about the market values of certain kinds of assets and the effects of changes in market values on their income. Because the board lacked sufficient political will to expand the requirement or even continue it, the members ended up saying that management

> . . . is encouraged, but not required to disclose supplementary information on the effects of changing prices. . . . Entities are not discouraged from experimenting with other forms of disclosure. (par. 3)

Based on our analysis, we are confident that the markets will reward any managers who legitimately attempt innovation in this area by trying to provide depictions of these relevant facts that are more reliable than data that financial analysts can gather on their own from less reliable secondary sources.

The second recommendation is found in SFAS 95 on the cash flow statement. As we described in Chapter 4, the FASB was unable to muster a majority of four members to require managers to use the direct method of reporting operating cash flows, despite the fact that there was a great deal of support for this mandate from financial statement users. Instead of requiring it, the board ended up suggesting that managers use the direct method while permitting them to use the indirect as an acceptable option. It's reasonable to think that managers who are responsive to expressed needs in other kinds of marketplaces would try to meet that demand and earn a reward. However, that supposition turns out to be false and cash flow reporting practice does not coincide with the preference. In fact, based on the annual surveys conducted by the American Institute of Certified Public Accountants, managers of 99 percent of public U.S. companies use the indirect method.[2] The financial statement users' frustration with this choice was expressed in these words by the Financial Accounting Policy Committee of the AIMR in *Financial Reporting in the 1990s and Beyond*:

> . . . [T]he cash flow statements that have appeared in published financial reports are much less useful than we might have expected . . . [because] almost no public company presents its cash flows from operations using the direct format; virtually all use the indirect format. (p. 65)

The analysts on the AIMR committee went on with these compelling words to display their disappointment with managers' stonewall resistance to providing the information that financial statement users demand:

> Although FASB has not seen fit to mandate the direct method, and neither has the IASC, both endorse it as the preferable method. Nothing other than inertia prevents progressive business enterprises that seek favor with analysts from adopting the direct method. We reiterate: not only is the direct method permitted, users of financial statements prefer it. (p. 67)

Managers should have no doubt that the markets want to have this unreported information, and it would behoove any of them to provide it and thereby move further into the circle representing the capital markets' demands.

We have already described the FASB's third recommendation several times. Specifically, the members of the FASB did not believe they had enough political power to require reporting stock options expense on income statements. As an escape from the pressure, five of them voted for SFAS 123, which strongly encourages managers to put the expense on the income statement but allows them to leave it off and merely disclose a pro forma earnings number in the footnotes. The members of the AIMR committee also spoke forthrightly on this topic:

> . . . [W]e strongly believe that stock options have value, that they are used to compensate managers, and that they should be recognized and measured as compensation expense in the financial statements. (p. 47)

These thoughts make it clear that these influential capital market participants have a demand for the expense treatment. However, virtually no managers of public companies have responded to it but have chosen instead to supply the markets with the footnote information.[3] By now, we think everyone reading this book ought to be able to see that tucking these relevant facts away in the notes does not prevent the markets from getting to the information or reacting to it. In fact, it is plausible that management's decision to be less than forthcoming has created a lack of trust and actually caused stock prices to be discounted.

These three examples show how managers could easily move their information sets into greater congruence with the markets' demands. These first steps are especially good ideas because they are already included within GAAP and should not create any special issues for auditors. Further, the FASB has already completed a lot of research into the markets' wants and needs, with the result that management does not have to waste time duplicating their efforts.

Of course, many other innovative possibilities for voluntarily improved financial reporting are outside the current limits of GAAP, including publishing supplemental financial statements and more information about off-balance-sheet items, financial instruments, inventory, and business segments. The only real constraint is management's ingenuity in discovering and servicing investors' needs while telling the truth.

WHAT ABOUT GAAP?

In the 1930s, when Congress set out to regulate the U.S. capital markets, it set in motion the creation of another set of financial information in addition to the two circles we have just described. We're talking about generally accepted accounting principles, of course, and their existence means that financial reporting is more complicated than simply moving the management circle over into the users' circle.

We think the diagram in Figure 6-5 is a more complete representation of today's regulated reporting environment. It differs by the addition of a third circle representing GAAP.

As we described in Chapters 4 and 5, the FASB and its predecessors have often given short shrift to the markets' demands for information while trying to meet the disparate but nonetheless intense political demands of managers, auditors, and regulators. As a result, we see that there is only a small overlap between the information required by GAAP and the markets' needs.

To explain the diagram more completely, the area enclosed by the left and upper circles (Areas ① through ⑥) represents all public information that managers report, both by mandate and by volition. In contrast, Area

FIGURE 6-5

The Intersections of Supply, Demand, and GAAP

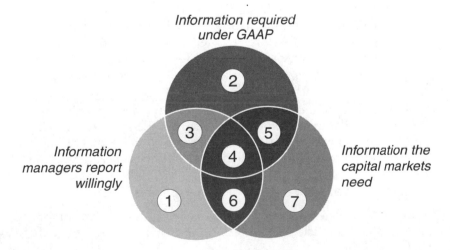

Information required under GAAP

Information managers report willingly

Information the capital markets need

⑦ represents the capital markets' unsatisfied demands that market partic-ipants must satisfy for themselves by turning to unpublished private information. Whether those needs are fulfilled somewhere else or not at all, managers who withhold useful information force investors to invest under greater uncertainty with the negative consequences of higher capi-tal costs and lower security prices.

Let's look more closely at the specific subsets in the diagram.

- Area ① represents information that no one needs and that no one has mandated. The cost incurred by managers in producing it is a total waste of the stockholders' money.

- Area ② represents managers' wasted effort in reporting informa-tion they don't want to supply but have to because it is required by GAAP even though the markets don't demand it. As such, it encompasses the greatest failures of the standard-setting process. Any cost incurred by the FASB or one of its predecessors in creating these practices was also an unnecessary waste.

- Area ③ symbolizes jointly wasted efforts by both managers and standard setters. Even though managers are happy to report this required information, the capital markets simply have no use for it. This area represents the information produced when the FASB compromises with the preparer constituency without incorpo-rating the users' needs.

In contrast, Areas ④, ⑤, and ⑥ represent reported information that meets the markets' needs. Each component has its unique character.

- Area ④ is "no-brainer" territory because management has wisely chosen to submit to being required to report this information that the markets need.

- Area ⑤ represents information that the markets need but get only because the FASB has enacted rules to force managers to provide it. This area represents the few situations in which the standard-setting process has actually succeeded in moving practice into the users' circle.

- Area ⑥ represents useful information that managers willingly report without being forced. As such, it is the domain of Quality Financial Reporting. Alas, we are inclined to think that this portion of the diagram is very small in today's financial reporting culture.

One More Point, One More Time

Throughout the book until now, we have made the point that compliance with GAAP is insufficient for meeting the markets' needs for reduced uncertainty. We find that Figure 6-5 clearly illustrates that point. Complying with GAAP provides the markets with only the information represented by Areas ④ and ⑤ but leaves unsatisfied the users' demand for the large amounts of information represented by Areas ⑥ and ⑦. This failure to communicate useful information produces uncertainty, high user processing costs, and eventually lower security prices.

A NEW STRATEGY

The diagram in Figure 6-6 modifies the previous one to describe the Quality Financial Reporting strategy of satisfying the markets' demand for useful information. Specifically, this strategy aims to merge the management and GAAP circles into the markets' circle.

For one thing, we see that this strategy will allow managers to reduce and eventually avoid the wasted efforts and costs of producing the useless information represented by Areas ①, ②, and ③. At the same time, it will also expand the useful public information represented by Areas ④, ⑤, and ⑥. Not by accident, this double convergence on the users' circle will reduce the markets' dependence on the less reliable and more expensive private information represented by Area ⑦.

Because the FASB is responsible for expanding Areas ④ and ⑤, we believe that it will provide a better service to the capital markets in particular and society in general by focusing its efforts on discovering unsatisfied financial statement users' needs. At the same time, it should do

FIGURE 6-6

Another Strategy for Meeting More of the Demand

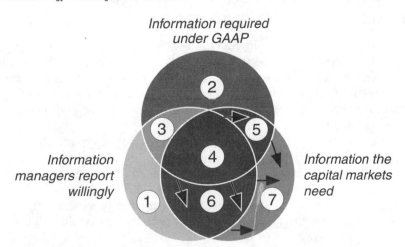

nothing to require managers to supply information that the markets don't demand. In our fantasies, we imagine the board's acting to rescind the old rules that create Areas ② and ③. On the other hand, we think a more realistic vision for the future will find QFR-minded managers actually helping the FASB's efforts to expand Area ④ while squeezing out Area ⑤ because they will see that it makes sense to meet those market demands without coercion. We speculate more about the standard-setting process under the QFR paradigm in Chapter 18.

Finally, QFR managers will greatly expand their efforts to provide the information in Area ⑥ without waiting for the FASB to act. In fact, we believe that increasing the contents of this area is the ultimate objective of applying Quality Financial Reporting. This behavior will occur when managers realize that they can reap lower capital costs and achieve higher stock prices by reaching out voluntarily to the markets more effectively than their competitors instead of withholding useful information or grudgingly reporting only the bare minimum required by GAAP. Once managers get a vision of these economic incentives to adopt QFR, they will have latched onto a force for change that is more powerful than the limited political power that now resides in the FASB and the SEC. We are convinced that the rewards for successfully competing in the markets for cheaper capital will stimulate much more innovation and progress more quickly than any protracted due process could ever hope to accomplish.

At the same time, managers who pursue the QFR strategy will reduce the markets' inefficient dependence on the private information symbolized by Area ⑦. The eventual result will be to make everyone better off.

WHY QFR MAKES MORE SENSE THAN THE STATUS QUO

To claim the advantages of lower capital costs and higher security prices, it now seems obvious to us that essentially all managers would want to voluntarily increase the quality and quantity of information in their financial reports. Doing so will build bridges to the capital markets and open up access to the advantages produced by creating a better relationship and reducing uncertainty.

In contrast, we think the status quo strategy pays off only in the highly unlikely situation that managers could somehow use GAAP accounting to consistently fool investors and creditors and lead them to accept a return that is too low for the real risk. Enron has shown that this outcome is no more than remotely possible for the short term; managers have nothing more than an incredibly low probability of pulling it off over any longer period.

Furthermore, we have to challenge an ethical framework that justifies acts by managers to use corporate resources to produce financial reports that deliberately attempt to mislead stockholders or otherwise fail to inform them. Even without invoking this moral principle, we think it is virtually certain that managers who are known for trying to mislead the markets surely end up creating more risk for investors and lowering stock prices instead of increasing them.

In summary, the most certain route to lower capital costs uses Quality Financial Reporting to proactively explore ways to satisfy the markets' needs while eliminating unproductive reporting efforts. It is no longer good enough (if it ever was) to wait complacently for the bureaucratic processes of the FASB and the SEC to create useful new reporting methods. They have never been successful at doing so in the past, and no one should expect them to be nearly as motivated, innovative, or nimble as managers in hot pursuit of lower capital costs. The following section expands on these thoughts.

THE WRONG ROLE FOR REGULATORS

Although we certainly have some ideas that managers can apply to produce more useful financial reports, we insist that it would be totally presumptuous of us to state what we think all managers must do to meet the capital markets' needs for reduced uncertainty. If we were to take that authoritative stance, we would fall into the same trap that has put managers and their accountants into their unhealthy codependency with regulators and standard setters. Instead, we think decisions about new and possibly more useful reporting techniques and topics should be made by individual members of the vast army of managers who will actually *want* to prepare high-quality financial reports that will help them compete in the markets, reduce their capital costs, and boost their stock prices. They are in the best position to know what kind of uncertainty exists about their business and what information they have or could get that would reduce the markets' doubts and promote demand for a lower rate of return.

As we have said, we think a major cause for the deplorable situation of GAAP's limited usefulness is that accountants and managers have contentedly waited on authoritative bodies to produce innovative ideas. Our experiences working for the FASB and SEC have given us the personal insight that one primary purpose for political institutions and processes is to prevent change. Failing to reach that goal, the system then falls back to the secondary goals of slowing down change and minimizing its effects. This analysis reveals the virtual hopelessness of depending on standard setters to bring about true innovation that would increase the amount of useful information in financial statements.

Nonetheless, managers and accountants have trusted in GAAP and the lawgivers to define quality for so long that they may have literally lost sight of the possibility of doing anything different. Perhaps no one knows better than us that many of our academic colleagues also lack imagination; thus, it's quite possible that the current generations of managers and accountants have never been taught or even exposed to the idea that different accounting methods could convey really useful information to financial statement users.

As confirmation of this shortfall in education, Paul Miller had the privilege in 1997 of interviewing Professor Merton Miller of the University of Chicago. During the course of the videotape session, Paul asked the Economics Nobel laureate to speculate about why it seems that virtually all managers do not comprehend that they face higher capital costs when they fail to reduce uncertainty as much as they could by providing more information. Without hesitation, he responded by saying with a smile, "Because you accounting professors have never taught them!" Based on our own classroom experience and what we read in standard textbooks, we are convinced that he was right. Indeed, one of our motives for producing this book is our perception of the nearly universal lack of awareness of the linkage between information quality and the cost of capital.

Our ultimate point in this arena is that QFR involves turning managers loose to find their best practices for fully informing the capital markets. However, our thoughts must not be twisted to become a call for deregulating the financial reporting system.

SOME THOUGHTS ON REGULATION AND DEREGULATION

Of course, one public goal for regulating the capital markets is to discourage and prevent fraudulent financial reporting. Achieving this purpose is difficult because its roots lie in the hearts and minds of those who justify their taking of wealth from others by deception. As former SEC chair Arthur Levitt recently advised us, "There are a lot of bad guys out there, really bad guys," and who should know better than he does? If frauds are that deep-seated, then they probably cannot be prevented by creating more rules. Instead, what is needed to diminish the frequency of fraud is a revolution in the way managers think about truth telling. In a sense, this is what QFR is all about—liberating managers to find creative ways to get more of the truth into their financial reports and thereby increase their usefulness. At the same time, they will also benefit from taking out the untruths that currently are presented there. .

Lest anyone misunderstand where we're headed, we need to clearly distinguish QFR from proposals made in the 1970s and 1980s for deregulating the capital markets, including financial reporting practices. The gist of those arguments is not too different from QFR in that they asserted (1) that managers have significant economic incentives to tell the truth and (2) that the markets can use the pricing mechanism to levy penalties on miscreants who use falsehoods to try to wrongfully take money from capital market participants. While we understand these writers' enthusiastic support for the markets' ability to penalize the deceivers, we suggest that they may have overlooked a couple of major points.

First, a high degree of regulation is deeply embedded in the capital markets, not just in the U.S. but around the world. It didn't just pop into existence overnight at the whim of a few ambitious regulators and powerful legislators. In fact, it has been built up slowly and steadily over at least seven decades. As a result, it is thoroughly woven into the tapestry and there can be no realistic probability that it could ever be undone. (It certainly cannot be unraveled on the basis of the arguments of two academic accountants like us.)

Second, in order for the markets to be able to punish specific deceivers, the capital market participants must know that they have been deceived and who was responsible for the deception. However, those discoveries are unlikely to be made until after the damage has been done. As a result, arguing for sole reliance on the market mechanism for enforcement means that individual investors will suffer losses while the perpetrators are free from any official sanction. While the miscreants may be unable to reenter the markets in the future, they will still have their misbegotten riches to keep them comfortable. Granted, the harmed parties could initiate litigation to recover their losses, but one would have to be severely overoptimistic to suggest that the court system will guarantee swift and complete retribution for the harm done. In short, we think huge costs would be imposed on society if deregulation were to occur, primarily because the capital costs for all companies would be elevated by the higher risk for investors that they could incur losses without any effective recourse against those who deceived them.

Therefore, just in case anyone thinks so, we state unequivocally that our advocacy for QFR is *not* a call for deregulation. Instead, it is a call for a more intelligent response to regulation by managers so that they will not terminate their reporting efforts as soon as they meet the regulatory minimums. Those minimums do serve the important purposes of creating confidence in the markets and providing for justice to be done. We do not think those advantages should be sacrificed by deregulating the practice of financial reporting.

In fact, we think that a widespread adoption of QFR would result in more calls for tougher regulation against those who try to deceive. Perhaps no one would benefit as much from more effective regulation as those managers who choose to provide high-quality information because the tougher regulations would be likely to expose the fact that some of those managers competing in the markets are playing fast and loose with the truth while trying to look like they're producing sound financial reports. The consequence would have to be a lower level of perceived overall risk and a lower market-level cost of capital.

A CLOSING INTERNATIONAL THOUGHT

Before finishing up this chapter, we want to make one more point about deregulation. In the increasingly global capital markets, few clear-cut authorities exist for governing international transactions or for prosecuting perpetrators of fraud. In effect, the global markets are unregulated and probably beyond regulation because of the immense obstacles to establishing an international authority that replaces existing national sovereignties. This situation clearly makes international investing more risky.

Therefore, just about the only managers who have been inclined to enter into these alligator-infested waters are (1) those who think they can make a killing by deception and then escape retribution and (2) those who have already established an ironclad reputation for honesty and fair dealing that allows the markets to trust their financial reports.

When we look at the situation from this perspective, we think that the global markets offer especially ripe opportunities for those managers who want to use QFR and do other things to develop a legitimate reputation for truth telling and trustworthiness. Because of the presence of multiple authorities, each of which has produced its own requirements reflecting its local political situations, managers will benefit from focusing single-mindedly on simply doing those things that inform the markets about what has really happened instead of manipulating their images within the constraints of the rules.

We think this opportunity exists despite the creation of the International Accounting Standards Board and the setting of a goal to establish truly international and universal accounting principles. Because the IASB's due process will be even more politically complex than the FASB's process, it is virtually certain that international standards will not get any closer to rules that will require managers to supply more of the useful information demanded by financial statement users. As a result, there will still be a huge unmet demand from the global capital markets for useful information. That demand will be met only when managers voluntarily go beyond the minimum levels required by GAAP, whether the rules are created in the U.S., in another country, or through international efforts.

NOTES

1. If one is looking for a good outcome from the Enron disaster, it may very well occur in the form of dissatisfaction with the status quo of the system. In fact, we hope it does, because we think that Quality Financial Reporting offers the best alternative.

2. These surveys are published by the AICPA under the title *Accounting Trends and Techniques*.

3. As near as we can tell, Boeing and Winn-Dixie are the only large public companies with managers who have chosen to use the preferred method.

CHAPTER 7

Financial Analysts Speak Their Minds

Up to this point, we have mostly relied on common sense, economic reasoning, anecdotes, and extrapolation from other situations to describe the value of the Quality Financial Reporting strategy for achieving lower capital costs and higher stock prices.

In this chapter and the next two, we want to pause and substantiate our thoughts by showing what others have said and what they have discovered through empirical research. We don't think these additional comments are essential for proving the truthfulness of our assertions, but they should provide comfort to readers who are rightfully skeptical about what a couple of academic accountants have to say, especially since what we have suggested is so different from common practice.

THE AIMR MONOGRAPH

In 1993, the Association for Investment Management and Research[1] (AIMR) published a significant but infrequently cited monograph written by Professor Peter Knutson. It was produced under the direction of the AIMR's Financial Accounting Policy Committee for the purpose of presenting the collective views of the organization's members on a wide range of financial reporting issues. This book, entitled *Financial Reporting in the 1990s and Beyond*, presents a hard-hitting and intelligent analysis of the then current state of financial reporting and makes many recommendations for ways that accountants and managers could do a better job. The committee members, it should be noted, were generally top-level financial analysts, with some representation from accounting and finance academicians.

This monograph is significant because it represents an input from the seldom outspoken financial statement user constituency. It is also significant because it defines in many places the needs and wants of this constituency. If we are correct in asserting that management will benefit from joining in partnership with the capital markets, then these expressed desires would constitute a beginning point for identifying how to meet those needs and wants. To describe our point another way, if financial reporting is ever going to change from being supply-driven to being demand-driven, don't managers and accountants need to learn what the financial statement users demand?

Before going into specific items from the AIMR monograph, we want to point out that the members of the FASB were all made aware of it and went on to show great respect for its contents. In fact, one of the AIMR committee members, Tony Cope, was subsequently appointed to the FASB.[2] This positive attitude toward the report displayed by high-level standard setters should help lend credibility to its contents.

This chapter presents more than 50 brief excerpts from the monograph that confirm the points that we have made in the prior chapters.

THE CAPITAL MARKETS ARE MARKETS

Our first and perhaps most fundamental assertion in our assessment of the present dismal state of financial reporting is that many managers have overlooked the fact that the capital markets are markets just like the labor market, the product and service market, and the company's supply chain. We have gone on to suggest that management will experience great benefits if it changes its approach and begins to see the capital markets as potential partners instead of necessary evils or adversaries. The AIMR monograph offers several comments that illuminate this idea and lend it more credence.

Investors Have Needs to Be Addressed

The following quotation makes it very clear that this group of sophisticated users believes that their demands should be addressed when management puts together its financial reports:

> If financial statement users demand information in a particular form, then it should be provided. If the costs of providing such information truly are prohibitive, the demand will cease as investors refuse to absorb the decrease in the value of the securities they hold. (p. 67)

The committee's point is that economic forces are at work in the form of demand for useful information. It makes no sense for managers to conclude that the cost of providing the information is prohibitive until they know how much it is demanded. But, because accounting has been in a supply-push mode for decades, most managers and accountants analyze these sorts of issues in terms of what they can produce and publish instead of what is demanded. We think a major attitude change is long overdue, and this comment from these statement users shows that they agree with us.

The Social Benefit of Quality Financial Reporting

The AIMR makes quite a few comments distinguishing the practice of financial reporting from the practice of financial analysis. This one makes it clear that the committee members want management to provide information that analysts can use to reach their own conclusions:

> The function of analysis is to allow those who participate in the financial markets to form their own rational expectations about future economic events, in particular the amounts, timing, and uncertainty of an enterprise's future cash flows. Through that process, analysts form opinions about the absolute and relative value of individual companies, make investment decisions or cause them to be made, and thereby contribute to the economically efficient allocation of capital and clearing of the capital markets. (p. 1)

This comment also reinforces our assertion that managers' widespread adoption of QFR will serve the public's interest in having markets that create and allocate capital efficiently.

The Capital Markets Are Efficient

Another foundation for QFR is the observation that the capital markets are highly efficient in collecting and processing information in the quest for wealth. If the markets are efficient, then management will achieve nothing but wasted effort and higher capital costs by trying to manipulate the company's financial image instead of just telling the truth. This quote confirms that a belief in the markets' efficiency is not a matter of faith but evidence:

> During the past 25 years or so, a great literature has been created that supports the hypothesis that financial markets are, to one degree or another, efficient. *How* efficient is a matter of debate among both practitioners and academics even today. In its most basic form, the efficient market hypothesis (EMH) states that information is quickly impounded in stock prices. The implications are that one cannot profit by having access to information that also is available to others. The evidence supporting the EMH is voluminous in the literatures of economics, finance, and accounting. There also is abundant literature that points out anomalies in the EMH. The degree to

which market efficiency actually exists is a matter that will continue to be debated for some time to come.

What we all may agree upon is that information does affect stock prices eventually. The corollary is that markets could not possibly be efficient if information were not available. . . . therefore, no matter how efficient or inefficient a financial market may be, information is its lifeblood. (p. 12)

The source of the markets' efficiency is also described in this short passage:

In sum, if markets are efficient, they are made so by the work of financial analysts who continually are seeking to find discrepancies between price and value and who advise on portfolio transactions accordingly. This moves market prices toward price-value equilibrium. (p. 14)

If managers cannot bring themselves to actually believe that the markets are efficient, they might as well act like efficiency exists. Otherwise, they are hoping that they will be among the very few who successfully fool the markets. Even if they could be in that small group, they wouldn't be able to sustain the ruse for very long.

On the other hand, if the markets are not very efficient, then we think it makes even more sense for managers to use Quality Financial Reporting to distinguish their reporting practices from those used by others. Specifically, if inefficiency were to reign, two conditions would be created. First, the markets would know that they were inefficient and go on to discount virtually all stock prices for the high degree of risk that would apply across the board. Second, inefficiency would lead to some securities being overvalued and others being undervalued. (While it might seem desirable for management to milk that inefficiency by trying to get and stay in the overvalued condition, it turns out that being there is not advantageous.[3]) If a management could give its financial reports a positive distinctive for completeness, candor, and trustworthiness, the demand for the company's stock and its real value would be increased. This outcome would be especially likely in an inefficient market because of the low overall quality of public information. In other words, market inefficiency would actually increase the advantages to be gained by pursuing QFR.

Who Are the Financial Statement Users?

Chapter 3 explains our view that the regulators' focus on individual investors is politically useful but unrealistic. Instead, managers need to understand and directly serve the needs of sophisticated financial analysts and then watch as the processed information flows down to the individuals. Thus, they should not hold back financial and other relevant factual details that the analysts need. Nor should they assume that they can drive market prices higher by choosing financial reporting policies that accentuate the good news while hiding the bad news. The committee affirmed this thinking with these words:

> A notable consequence of the rise of institutional investors is the increased need for financial reports written for and directed to the professionals who actually select or otherwise recommend the securities owned by institutions. They should be viewed as the primary audience for financial statements. The needs of individual investors are often cited in discussions of financial reporting. But the acumen, cognizance, and savvy of individual investors is often underestimated. It would be scandalous to deprive professional investment advisers, portfolio managers, and other financial analysts of information they need on the flimsy grounds that those data might confuse individuals who do not understand accounting. (p. 32)

This understanding that the most influential audience is smarter than average should also make managers conscious of how wise it is to satisfy these users' needs by making the public information complete and otherwise easier to consume. The AIMR used its discussion of the cash flow statement to warn managers of the fallacy of avoiding their own preparation costs by imposing processing costs on the financial statement users:

> . . . [I]f the [cash flow] reconciling items "can easily be evaluated by an analyst," they can even more easily (and accurately) be evaluated by the reporting enterprise. Not only that, but evaluation and adjustment, if done by the reporting enterprise, need be done only once, thus saving the greater efforts of and lesser accomplishments by the scores of individual analysts who may follow that firm. (p. 66)

This shifting by management of its efforts and preparation costs to users inevitably leads to discounted stock prices and a decline in the firm's market value greatly in excess of the management's one-time preparation costs. We describe more details about the trade-off between preparation and processing costs in Chapter 10.

Back to the Basics

We also asserted that the purpose of financial reporting is to put useful information in the hands of investors and creditors. The AIMR committee also endorses this objective:

> . . . [W]e must keep in mind that the primary purpose of financial reporting is to provide information that is valuable to financial statement users; it is not merely to produce reports that comply with a variety of arcane requirements nor to provide employment to accountants. Therefore, those who use financial statements should have a major voice in determining their form and content. (p. 78)

Of course, the FASB expressed this objective before either we or the AIMR report came along. The committee also endorsed the FASB's summary of what users need from the information in financial reports:

> ... [F]inancial analysts seek to prognosticate the amounts, timing, and risk attached to a firm's future cash flows—either directly or through such surrogates as earnings forecasts. (p. 17)

We have more to say later in the chapter about the users' focus on the future as opposed to accountants' common fixation on the past.

THE FOUR AXIOMS

In Chapter 1, we laid out our fundamental theory by describing these four axioms:

1. Incomplete information creates uncertainty.
2. Uncertainty creates risk for investors and creditors.
3. Risk makes investors and creditors demand a higher rate of return.
4. A higher rate of return for investors and creditors is a higher cost of capital for the firm and produces lower security prices.

From this perspective, it can be seen that the fundamental goal of financial reporting should be the elimination of as much uncertainty as possible. The AIMR committee said much the same thing when it explained the difference between financial reporting and financial analysis:

> The amounts and timing of future cash flows are in most cases uncertain to various degrees. It is the function of analysis to deal rationally with that uncertainty. It is the function of financial reporting to provide data useful to analysts making assessments of an enterprise's future cash flows and its values today. (p. 19)

The committee also acknowledged the relationship between reduced uncertainty and lower capital costs with this comment on the advantage of management's spending more money to get better audits:

> We expect that even if audit cost were to increase, it would be partially or wholly offset by the decreased cost of capital resulting from higher quality and more reliable information being made available to the financial markets. (p. 59)

Again, it seems clear that it is futile for managers to expect to be able to cut costs to "save" money in preparing and auditing financial reports and then go on to also obtain a lower cost of capital. Don't we all know that we can't buy a discount fare and fly first class? We describe audits and audit quality in more detail in Chapter 13.

THE SEVEN DEADLY SINS OF FINANCIAL REPORTING

In Chapter 2, we described the following seven mistakes that managers often make when engaging in financial reporting:

1. Underestimating the capital markets
2. Obfuscating
3. Hyping and spinning
4. Smoothing
5. Minimum reporting
6. Minimum auditing
7. Preparation cost myopia

The AIMR committee commented on each of these sins.

Underestimating the Capital Markets

One only has to read the monograph to grasp that the capital markets are both efficient and populated by highly intelligent analysts. Once that point is internalized, the tendency to underestimate the capital markets will evaporate.

For example, the committee used these words to address the ability of the markets to ferret out relevant information from a variety of sources:

> Sometimes it is asserted that financial statements do not contain new information. Analysts hope that assertion is true. If it is, that means that both the companies and the analysts who follow them have done their job successfully in making the market as efficient as can be. When a financial statement contains a "surprise" or two that causes a market price to change, one usually may conclude either that the analyst lacked perspicacity or that the company engaged in duplicity. (pp. 12–13)

In other words, the committee expects the markets to be so efficient that surprises arise only when analysts don't do their homework or a trusted management tries to pull off a trick or other deception. Surely, such tricks will taint the management's reputation (perhaps even for years) and raise the risk of doing business with the company. In the case of Enron, the deception was massive, perpetrated by a trusted management, and not reported by a reputable auditor. As a consequence, the fallout may have been sufficient to drag down the entire market because of the possibility that similar conditions exist for other significant companies.

Obfuscation

With regard to obfuscation, the AIMR committee offered up this succinct guideline:

> Financial reports have to be understandable. (p. 20)

The members also made these cogent comments:

> . . . [W]e could and do expect a better effort on the part of enterprises issu-
> ing financial reports to make their affairs more understandable to the
> investment analysts and advisors who simply are unable to devote major
> portions of their time to digesting imposing new pronouncements on
> abstruse accounting topics. (p. 79)

> . . . [R]isks are at least to be disclosed under the provisions of FASB State-
> ment 105 [for financial instruments], but the disclosures are scattered
> throughout the financial statement notes and are completely understood
> only by relatively sophisticated and tenacious financial statement readers.
> (p. 30)

In other words, managers have no positive payoff in the common practice
(intentional or otherwise) of putting out financial reports that are difficult
to decipher; however, they do have a lot to lose. This gamble is not worth
taking.

Hyping and Spinning

With regard to managers' tendencies to exaggerate to make themselves
look good, the analysts made these confirming observations:

> Companies send out press releases, hold analyst meetings, and otherwise
> see that news affecting them is presented in the most favorable light.
> (p. 12)

> We have observed, without surprise, that the existence of choices has intro-
> duced bias into financial reports. Any sensible financial manager, given a
> choice of methods, must select the one that makes his or her firm look best,
> if for no other reason than not to appear irrational to those who provide
> capital to the firm. (p. 71)

Here are two more comments:

> For financial reports to be useful, they must be trustworthy. (p. 34)

> Many companies entertain analysts, usually in groups, so that the compa-
> nies may present their stories in the most favorable circumstances. One of
> the tasks of an analyst is to sort through all of the favorable information to
> discover and weigh the facts that are most germane to assessing a com-
> pany's future prospects. (p. 15)

It seems to us that managers who know that their audience doesn't trust them to tell the truth should want to go an extra mile to ensure that this attitude is dispelled before making any claims about the company's past results, current condition, and future prospects.[4]

Smoothing

The AIMR financial analysts said quite a few things about the sin of smoothing, and not one of them is complimentary. The consistent theme is that they just want to have the facts so that they can do the analysis without having to undo the effects of management's elaborate attempts to make volatile results look nonvolatile. This comment is the most to the point:

> We believe that financial analysis is best served by financial reporting that reports transactions as and when they occur. If there is smoothing to be done, it is the province of analysts to do it. If there are financial reporting anomalies that are attributable to seasonality, it is far better to report and explain them than to conceal them with undocumented smoothing. (p. 58)

The following comments, which were made in the context of describing market value accounting for financial instruments, will probably shock managers who think analysts *automatically* abhor volatility:

> No matter how well mark-to-market accounting could be implemented and applied judiciously to matched assets and liabilities, it still would increase significantly the volatility of reported earnings. Some argue that the volatility exists and that a primary benefit of mark-to-market accounting is that real volatility would be revealed. We agree. . . .
>
> As financial reporting is practiced today, financial managers have much discretion over the recognition of changes in value by astute timing of exchange transactions and by the adoption of artful allocation procedures. Mark-to-market accounting would take away much of that discretion. Even where the relative influence of market value changes is small overall, at the margin it has the propensity to make earnings exceedingly unpredictable, a disconcerting fact for enterprises trying to minimize their capital costs by reporting smooth and growing earnings.
>
> Some analysts are quite willing to accept the increases in reported income volatility that would be produced under mark-to-market accounting. Many even would welcome it. They argue that the effects on a particular enterprise of general economic conditions and financial market movements are relevant and vital to their assessments of the enterprise's economic status and progress over time. (pp. 43–44)

These thoughts are clearly contrary to the conventional wisdom. Of course, one of our objectives in writing about QFR is to stand convention on its ear.

Minimum Reporting

Two of our chief claims in the prior chapters are that managers are sorely mistaken if they think (1) that it is enough to report only the least amount they are required to report and (2) that the FASB and SEC can be depended on to define requirements that are sufficient to adequately reduce investors' uncertainty. The AIMR committee had this to say about those attitudes:

> We worry that the purpose of a standard can be thwarted by a grudging compliance with only its technical requirements. We look in financial reports for information—and often its provision requires explanations that go beyond the minimum reporting requirements contained in a standard or checklist. (pp. 20–21)

The analysts have made it clear that they don't consider the minimum to be enough.

The next statement takes the FASB off the hook for not having enough political power to make unwilling (and unwise) managers do what they ought to know is good for themselves:

> Some investment analysts have even begun to question whether those who prepare financial reports understand the purpose for which a particular standard was issued. The FASB and the SEC set *minimum* disclosure requirements. There is no proscription on relating more or explaining that which is disclosed. We should not blame the FASB because it cannot mandate a willingness on the part of managements to decipher and illuminate their affairs. (p. 79)

If analysts say that minimum reporting isn't getting the job done, then managers should wake up to that fact and start providing the needed and desired information voluntarily without waiting for a dysfunctional political process to produce mandatory requirements that will magically lead to lower capital costs. This volitional expansion above and beyond GAAP is the essence of Quality Financial Reporting.

Minimum Auditing

The next sin that managers often commit is denigrating the contribution of auditing to the usefulness of externally reported financial information. The whole idea behind auditing is to reduce uncertainty, but many managers don't seem to grasp that point. Neither do a lot of auditors, with the consequence that typical audits are not really value-adding activities.

Although the following comment was offered in a discussion of the issues related to financial reporting by non-U.S. companies audited by non-U.S. audit firms, it should serve as a clarion call to managers who think it is a good idea to have a friendly and pliant auditor who does not object very often:

> In particular, we regard independence as an essential prerequisite to attestation. (p. 25)

The AIMR analysts also went so far as to propose an evolution in auditing away from focusing on the numbers in the financial statements to having the auditors attest to the suitability of the processes used by management in preparing financial statements. They said:

> [The role of external auditors] should be to assist enterprises to establish procedures and routines that minimize the time taken to get reports prepared and lessen the probability of material errors or misstatements. (p. 58)

They went on:

> . . . [W]e envision external auditors being substantially more involved with the functioning of the internal systems that produce financial data for external consumption. . . . In short, we believe that too much attention is paid to the numbers and too little to the process that produces them. (p. 59)

They concluded the discussion with the following words, quoted earlier in this chapter:

> We expect that even if audit cost were to increase, it would be partially or wholly offset by the decreased cost of capital resulting from higher quality and more reliable information being made available to the financial markets. (p. 59)

We have more to say about audits and auditors under QFR in Chapter 13.

Preparation Cost Myopia

It turns out that the AIMR committee denounced the management sin of focusing on the out-of-pocket costs of preparing financial statements and financial reports without considering the benefits. These users' statements should be enough to cause managers to rethink their old habits of always looking for the cheapest way to get by with doing the least.

The following comment is especially meaningful because it greatly expands the breadth of the costs that ought to be included in management's analysis. The main point is that the total costs include both management's costs of producing information *plus* users' costs of processing information. A second major point is that cutting the first costs invariably causes the second to increase. The eventual results are higher capital costs and lower security prices. Consider these words:

In particular, it is the providers of financial statements from whom the claim of excessive cost is heard. We can respond by asserting that the cost to them, high as it may seem, is still less than the benefit to financial statement users of (1) minimizing the cost of providing the data by having the firm do it once and provide it to multitudes of users who otherwise would individually have to replicate the firm's effort; (2) having the firm as the source of information thus obviating the need for analysts to scavenge for less reliable data from secondary sources; and (3) making available an additional source of information that confirms or denies other sources. (p. 81)

In the following statement, the committee makes three strong points on the managers' myopia in not looking outside the confines of their own budgets:

. . . [W]e need to consider who bears the cost of providing the information that appears in financial reports. In one very real sense, there is no added compliance cost to financial statement preparers. Their salaries remain unchanged and may even be enhanced as the scope of their responsibilities is enlarged. The costs are paid out of general corporate funds and, ultimately, are borne by the firm's investors, the users of financial statements. The cost of information is one of the prices we pay for efficient financial markets. (p. 82)

In other words, the analysts ascribe little credibility to management objections about compliance costs. After all, it isn't the managers' money.

The committee also went on to address the issue of just who pays for and who benefits from improved reporting:

We argue that users of financial statements are also the owners of the enterprises being reported upon, and it is the users who, in addition to receiving the benefits, ultimately bear the cost of providing financial reports. (p. 6)

Investors are the ones who suffer both the cost and reap the benefits of improved financial reports. We would hope that company managers, who are their agents, should not confuse their own personal interests with those of their principals. (p. 82)

With these thoughts, the committee again destroyed another piece of conventional wisdom, specifically the old chestnut that there is a fundamental unfairness in having preparers incur costs while investors reap the benefits. In fact, as owners of the reporting companies, it is the investors who both pay and reap. And, for good measure, the committee reminds us that management is always to be considered to be the agent for the owners and not the other way around.

GAAP AREN'T GOOD ENOUGH

We used Chapters 4 and 5 to explain the political nature of the process for creating GAAP and showed numerous examples of specific situations in which it produces financial reporting standards that are compromised and otherwise not up to the task of fully informing investors and creditors in the capital markets. The AIMR committee also expressed its own disappointments with the quality of information produced by complying with the accepted principles.

One point was the members' view of the kind of information that they consider to be useful:

> In an ideal world, the most relevant accounting data would be those that reported assets and liabilities in a way that would allow analysts to impute the future cash flows emanating from them individually and collectively. (p. 33)

This stance means that the information reported in the financial statements about assets and liabilities should help users anticipate future cash flows. Thus, the committee was endorsing the same objective adopted by the FASB. However, the monograph states that the focus on the past in GAAP financial statements does not produce that result:

> Financial statements express net worth as the surplus of total assets over total liabilities. Because [GAAP measures of] assets and liabilities are both the result of *past* transactions and events, so is the accounting measure of net worth. (p. 17)

The committee also expressed frustration that GAAP cause accountants to produce reports based on carefully verified but irrelevant facts that don't help analysts reach their objective:

> Certainly financial analysts desire information that is both relevant and reliable, but their bias is towards relevance. In a phrase, analysts prefer information that is equivocally right rather than precisely wrong. Inexact measures of contemporaneous economic values generally are more useful than fastidious historic records of past exchanges. (p. 33)

In addition, the committee members described another disconnect between GAAP and their needs for valid and otherwise useful information:

> In many cases, we see accounting that differs because of the form of the underlying transaction, not its substance. Concurrently, we see differences in substance that are not reflected in the accounting. (p. 28)

In other words, these financial statement users agree that GAAP aren't good enough.

Specific Shortcomings

In addition to general criticisms, the AIMR committee also described several specific shortcomings in GAAP. Early in the report, one of our own pet peeves is mentioned:

> If we are to have financial statements in the traditional form, they ought to include what they purport to contain. For example, many so-called "off balance sheet" items should be on the balance sheet. (p. 20)

To our way of thinking, this assertion is a no-brainer. The only reason for managers to engage in off-balance-sheet-financing is to try to fool users of financial statements into believing that they are not as far in debt as they really are. (In any other setting, wouldn't that action be called lying?) Once this behavior is uncovered, a taint of untrustworthiness is attached to the management and the resulting uncertainty will tend to produce higher capital costs, just the opposite of what the managers wanted to bring about.

Another area of practice criticized by the AIMR is accounting for business combinations. This lengthy comment hits several nails right on the head:

> Many people believe that existing values (in a combination) can be [recognized] only when a transaction takes place, a major premise of accounting as practiced today. For example, when Firm A is purchased by Firm B, it is the assets and liabilities of Firm A that are recorded at their fair value, not those of Firm B. That is because those values are considered to have been validated by a transaction, even though the transaction was at a single price for the entire firm and cannot be a reliable measure of the specific value of any of its components. One could then argue that whatever techniques are used to place values on the individual assets and liabilities of Firm A could be used to restate the assets and liabilities of Firm B. If not, then we perhaps ought not to apply them to Firm A.
>
> An even more difficult situation arises when Firm B acquires less than total ownership of Firm A. Under current practice, only the proportionate share of Firm A's assets and liabilities owned by Firm B are revalued, but all of Firm A's assets and liabilities—partially revalued, partially not—are consolidated with those of Firm B, none of whose assets and liabilities have been revalued. What a mélange! The result is a combination of historic and current values that only a mystic could sort out with precision. (p. 28)

Despite several years of effort on updating GAAP for combinations, the best the FASB could do in 2001 was to issue a new standard (SFAS 141) eliminating pooling, which added book values of both companies, while perpetuating the purchase method, which can produce the indecipherable "mélange" that the AIMR complained about. This point reinforces our observation that managers should not sit around waiting for the FASB and

SEC to produce innovative solutions to old problems. Despite the passage of 30 years and the accumulation of a tremendous amount of knowledge about the capital markets and how they make decisions, the FASB's best effort on combinations was to endorse the APB's decision from 1970 that purchase accounting is better than pooling. The FASB never really got around to discussing the issue of whether new basis accounting might be better, and may have never even considered the possibility that accounting for all companies with market values at all times might provide the most useful information for assessing future cash flows. We think the AIMR has helped make our case on how unwise it is to expect the regulatory system to create innovation and keep financial reporting practice on the leading edge.

One thing that the FASB did change about purchase accounting was its treatment of so-called goodwill—the amount of the purchase price paid in excess of the estimated market values of the identifiable assets of the acquired company less the market values of its liabilities. The FASB did away with amortizing that cost over a predicted "useful" life and introduced the practice of leaving the goodwill's cost balance on the books until management encounters sufficient evidence to show that its value has been impaired. In creating this policy, the board completely disregarded the AIMR's preferred treatment, as described in these three quotes:

> . . . [W]e recommend that purchased goodwill be written off at the date it is acquired. We believe that it is an important number, but only to depict a value at a particular date—a value that undoubtedly is subject to rapid and sizable potential change thereafter. . . . Therefore, we recommend banishing goodwill from an enterprise's list of assets, but preserving a record of it by having it show as a separate and distinct reduction of shareholders' equity. (p. 4)

> Once it has been established for the record how much was paid to acquire goodwill, it ought to be removed from the list of assets forthwith. (p. 49)

> Goodwill should not be recognized except briefly as it is determined by the exchange price for an entire enterprise because (a) its determination (except at the rarely-encountered moment of an exchange) is the stuff of financial analysis, not accounting, and (b) its value at that moment is fleeting and has no necessary or causal relationship to its value in the future. (p. 52)

In effect, the analysts said that they don't want to bother with removing the goodwill balance from the financial statements. They would just as soon management would take it away because they cannot use the cost balance to predict future cash flows. With respect to finding convergence between the views of the FASB and the user constituency, we think there is a large gap in GAAP.

The AIMR also expressed its frustration with accounting for another GAAP intangible called *software development costs:*

> FASB Statement 86 sets standards for accounting for the cost of computer software to be sold, leased, or otherwise marketed. Its reasoning is in accord with traditional accounting thought, but its result is to place on the balance sheet as an asset an amount that depicts neither the value of the software nor the total cost of developing it. (p. 30)

Again, the committee members are faulting GAAP (and the FASB) for putting a useless number in the financial statements that they have to go to the trouble of removing. At the same time, they are expressing their frustration at not having access to information they want to have.

The committee emptied both barrels on the bias inherent in "lower of cost or market" methods and accountants' focus on "impaired" assets:

> . . . [A]lmost all [financial analysts] would agree that so-called "lower of cost or market" methods are neither informative nor useful. . . . The best argument that can be made in favor of lower of cost or market is that it does reveal market values when they are lower than cost, thus divulging important information on certain asset impairments. (p. 34)

> Not only do we need standards that make asset impairment writedowns more predictable, we also find it peculiar that many accountants deem writedowns to be good because they are "conservative" whereas writeups are not. It seems to us that whatever criteria are applied to determine writedowns would be every bit as verifiable and useful if also applied to writeups. (p. 28)

This same criticism can be applied to even freshly minted standards, especially the "impairment" treatment of goodwill in SFAS 142, issued by the FASB in July 2001, and the lower of cost or market treatment for long-lived assets imbedded in SFAS 144, which was published in August 2001. The only usefulness in this general downward bias is its protection for auditors.

The AIMR was not reluctant to disapprove of the generally accepted orientation toward measures based on past transactions:

> In many . . . facets [of the FASB's financial instruments project], we are being forced to face up to the deficiencies arising from application of historic cost accounting to financial instruments. (p. 31)

> Historic costs are sunk costs and there is little disagreement [among analysts] that they are often irrelevant to financial decisions. (p. 33)

> Historic costs, even more so lower of cost or market procedures, tend to introduce bias in favor of buyers of securities by suppressing good news while revealing the bad straight away. The absence of adjustments to reflect price changes, even as supplementary information only, in North American

accounting standards institutes a bias that varies in proportion to (1) the
rate of price change, (2) the dispersion of those changes among the various
goods and services traded, and (3) the holding period for assets whose
prices change. (p. 37)

Nonetheless, the analysts were generally pragmatic about the traditional
emphasis on cost measures and several times indicated their reluctance to
endorse a wholesale abandonment of the familiar and its replacement by
the unfamiliar. A QFR management can deal with this situation with
extensive supplemental disclosures, as the FASB recommended in SFAS
89. Few if any members of today's management corps have done so, however.

Despite this reluctance, the AIMR committee members had fresh
memories of the FASB's struggles in the early 1990s trying to require management
to use market values instead of applying lower of cost or market
for reporting on investment securities held by the reporting entity. As
described in Chapter 5, the board was hammered in the political process
over its initial efforts for mark-to-market accounting, and compromised
by first creating three portfolios and then specifying different asset and
income measures for each of them. The AIMR was obviously not pleased
with this solution:

> [The] recently issued FAS 115 goes part of the way by requiring marketable
> equity securities to be reported at market value, but using historic cost as
> the basis for recognition of gain or loss [from sale] for most such securities.
> We support the valuation but not the gain/loss recognition provisions of
> FAS 115. (pp. 40–41)

In fact, the committee had a great many comments on the desirability
of current market value information for all assets and liabilities. We
will present a large number of them in Chapter 15, which covers the topic
of value-based accounting in more detail.

How Slow Can It Go?

In closing this section on GAAP, we want to include one more quote from
the AIMR, this time on the rate of change in practice:

> The financial reporting process is most useful when it goes beyond the past
> and present to include management's views of its future strategies, plans,
> and expectations. For example, management currently is required in the
> MD&A section of its annual report to shareholders to report how the
> results of each of the past three years differ one from another. The SEC
> strongly encourages but does not require similar discussion of how management
> expects the results of future years to differ from those of the past.
> Why have managements been so slow to respond to this urging? We have
> seen some improvement recently, but the pace is glacial. (p. 21)

In contrast to the foot-dragging complained about here, managers who embrace the Quality Financial Reporting paradigm will be way out in front of the SEC in trying to gain an advantage over their capital market competitors by improving the quantity and quality of their disclosures.

TIMELINESS

Another characteristic of QFR is its encouragement of more timely reporting. The more quickly information is published, the more quickly uncertainty is removed, along with the concomitant risk. The inevitable result of more timely reporting is lower capital costs and higher security prices.

When the AIMR's report was being produced in the early 1990s, there was a lot of public discussion of proposals to actually *reduce* the frequency of public reports from four times a year to only two. The purported advantage was to eradicate management's focus on the short term by eliminating quarterly reports. This logic is short-circuited by the four axioms because they show that a longer delay between interim reports increases uncertainty and raises capital costs.

In response to the proposals, which were being seriously advanced, the AIMR felt obliged to defend quarterly reporting, as shown in the following series of quotations. The committee's comments need to be interpreted in their contemporary context, which was without the Internet and the World Wide Web. As far as the committee members were concerned, quarterly reporting was about the best that could be accomplished at the time. We now consider quarterly reporting to be too infrequent. With that idea in mind, here are several of their comments on timely reporting:

> We believe that financial markets, both domestic and foreign, are best served by frequent and even-handed dissemination of information to the public. (p. 24)

> In most other countries, financial reports are issued semi-annually; in a few countries, only annual reporting is the norm. Some people now advocate that the United States abolish its quarterly reporting requirement and regress to semi-annual or even annual reporting only. . . . AIMR unequivocally supports quarterly financial reporting and is opposed to any movement to eliminate it. (p. 24)

> . . . [F]inancial information is useful only when it is disseminated quickly, fairly, and widely because the digestion of such information by analysts is what makes the markets efficient. (p. 36)

Another factor in the historic context for these comments was a burgeoning movement in favor of retracting insider trading laws and penalties. The following three comments respond to that proposition with strength and clarity:

One of the major tenets of a free-enterprise economic system is that information is disseminated completely and fairly to all market participants.
(p. 90)

A collateral benefit of frequent financial reporting is that it diminishes
opportunities for trading on privileged information, a practice AIMR and
other responsible members of the investment community deplore. The
longer a company waits to release information to the public, the more
likely it is that the information will become known sooner to a small and
select group that can use it to trade for its own benefit. Even under current
disclosure rules, which many find draconian, financial information has
from time to time been intercepted or diverted on its way to dissemination.
(p. 36)

Financial analysis thrives on information. . . . [F]or capital allocation to proceed efficiently in our economy, information must be disseminated both
promptly and *publicly*. This applies to financial information, both in the
form of financial statements and otherwise, as well as to sources of all nonfinancial data that can affect perceptions of the value of companies. The
two conditions, promptly and publicly, are complementary. . . . [I]f financial information is not disclosed to the public promptly, it will become
known first to a small number of privileged "insiders," only later filtering
down to the public at large. Those circumstances place an onerous burden
on AIMR members, all of whom are prohibited from using material non-
public information by the AIMR Code of Ethics and Standards of Professional Conduct. (p. 52)

While the last sentiments may be unrealistic because of the tempta-
tion facing some analysts who gain access to inside information, the fact
remains that the widespread fear of the existence of this information creates uncertainty in the minds of capital market participants. By now, we
all know what that uncertainty does to risk, capital costs, and security
prices.

SUMMARY

This chapter has two objectives. The first is adding evidence that the need
for Quality Financial Reporting has emerged from the failure of managers
and accountants to see that GAAP and other forms of minimalist reporting fall extremely short of meeting the needs of financial statement users.
Thus, the QFR idea cannot be dismissed offhandedly as the fruit of the
imagination of a couple of accounting professors. The demand for better
reporting is quite clear.

The second objective is to put a long series of financial analysts'
thoughts on the plates of the managers and accountants who are reading
this book. For far too long, they have made oversimplified assumptions

about those thoughts, primarily for the purpose of rationalizing the GAAP compromises that have been reached to satisfy what they saw as their own interests in looking good in the financial statements (managers), incurring low compliance costs (CFOs), and protecting their own assets against recrimination (auditors). Those assumptions are seriously challenged by the contents of this chapter. We hope that this thought gets through to all of our readers.

NOTES

1. As briefly described in Chapter 2, the AIMR is the largest and most prestigious professional society of financial analysts, portfolio managers, and other investment professionals. Among its activities is the awarding of the Certified Financial Analyst (CFA) designation to expert financial statement users.

2. Cope resigned from the FASB in 2001 when he was named a full-time member of the newly formed International Accounting Standards Board.

3. The key to understanding this paradox is that an overvalued situation helps only those shareholders who sell their stock, while it hurts the new stockholders because they have paid too much as a result of the efforts of the managers who now work for them. Another disadvantage of overvaluation for managers is that it can increase the strike price of incentive options and decrease their value. This topic is discussed further in Chapter 8 through the advice provided by Warren Buffett and Professor Baruch Lev.

4. In response to Enron's huge surprises, the management of another corporation in the same line of business decided to distance itself from the failed company. As reported in *Fortune* (Nelson D. Schwartz, "Enron Fallout: Wide but Not Deep," December 24, 2001, p. 72), "Last month Mirant CEO Marce Fuller spent an hour and a half taking analysts in Atlanta and New York through each line of Mirant's balance sheet. This isn't a topic that would have been included in an analysts' meeting in the past, but there's going to be a lot more pressure on companies like ourselves to help people understand how we make money.' " We see a glimpse of QFR in this action.

CHAPTER 8

The Weight
of the Evidence

Based on what we have shown in the first seven chapters, we hope that only those who are most resistant to change are holding out against the advantages promised by Quality Financial Reporting. To try to persuade even more managers and accountants (and others as well), this chapter provides additional evidence that the ideas behind QFR are valid. While the previous chapter shows unequivocally that the members of the AIMR's Financial Accounting Policy Committee strongly desire more informative corporate reporting, it is important to understand that we and they do not stand alone in voicing this demand and encouraging change. These are some of the points that we try to make in the following pages.

As you'll see, we weren't the first ones to come up with some of the ideas. Of course, that fact does nothing to diminish their power and their potential for inducing managers and accountants to create their own change without waiting for someone to require them to start doing something different.

A second point is confirmation of our claim that many people have also been blind to the disadvantages of the status quo, to the point that they have not been able to comprehend the limitations of the traditional concept that it is sufficient and best to comply with GAAP and then stop. They are, as we have said, content to be dysfunctionally codependent with standard setters and regulators in stumbling around doing the same things without ever thinking innovatively.

A third point that we put forward is that some research has revealed that the truths inherent in the four axioms are borne out in the capital markets. This fact, at the very least, disarms critics of QFR who say that there is no empirical evidence to back them up. Now that there is some proof, we expect them to still dispute the axioms' validity, simply because they are afraid to change from what they have always done. We describe some of this evidence in Chapter 9.

Here are the sources we discuss in this chapter:

Survey-based studies

- The Jenkins Committee
- The ValueReporting Revolution
- Epstein and Palepu

Notable experts

- Baruch Lev
- Warren Buffett
- Neel Foster

There are, of course, a great many other sources, and certainly a lot more that we haven't come across yet. We're not trying to catalog every possible piece of evidence; rather, our goal is to present persuasive data that our ideas are sound and useful.

SURVEY-BASED STUDIES

From the beginning of this book, one of our themes has been an urging to managers to get in touch with capital market participants in the same way they have gotten in touch with their customers, employees, and supply chain partners. One step that has been taken is surveying participants to uncover their satisfied and unsatisfied needs and wants. In fact, a great deal of this kind of research has already been performed.

Before looking at three efforts in the area, we feel compelled to observe that while surveys are useful, their ability to uncover new ideas is limited. For example, we're not absolutely sure, but we're pretty confident in speculating that if someone had asked administrative assistants and typists 25 years ago what they would have wanted to help them do their work more quickly and neatly, they all would have started by suggesting ways to improve typewriters and correcting fluid. Not a single one of them would have come up with the idea of entering information into a computer's memory and then displaying it on a screen and making changes and corrections there instead of on the typed page. Nonetheless, word processors and laser printers came along and have almost completely replaced typewriters and correcting fluid. Our point is that just asking people what they would like to have will not always produce a vision of how to make things better.

In addition to the survey responses, we also use these discussions to show that even high-powered groups and astute individuals have missed the weaknesses in their financial reporting presentations because they could not get outside the paradigm of mandatory uniform reporting under a regulatory system.

The Jenkins Committee

In the early 1990s, the American Institute of Certified Public Accountants created a Special Committee on Financial Reporting and charged it with the task of identifying the kinds of information that managers should provide to investors and creditors and with recommending how auditors should be involved with that information. The committee worked for three years to produce its 1994 report, which is usually called the Jenkins Committee Report after its chair, Edmund Jenkins.[1] The report's official title is very much in line with QFR: *Improving Business Reporting—A Customer Focus.* The committee and its staff designed and implemented a variety of research plans to gather information about the needs and wants of users. It is also commendable that they made their database available to others to allow them to perform additional research.

However, the committee membership was dominated by practicing public accountants with a couple of corporate accountants and one academician. There were no users to be seen on the membership list. Perhaps this dominance explains why the results of the study are limited—in our view, they are stunted by the committee's apparent assumption that any change in financial reporting practice would have to be created by regulation, not by voluntary efforts going beyond GAAP. This sentence from the report includes some clues to that effect as it explains why the committee was afraid to ask financial statement users open-ended questions about what they might want to find in financial reports:

> Without the ability to evaluate the relative usefulness of information, . . . recommendations [for change] go too far, suggesting the need for information that does not improve the decision processes of users and thereby inflicting unnecessary costs on the reporting process. (p. 11)

In effect, this committee of mostly auditors made the same mistake as most of its predecessors by aiming to sort through the kinds of information that could be reported and identifying those that should be *supplied* instead of simply trying to figure out what the users *demand* and leaving the matter of supply up to those who do the reporting. A signal is also sent about their views and emotions in the words *inflicting unnecessary costs.* Only the more powerful can inflict unnecessary costs on the less powerful; thus, the committee members clearly saw that the content of financial reports inevitably depends on political power, and completely missed the possibility that economic incentives could motivate managers to willingly incur some new costs to voluntarily improve their reporting methods.

Just for confirmation, the same demand-driven, regulator-dependent paradigm is evident in this sentence:

> The accelerating pace of change today coupled with the long lead time necessary to effect improvements in business reporting require standard setters and regulators to anticipate the changing needs of users. (pp. 15–16)

While we probably felt this way ourselves in 1994, QFR has since given us a different point of view that shows how absurdly preposterous, even hopeless, it is for a group of accountants and/or auditors to sort through all the possible needs, come up with one set of designated useful information, and then develop enough political power to force every management to report it. This obsolete paradigm now reminds us of a committee of factory managers in a planned economy deciding what they are going to make and sell in the upcoming season according to the cost and ease of making the products without considering what consumers want and can afford. It makes so much more sense to allow individual producers to do their research and then take to market the products that they believe they can both produce and sell at a suitable profit.

Despite these flaws, we find that various aspects of the Jenkins Committee report confirm the QFR ideas that we have been presenting. For example, the following quotation summarizes what the committee discovered about users' assessments of common practices and supports our assertion that managers do not win the capital markets' confidence by manipulating their financial image within the constraints of GAAP:

> Users are very concerned about the reliability of information in business reporting. They believe that many companies' managements are not forthright in reporting problems and poor company performance, that much of the information they disseminate is too promotional, and that troubled companies take great pains to convey the impression that they are not seriously troubled. Although they have confidence in management integrity, users say managers commonly procrastinate about disclosing problems and many managers express a more optimistic view of their companies' situations than seems warranted by the users' own analyses. Users believe, for example, that management emphasizes non-recurring losses while burying non-recurring gains in continuing earnings. They also believe that management tends to double up when reporting bad news by also recognizing other losses that have occurred earlier but whose recognition has been deferred or losses whose current recognition will avoid the need to recognize expenses or losses in the future. (p. 32)

At the very least, this observation ought to puncture any thoughts by managers that their hyping, spinning, and smoothing are actually fooling anyone.

The committee also spent some time discussing the relationship between the reported information and the reporting entity's cost of capital. The report first asserted:

> Increased informative disclosure benefits users by reducing the likelihood that they will misallocate their capital. This is obviously a direct benefit to individual users of business reports. The disclosure reduces the risk of misallocation by enabling users to improve their assessments of a company's prospects. (p. 38)

The committee went on to say that improving users' ability to assess the future cash flows and make better decisions also has an

> . . . effect on the disclosing entity's cost of capital. The benefits to users are translated into lower capital prices, a benefit for companies. This takes place across the total population of disclosing companies and is therefore a reduction in the average company's cost of capital. (p. 38)

The committee went on to explain, without specifically invoking the four axioms, that higher-quality information produces a lower cost of capital, even if it reports bad news:

> . . . [W]hen the information indicates poor prospects, it means that the entity's economic risk is high, not that the increment in information is functioning to raise the price of capital. Getting a better understanding of the true economic risk would still lower the price of capital for the average company. (p. 39)

In other words, based on its surveys and other types of research, the committee confirms that reporting more complete information will lead to lower capital costs than reporting incomplete information. The committee lamented that there was no empirical proof of the proposition that "informative disclosure lowers the cost of capital." We'll address that issue in the next chapter.

There are, of course, a great many other points in this report concerning the kinds of information that the committee thought managers ought to be forced to report by new standards. Thus, the Jenkins Committee report could be a good source for those who would like to find out more about the kinds of things they could provide voluntarily.

In hindsight, it is regrettable that the committee members could not have glimpsed the QFR paradigm that relies on economic incentives instead of regulatory mandates to get management to go beyond the minimum limits of GAAP to supply what is demanded instead of supplying what the supplier wants or is forced to publish. Despite this limitation, we believe that the report supports the ideas we have been advocating.

The ValueReporting Revolution

After several years in development, the global accounting firm of Price-waterhouseCoopers (PwC) announced and then launched an initiative called ValueReporting that is very similar to QFR, although it tends to focus on reporting one new class of items rather than the wider spectrum of the kinds of useful information we think managers would benefit from reporting.

Under the leadership of Robert Eccles, a business professor at Harvard before affiliating with PwC, the project is an effort to encourage managers to report more information about their firms' specific performance measures (mostly nonfinancial in nature) so that users will not have to guess or otherwise make decisions while swimming in uncertainty. The rest of the four-person team identified with the project are Robert Herz (who was named chair of the FASB in 2002), Mary Keegan, and David Phillips. This group put together a book called *The ValueReporting Revolution* that was published in 2000 by John Wiley & Sons, Inc.

With these words from that book, the authors issue a call to arms that we think is pretty much in line with QFR:

> This . . . revolution has a name: ValueReporting. This is its manifesto: a call to managers to adopt a philosophy of complete transparency   to report information to the market on *all* the measures they use internally to manage. And that encompasses performance dimensions that other stakeholders regard as important as well, including social and environmental responsibility. (p. 5)

In addition to displaying the firm's idiosyncratic penchant for leaving out spaces between words in titles, this quote shows that the PwC team is working right at the heart of QFR and its reliance on the idea that management is better off when it reports openly and completely.

A key part of the background for the book was a large survey, which they described briefly as follows:

> In 1997 and 1998, PricewaterhouseCoopers surveyed hundreds of institutional investors and sell-side analysts in 14 countries. (pp. 3–4)

The findings showed some interesting results in terms of the low level of satisfaction with current financial reporting practices by both users and managers:

> Only 19 percent of the investors polled and 27 percent of the analysts found financial reports very useful in communicating the true value of companies.
>
> The preparers of these reports—the companies themselves—agree. Only 38 percent of executives in the United States felt that their reports were very useful. Even more dramatically, in a similar survey of the high-tech industry in the United States and Canada, only 7 percent of the investors,

16 percent of analysts, and 13 percent of company executives found reported information very useful in determining the true value of a company. (p. 4)

As an aside, we would like to know exactly which 16 percent of the analysts think GAAP are good enough so that we can avoid taking their investment advice and which 7 percent of the institutional investors feel this way so that we can avoid buying their mutual funds or allowing them to handle our pension plans.

These survey results also reveal a disconnect in the sense that up to twice as many managers as recipients attribute credibility to their financial reports. We think these statistics confirm our hypothesis that managers and accountants tend to be satisfied with the idea that financial reporting ought to be driven by supply rather than demand.

At various places in the book, we find support for our claims of the benefits of voluntarily adopting QFR and our vision for uncoerced initiatives outside the regulated reporting system:

> It is *inevitable* that a key contribution to solving a problem deeply embedded in the capital markets will come from the product markets. The market hungers for more—and more useful—information, delivered more quickly than ever. It *will* be satisfied. Entrepreneurs working inside garages and inside corporate behemoths will seize this opportunity to satisfy the market's hunger for information and will profit from doing so. (p. 7)

> Managers, who often have stock options and are only human, generally tend to place their company's worth higher than the market does. (What parents don't think their children are exceptional?) Perhaps they are right, and the market *does* in fact undervalue their company's shares. After all, these managers have information about their companies that the market doesn't. Only with such information could the market make a reasonable determination of stock value. (pp. 48–49)

These assertions support the four axioms:

> [The lack of] the right kind of information . . . leads to uncertainty and results in more conservative projections of revenues, earnings, and cash flows. Uncertainty can also increase the perception of risk, which results in a higher discount rate being applied to profit projections because of the higher cost of capital. The outcome is a lower stock price than might be justified if more and different information were available. (p. 49)

> In extreme cases, a lack of information about a company can cause an investor to avoid investing in its stock at all. A recent survey conducted for *Investor Relations Magazine* by Rivel Research Group provides the evidence. Of 1,700 investment professionals surveyed, 78 percent said they did not recommend or invest in a stock because of inadequate information. (pp. 49–50)

With regard to managers' needs for shaking free from their lethargic codependence with regulators and deep-seated resistance to imposed changes, Eccles et al. make these statements concerning voluntary reporting without waiting for new standards and rules:

> Shouldn't executives enthusiastically support any initiative that seeks to change the [earnings] game? Shouldn't they, in fact, work actively to change the game themselves? Couldn't they just say, "We're not going to play anymore," and start offering the market the information on nonfinancial measures and intangible assets it wants and needs?
>
> Certainly no one requires companies to provide such information, but no one says they can't. Managers who think their companies' stocks are undervalued, and most do, should be especially motivated to do this. And they should provide earnings information as regularly as possible to mitigate the event nature of quarterly earnings announcements as well. (p. 102)

> The brutal reality is that relatively little has been done to systematically address the need or process for providing the information the market wants. Instead, the inexorable activities of regulators and accounting standard-setters, particularly those in the United States, continue to generate more and more rules that further complicate a financial reporting model that many view as increasingly less relevant. Equally unfortunate, there are also strong, firmly constructed barriers to speeding up the process of developing a new reporting and disclosure model. (p. 103)

Concerning the wisdom of being first to escape the clutches of the status quo and embrace voluntary change, they say:

> Clearly, all the players can take some measure of responsibility for erecting institutional barriers to changing the very nature of corporate disclosure in terms of both content and process. Given the inevitability of such change, however, companies should follow the example of their predecessors, lead the process, and stay one step ahead of the regulators. After all, the market sees the need for the change and will force it to happen, with or without regulatory solutions. (p. 105)

The following comment reinforces our thesis that voluntary reporting is essential because the existing regulatory system is just not going to produce the kind of innovation that addresses the capital markets' needs:

> Regulators, professional standard-setters, and academics simply cannot *initiate* new reporting practices for new measures without support from the business community. The executives who run the companies that need the capital have responsibility for providing to investors the information they need. (p. 109)

Like us, the authors also have a vision for a great many benefits for all parties from improved disclosure. They backed their views up with a survey of what others believe, as described here:

> A PricewaterhouseCoopers global survey of institutional investors and sell-side analysts identified what those groups see as the five most important benefits of better disclosure: increased management credibility, more long-term investors, greater analyst following, improved access to new capital, and higher share values. (p. 189)

As a result, it appears to us that the ValueReporting and QFR revolutions are different routes to the same ending point. Furthermore, it also appears that a great many in the financial reporting community are ready for the change.

Finally, the Eccles group clearly agrees with our view that benefits will follow when managers embrace the capital markets as partners in the same way that they have embraced other markets:

> If management truly views shareholders as partners, and places creating value for them near or at the top of its primary responsibilities, then it should treat them as such. Management should give shareholders information on strategic plans and performance and actively solicit their feedback on both. If shareholders don't like the strategies and register dissatisfaction with the company's performance, management should listen to their complaints and quickly learn what has caused them. (p. 209)

Despite the similarity, this last statement also differentiates their approach from ours. We think they are expecting more than we do when it comes to managers' responsibilities. We are content to point out that the quest for higher stock prices provides sufficient mutual economic benefits to change managers' behavior without invoking higher-level responsibilities and duties. It's not that we don't agree that better reporting has a dimension of responsibility to it; we just think that the economic effects of truth telling have greater potential for changing behavior than appeals to a higher duty.

On the whole, we find little in this ValueReporting Revolution to disagree with, apart from this appeal to a higher sense of duty and a tendency to accept GAAP financial statements as satisfactory for reporting financial results and conditions.

Epstein and Palepu

Another survey provides additional evidence about the gap between acceptable financial reporting practices and what financial statement users want. In particular, Professors Marc Epstein and Krishna Palepu solicited opinions from a large number of financial analysts on questions about where they felt their needs were being met and where they were being left unsatisfied.[2] For example, they provide these overall summary statements of their results:

Most analysts do find annual reports an important source of information. The management discussion and analysis section and most other parts are well read and used. One notable exception is the balance sheet that analysts often perceive as irrelevant because of its reliance on historical costs and arbitrary write-offs of intangible assets. . . .

Footnotes seem to frustrate analysts the most. When asked which components of the annual report they often have a hard time understanding and which they would like explained more, star analysts rated the footnotes first. Thirty-five percent of the analysts have difficulty understanding the footnotes and 55% would like further explanation of the footnotes. Eighteen percent of the analysts had trouble understanding the statement of cash flows, and 34% would like further explanation of this financial report. (pp. 50–51)

Here, then, is more survey-based research evidence that mere compliance with minimum standards cannot be considered to be sufficient for meeting the capital markets' needs for useful information.

Epstein and Palepu don't quit after presenting their findings but go on to describe what they consider to be a promising financial reporting strategy for management to pursue:

The bottom line is that financial analysts want companies to be more forthcoming with their financial information and provide more voluntary disclosures that "tell the corporate story" to external users. They commonly believe that companies tend to provide only the information that is legally required unless they have additional good news they want to trumpet. If corporate disclosures are to be credible, full disclosure must occur in both good times and bad. A corporate communications strategy that recognizes the importance of open and honest communications to both financial analysts and shareholders is important to the fair valuation of a company's stock. (p. 51)

We are, of course, gratified to find these authors echoing the call for Quality Financial Reporting that we have been making since 1997.

NOTABLE EXPERTS

We also find support for QFR in the writings of other notable experts. The thoughts of three of them are presented here in support of Quality Financial Reporting. Surely there are others, but we are trying to present just enough to lend more credibility to what we have said.

Baruch Lev

Professor Baruch Lev, presently at New York University, has dedicated his academic career to the search for ways to improve financial reporting. At the time of this writing, he was working mostly on issues related to reporting useful information about intangible assets in the financial statements. His current work has been widely cited and accepted.[3]

It turns out that we have found support for QFR in some of Lev's earlier writings, especially a paper (entitled "Information Disclosure Strategy") that he published in the *California Management Review* in 1992. The article begins with this observation and question:

> Managers rarely devote to information disclosure the careful attention and thorough planning accorded to other corporate activities, such as production, marketing, and finance. For example, a study on the disclosure activities of 100 of the largest U.S. public companies revealed that 55 companies made fewer than four voluntary disclosures during the seven years 1981–1987, and only 16 companies made at least one voluntary disclosure a year. Is such modest disclosure activity due to managers' belief that the consequences of information releases are not significant and lasting? . . .
>
> Whatever the reasons for the modest disclosure activity, economic theory and empirical evidence demonstrate that such restraint is in general detrimental to the company and its stakeholders. Specifically, evidence indicates that the consequences of most voluntary disclosures are significant and long-lasting . . . (p. 9)

These thoughts leave no doubt that we're not alone in our puzzlement over the current management behavior of deliberately withholding virtually any financial information that is not required to be disclosed.

Lev goes on to make the same connections that we offered in the prologue:

> . . . [C]apital market efficiency does not negate the benefits of information disclosure, rather it enhances them; and despite the existence of extensive disclosure laws and regulations, there is considerable leeway for voluntary communications. Most importantly, disclosure activity does not differ in principle from other corporate activities, such as investment, production, and marketing. Disclosure shares with these activities the fundamental characteristics of providing benefits and incurring costs, and it therefore warrants the careful attention and long-term planning accorded to any major corporate activity. Hence the need for an information disclosure strategy. (pp. 9–10)

Lev makes the following statement that agrees with our claim that a QFR strategy is essential for getting the capital markets to fully value a company's stock:

> Without an active, well planned and executed disclosure strategy there is no assurance that the intrinsic value of the company and its potential will be fully appreciated by outsiders (investors, suppliers, customers). (p. 12)

He jumps to the fourth axiom about capital costs with this statement:

The information disclosed by a company and sometimes the absence of disclosure, affect outsiders' perceptions of its economic condition and future prospects. These perceptions, in turn, affect key decision variables, such as the company's cost of capital . . . (p. 13)

He makes a great point when he suggests that smaller companies are more likely to benefit from a coherent disclosure strategy:

Information disclosure can create value in two ways: directly, by narrowing the information gap (asymmetry) thereby decreasing investors' uncertainty about the firm (agency costs); and indirectly, by enhancing value-creating activities through a reduced cost of capital and improved suppliers' and customers' terms of trade. It is important to note that the detrimental consequences of the information gap and agency costs are particularly pronounced for companies which for certain reasons (small size, unconventional business, restricted analyst following) are not prominent in the public's mind set. Consequently, the benefits of a disclosure strategy will be particularly large for such companies. (p. 16)

One stumbling block that may discourage some managers from embracing QFR is the apparent advantage of being in the situation where the capital markets have imputed a value to their company's stock that is higher than its inherent (or "intrinsic") value. It is tempting for them to think that they might be able to get to and then stay in this seemingly enviable position by carefully crafting (hyping and spinning) the financial news about their companies. Lev punctures this myth by pointing out that overvaluation is not optimal because it is disadvantageous to new stockholders (the owners that management now works for) and favors the old owners who sold the stock. It can also be disadvantageous to managers, as he describes here:

. . . [A] temporary overvaluation will increase the exercise price of employee stock options granted during that period, thereby reducing the incentive effects of such options as well as future employee gains. A temporary misvaluation is, therefore, not an excuse for inaction, since managers have an implicit responsibility to investors to continually maintain market values as close as feasible to intrinsic ones. (pp. 17–18)

With those latter words, he condemns the sin of telling tall tales to boost stock prices, and he does it without making an ethical judgment.

Lev also asserts that frequent reporting of high-quality information will help prevent stock price volatility:

An even flow of credible information, as opposed to infrequent releases of highly surprising news, will decrease the volatility of security prices *over time*, further improving the risk and liquidity characteristics of securities. (p. 19)

With regard to the strategy of staying silent, he says:

> ... [T]hose who seek solace in a "no voluntary disclosure" policy should be aware of a fundamental attribute of information in a competitive environment: *no news will generally be perceived as bad news.* (p. 21)

He goes on to explain in more detail:

> The impact of voluntary disclosures will depend, to a large extent, on the *credibility* of management. Maintaining credibility requires a commitment to *ongoing* communication with outsiders, rather than haphazard disclosures under duress. Credibility is predicated on a *long-term*, consistent disclosure strategy, where bad as well as good news is disclosed. Managers should recognize that the costs to financial analysts and institutional investors of disappointments are generally higher than their benefit from positive surprises. This asymmetry calls for considerable care and forthrightness in disclosing events which might negatively affect the company's operations along with an elaboration of the actions taken to deal with these events. In general, the strategy should be aimed at minimizing investors' surprises, particularly the negative ones. (p. 26)

After reading all this confirmation in a paper that predates our own discovery of the four axioms, are we threatened by the fact that Lev was apparently advocating Quality Financial Reporting strategies before we came along? Not in the least, because the truths behind QFR have been known for a long time, even before he found them. We are not concerned because our goal in producing this book is to expose these ideas to a lot of people in a way that persuades as many as possible that the status quo is killing them, hampering the capital markets, and holding back the economy. If our life's goal was to win a Nobel prize, we would have studied medicine, physics, or economics instead of accounting.[4]

Warren Buffett

When looking back over the twentieth century, surely one of the global giants of business and investing is Warren Buffett of Omaha, Nebraska. His life story has been told countless times in book after book and article after article. Through his single-minded focus on investing in quality holdings, he has accumulated a personal estate that is second only to that of Microsoft's Bill Gates. While his fortune for a while lagged compared to some Internet figures, he was standing tall after the bubble burst.

Of course, many investors hang on his every word and mimic his investing moves. Others give up trying to beat him and just buy shares in Berkshire Hathaway and ride on his coattails. Those who have been doing it for awhile have done pretty well, given that the Class A shares of his company were trading in the price range around $75,000 each in 2002.

Many people have kicked themselves for not getting on this bandwagon in the early days.

Long known for his unusual combination of "old-fashioned" fundamental financial analysis focused on building wealth with a relatively modest lifestyle that understates his success, Buffett has another quirk that has endeared him to many. It has also boosted the value of Berkshire stock and, naturally, the value of his estate.

This unusual habit is that he, strangely enough, is committed to telling the truth in his company's financial statements! He personally writes the annual report and doesn't hesitate to take blame for failures while calling his successes the results of uncanny luck. His report is totally devoid of the slick photos, shiny paper, and copious self-serving statements that characterize annual reports issued by other managers. He was also quick to embrace the Internet as a way to distribute financial and other news about his company so that everyone has the opportunity to get it at the same time. In effect, Buffett has practiced Quality Financial Reporting long before we gave it a name and formulated its concepts. After all, his business is investing and he has encountered the dark side of financial reporting time and time again. He knows better than to follow the herd over the cliff.

We could go on, but space limits us, so let's look at some of Buffett's thoughts. The source is a set of materials that he first distributed in 1996 and updated in 1999. It was occasioned by his decision, against his usual practice, to issue a Class B stock because the price of the Class A stock had reached such high levels that many investors could not muster enough cash to buy even one share, much less a round lot. Because he knew that this move would bring in a large number of new investors who did not know him as well as his old partners, he prepared what he called "An Owner's Manual" to describe his philosophy, his approaches to implementing that philosophy, and various other topics to help these new owners understand what he would be doing with their money.[5] This manual includes more than a few comments about Buffett's approach to financial reporting and how it differs from other managers' practices. His words leave no doubt that he endorses the concepts that undergird QFR.

With regard to the advantages of straight talking over hype and spin, Buffett says:

> Over time, practically all of our businesses have exceeded our expectations. But occasionally we have disappointments, and we will try to be as candid in informing you about those as we are in describing the happier experiences.

Buffett also doesn't trust GAAP to tell the whole story, and makes a promise to do the best he can to increase wealth despite GAAP:

Accounting consequences do not influence our operating or capital-allocation decisions. When acquisition costs are similar, we much prefer to purchase $2 of earnings that is not reportable by us under standard accounting principles than to purchase $1 of earnings that is reportable.

Here is an extraordinary insight into his own approach to decision making that reflects his empathy for his stockholders and their tolerance for risk:

The financial calculus that Charlie [Munger, his longtime friend and business associate] and I employ would never permit our trading a good night's sleep for a shot at a few extra percentage points of return. I've never believed in risking what my family and friends have and need in order to pursue what they don't have and don't need.

An earlier quote in this chapter refers to managers' tendency to believe that the markets have not fully valued their companies' stock; we also saw what Baruch Lev had to say about the disadvantages of misvaluation. Notice how Buffett's thoughts on this point differ from what many other CEOs say:

When we sold the Class B shares, we stated that Berkshire stock was not undervalued—and some people found that shocking. That reaction was not well-founded. Shock should have registered instead had we issued shares when our stock was undervalued. Managements that say or imply during a public offering that their stock is undervalued are usually being economical with the truth or uneconomical with their existing shareholders' money: Owners unfairly lose if their managers deliberately sell assets for 80¢ that in fact are worth $1. We didn't commit that kind of crime in our recent offering and we never will.

He also makes this proclamation to distance himself from the usual mindset of CEOs:

We also believe candor benefits us as managers: The CEO who misleads others in public may eventually mislead himself in private.

With respect to his own commitment to straightforward and complete reporting, Buffett says:

We will be candid in our reporting to you, emphasizing the pluses and minuses important in appraising business value. Our guideline is to tell you the business facts that we would want to know if our positions were reversed. We owe you no less. Moreover, as a company with a major communications business, it would be inexcusable for us to apply lesser standards of accuracy, balance and incisiveness when reporting on ourselves than we would expect our news people to apply when reporting on others.

With regard to playing games within the confines of GAAP, Buffett makes this pledge, invoking a golf analogy like we did:

At Berkshire you will find no "big bath" accounting maneuvers or restructurings nor any "smoothing" of quarterly or annual results. We will always tell you how many strokes we have taken on each hole and never play around with the scorecard. When the numbers are a very rough "guesstimate," as they necessarily must be in insurance reserving, we will try to be both consistent and conservative in our approach.

His acceptance of the idea that we convey in the four axioms (that complete information reduces uncertainty, risk, and the cost of capital) is revealed as he describes his own commitment to full disclosure:

> We will be communicating with you in several ways. Through the annual report, I try to give all shareholders as much value-defining information as can be conveyed in a document kept to reasonable length. We also try to convey a liberal quantity of condensed but important information in our quarterly reports, though I don't write those (one recital a year is enough). Still another important occasion for communication is our Annual Meeting, at which Charlie and I are delighted to spend five hours or more answering questions about Berkshire. But there is one way we can't communicate: on a one-on-one basis. That isn't feasible given Berkshire's many thousands of owners.

Somehow, we get the feeling that he really would like to be able to sit down with each of his stockholders and tell them what they need to know.

Buffett was way ahead of the SEC and its Regulation FD (for Fair Disclosure); he is still also way ahead of FD's opponents, who insist that it has hampered their ability to deal with the capital markets:

> In all of our communications, we try to make sure that no single shareholder gets an edge: We do not follow the usual practice of giving earnings "guidance" or other information of value to analysts or large shareholders. Our goal is to have all of our owners updated at the same time.

Buffett's faith in the role of information in the capital markets is revealed in this proclamation that telling the truth fully and completely helps ensure a fair price for a stock:

> Obviously, Charlie and I can't control Berkshire's price. But by our policies and communications, we can encourage informed, rational behavior by owners that, in turn, will tend to produce a stock price that is also rational. Our it's-as-bad-to-be-overvalued-as-to-be-undervalued approach may disappoint some shareholders. We believe, however, that it affords Berkshire the best prospect of attracting long-term investors who seek to profit from the progress of the company rather than from the investment mistakes of their partners.

In case it isn't obvious, we are both Buffett fans. Nonetheless, we think that even he could reap a lower cost of capital and still higher stock values by going further than he does to provide supplemental information about the fair market values of Berkshire's assets and liabilities. After all, the FASB recommended this practice a long time ago in SFAS 89. We also chide him for not following the board's recommendation with regard to reporting the company's operating cash flows with the direct method. With regard to reporting stock options, he is off the hook with us because he never issues them to anyone (not even himself), and he does not have to decide whether to put the expense on the income statement or in the footnotes.

With regard to options, we want to share another Buffettism, this time from his 1993 annual report, which was distributed during the period when the FASB was embroiled in the huge controversy over accounting for them:

> If stock options aren't a form of compensation, what are they? If compensation isn't an expense, what is it? And, if expenses shouldn't go into the calculation of earnings, where in the world should they go?

As if that isn't enough to condemn all who play games with the financial statements, Buffett also referred to the stock options issue as "the most egregious case of let's-not-face-up-to-reality behavior by executives and accountants." Yes! Yes! Yes!

Finally, we want to repeat a quote from Buffett that we presented back in Chapter 2:

> If I pick up an annual report and I can't understand a footnote, I probably won't—no, I *won't*—invest in that company because I *know* that they don't *want* me to understand it.

As one who stands on both sides of capital markets as investor and investee, and as one who has enjoyed phenomenal success, apparently without losing his common sense, Buffett wins our first ever QFR Practitioner of the Year Award.[6] We commend his example to all of our readers who are still harboring a fear that making a good effort to just tell the truth in financial reporting will produce bad results.

Neel Foster

Yet another perspective on financial reporting comes from John M. (Neel) Foster, a member of the Financial Accounting Standards Board since 1993. Foster's background is a bit unusual and worth describing. An economics graduate of Colorado College, he found that he needed additional preparation for a career in accounting, and took the equivalent of a major's coursework in two semesters at the University of Colorado at Colorado Springs. He then went to work at Price Waterhouse in Houston, but left the firm after several years (like a great many others who try public accounting). He soon landed on his feet at a new startup (called Compaq

Computer Corporation) and stayed with the company until 1993. Although he was nominated to the FASB by the Financial Executives Institute (now known as Financial Executives International), his record on the board shows that he displays nothing like the typical preparer's objections to progress. In fact, he has cast dissenting votes on a great many standards because they fell short of the level of reform that he felt the board could and should have achieved. (Included among them is his dissent to SFAS 123 on options.)

In the February 27, 1998, issue of *Status Report*, the FASB published the text of Foster's speech at a University of California conference on financial reporting. Many of his words constitute a strong endorsement of QFR, and it seems to us that it might be more persuasive to hear them coming from his dual perspectives as a corporate accountant and a standard setter.

Near the beginning, he says the following, almost as if he had read our script:

> Numerous academic studies have concluded that the more information there is in the marketplace, the lower the cost of capital. When you think about it, although it is nice to have the empirical support, you don't really need the academic studies to reach this conclusion—it's intuitive.
>
> . . . [An] example where uncertainty results in a higher cost of capital can be seen in the marketplace every day—junk bonds yield significantly more than Treasury bills. Obviously, the reason junk bonds have a higher yield is that there is more uncertainty about whether you will get back an investment in junk bonds.

As if he was reading the four axioms, he also said:

> The more information you have about something, the less uncertainty there is and, consequently, the lower the premium you will demand for your investment. In other words, better disclosure results in a lower cost of capital.

He went on to lament the kinds of responses the board receives from corporate managers and their accountants:

> It is pretty clear from the actions of some of the people who prepare financial statements that they aren't buying the argument about more information [reducing the cost of capital]. First, it's apparent from the resistance that we get at the FASB every time we propose to issue a new standard. We often get responses to our Exposure Drafts that are similar to what you would expect if you asked turkeys to vote for Thanksgiving. And recently the buzz words "disclosure overload" have become very popular—talk about an oxymoron. How can anyone who is a thoughtful investor be overloaded with information about his or her investment or prospective investment?

As to the common sense behind more complete financial reporting, Foster describes the beliefs of another business executive:

> George Hatsopolous, the chairman of Thermo Electron, which is an extremely successful technology company, once observed that most of the CEOs he knew were always complaining that the market didn't understand their companies and consequently their shares were underpriced. He allowed that if that was true, whose fault was it? Clearly, if the market didn't understand their companies it was because *they* were not adequately telling the story.

These thoughts are nearly perfectly aligned with what we have been saying.

Foster went on to comment on the effects that would ensue if the SEC acted to allow international accounting standards to be suitable in U.S. capital markets for both foreign and domestic companies.

> . . . I believe that if IASC standards were to become acceptable for filings in the U.S. and were judged to be less rigorous than U.S. GAAP, those companies that used them would quickly find out that they didn't have comparable price/earnings ratios to those companies that did use U.S. GAAP. They would be penalized by the market because there would be more uncertainty associated with them.

In effect, he confirmed that minimum reporting accomplishes nothing short of greater uncertainty and smaller stock prices.

With regard to managers' tendency to use public policy goals to encourage the FASB to create standards that will allow them to look good and achieve some benefit, he weighed in with thoughts similar to ours:

> The costs and benefits of transactions exist whether or not they are recognized and reported in financial statements. Concealing the financial impact of certain transactions from those who use financial statements may benefit a company in the short run. However, over the longer term it will ultimately increase the company's cost of capital to a higher level than it would have been without the concealment. And on a macro basis, it can only lead to inefficient economic decisions and misallocation of resources.

We find nothing to disagree with in this statement, except the suggestion that winning a temporary price boost above intrinsic value would benefit a company.

Foster's thoughts can be summarized with this last quote:

> My point is that if you believe in free markets, the requirement for neutral, credible, and reliable financial [reporting] that presents that information as faithfully as possible should be just as dear to your heart.

There, he said it. The best policy is to do the best you can to tell the truth, the whole truth, and nothing but the truth. Two out of three is just not good enough. Further, the benefits of pursuing QFR reach beyond the impact on the company and its managers and owners—indeed, the whole free capital market system would flourish at unimaginable levels if it were to be flooded with greater quantities of more useful information. We're encouraged about where these words came from. Wouldn't it be interesting if there were six more at the FASB who think like Foster does?

SUMMARY

There are obviously a great many other sources we could find for support. We could also find, if we cared to look, a great many sources where people argue that providing more information has bad effects on stock prices, that preparation costs are too high to allow QFR to occur, that stockholders have no right to know what's going on, that the market wouldn't know what to do with more information, that market values are irrelevant, and that stock option expense is not really an expense. We don't believe any of those things and we're not going to waste precious space in our book to debunk them. Let others try to refute our arguments on their pages, not ours.

NOTES

1. Jenkins went on to be appointed chair of the FASB in 1997.
2. More details are presented in their paper, "What Financial Analysts Want" (*Strategic Finance,* April 1999).
3. For more information about Lev's ideas, read, "The New Math," *Barron's,* November 20, 2000, pp. 31–36.
4. A well-known fact of science is that Copernicus is given credit for establishing that the earth and planets orbit the sun instead of the planets and the sun orbiting the earth. His book, *On the Revolutions of the Heavenly Spheres,* was published in 1543, while he was on his deathbed. However, the structure of the solar system was in fact carefully described by the Greek philosopher/ astronomer Aristarchus in the third century BC, essentially 1800 years earlier. The Copernican theory should be called the Aristarchian theory, but isn't. Historical scholarship also shows that Copernicus seems to have pinched the idea from others who had been writing in the decades before his book was published. Such are the winds of fame and fortune.
5. "An Owner's Manual" is available on Berkshire-Hathaway's website (www.berkshirehathaway.com).
6. For that matter, he could be QFR Practitioner of the Twentieth Century.

CHAPTER 9

Academic Research–The Empiricists Strike Back

This chapter is the third of three that addresses the kind of evidence that supports our arguments in favor of Quality Financial Reporting. Chapter 7 quoted extensively from statements written by knowledgeable financial analysts and Chapter 8 described the views of many other kinds of capital market participants. This chapter ventures into the esoteric and not very well publicized territory of academic research in accounting and finance. Among those who don't understand it, this research often seems to be an effort to question the obvious, with extra points given for obscure writing and complex math. Among those who do understand, there is often a tendency to overstate its significance and to go into rapture over the methodology. Perhaps it is no surprise that we think there is a middle ground, and we'll try to tread there while we look at some fairly recent efforts that address issues related to the four axioms of QFR. Before getting into specific papers, we want to explain more about empirical research.

EMPIRICISM

In earlier days when philosophers roamed the face of the earth, there was an ongoing debate about whether reality is what we observe or something more pure that is distorted and polluted by the physical world. Those who withdrew from physicality (most notably Plato) sought to develop understanding of perfection on the basis of reason in order to avoid that pollution. Others (most notably Aristotle), called *empiricists*, took the opposite route and asserted that the only reality can be that which is observed with the senses. Naturally, the members of the two groups were always trying to outdo each other, and nobody ever agreed with anyone from the other side. These debates have continued for millennia, with no real resolution in sight. Amazingly enough, people have still continued to be born, be educated, make a contribution to society, and die, all without knowing the answer to this dispute. Apart from that bit of cynicism about philosophers, what is our point?

What we are getting at is that many people still insist that they need real evidence of real events and conditions before they will believe and act on a proposition. In fact, this approach to learning has been imbedded in science for centuries. It has also become imbedded among academic accountants over the last 30 years or so. According to this point of view, great value is placed on evidence that is based on real experiences. This is the essence of empiricism.

Besides academic accountants, we have also found another group that attributes great value to empirical accounting research. It consists of managers, auditors, and accountants who have run out of good common sense arguments and who know that the research literature hasn't addressed a debate that they are about to lose. Under these conditions, they utter the cry: "It hasn't been proved by empirical research!" Strangely enough, they are often the most vocal in rejecting the concept of capital market efficiency, even though it has clearly been supported by more empirical research than any other theory in accounting and finance. They like empirical research when its findings support their biases or when it doesn't exist. However, they tend to ignore it when it goes against those biases.

Why do academics attribute so much value to empirical research? That's a hard question to answer, but the root of the explanation has to do with the intellectual discipline of not taking anything for granted, no matter how obvious, and of continually pushing the envelope on research methods. It also helps that the most prestigious journals publish this kind of research, so professors have economic and psychological reasons for doing it. Thus, by training and by predisposition, academic empiricists feel challenged when they encounter axiomatic statements like those we have asserted, namely that greater quantities of useful information will lead to lower capital costs and higher stock prices. The previous chapter described the Jenkins Committee report, which also included some similar assertions. Like a duck going after a June bug, some empiricists have decided to see whether they can find evidence involving large numbers of situations to assess the validity of the basic principles we have called axioms.

This chapter briefly describes some of these efforts. On the whole, we believe that the findings support the common sense that we and others have advocated. As a result, we do not believe that progress toward QFR should be halted for lack of empirical evidence.

METHODOLOGY

There are many different ways to construct empirical studies, and it would be ludicrous for us to try to catalog all of them here. However, there is a common thread among many of them that might be called the stimulus-response model. As shown in Figure 9-1, when something happens (the *cause*, or the *stimulus*), something else happens in turn (the *effect*, or the *response*).

The objectives of the research are to determine whether there really is a response to the stimulus, and if so, to assess the relationship between the magnitudes of the stimulus and the response. The ultimate goal is to predict future responses to future stimuli.

There are abundant challenges with the kinds of phenomena involved in financial reporting and capital markets because of the multitudes of stimuli and the various responses that all occur at the same time. Although it is still oversimplified, the diagram in Figure 9-2 is bit more representative of the situation.

As a result, nobody ever sets out to explain all the stimuli and responses. They simply try to narrow the problem down so that they can look at one cause (or several causes) and one effect. In these circumstances, finding that a particular piece of information explains only 2 or 3 percent of the variation in stock prices would be quite a discovery.

There are a lot of possible ways of filtering out the stimuli and responses, and we again cannot possibly begin to describe them all. The general quest begins by identifying a large group of events or conditions. For example, it's obviously much better to look at accounting numbers and stock prices for hundreds or even thousands of companies and dates instead of only a few. Furthermore, it also matters which companies are observed. In general, it helps to look at similar companies in order to cut down on the possible sources of extraneous variables. To put it another away, focusing on a homogeneous group reduces the number of stimuli to be filtered.

Another research issue is finding a way to measure the magnitudes of the stimulus and the response. In some cases, it isn't possible to mea-

FIGURE 9-1

The Basic Research Model

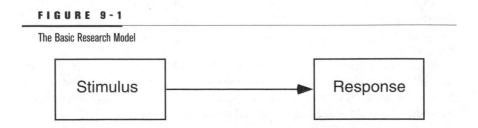

FIGURE 9-2

The Real-World Model

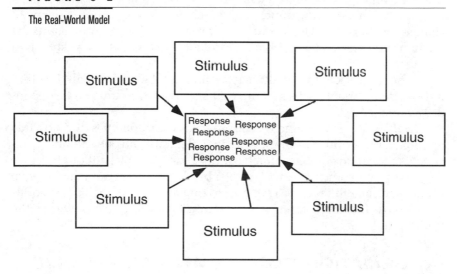

sure one or the other directly, with the consequence that the researchers choose a surrogate, or substitute, variable, usually because there is good reason to believe that its variability parallels the variability of the real thing. This situation is represented by the diagram in Figure 9-3.

The researchers hope that the more easily observed surrogates are so closely related to the real phenomena that they can learn something about the relationship between the latter.

The measurement effort also requires work to quantify the variables so that they can be mathematically manipulated and analyzed with statis-

FIGURE 9-3

The Surrogate Research Model

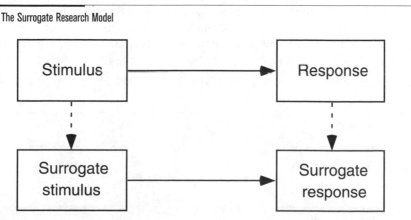

tics. One especially common analysis is *correlation and regression,* which attempts to quantify how much a given change in the stimulus seems to change the response. Using statistical terms, the idea is to measure the relationship between the *independent* and *dependent* variables, as shown in Figure 9-4.

The real trick in this analysis is to filter out the effects of all the other independent variables (the stimuli) that also affect the value of the dependent variable.[1]

Suffice it to say that no one appreciates the difficulties of doing this research quite as much as those who do it. Similarly, no one should appreciate its limitations quite as much as those same people, although, as we suggested, sometimes researchers get a bit too excited about what they've found, and sometimes those who are looking for proof of their pet theories go overboard. In both cases, they may attribute too much power to the findings.

INFORMATION QUALITY AND ITS RESULTS

We have intended this brief discussion to prepare the way for looking at some recent research that examines the axiomatic relationship between information quality and the cost of capital for the reporting company. Figure 9-5 represents that proposition.

The challenges of doing the research are many. To begin with, the researchers must find a way to assess the quality of the information. This task may involve their relying on work performed by others or on their gaining access to real original data and doing their own assessment. On the other side, they must find a way to measure the capital costs and relate them to the reported information. If, for example, the Federal Reserve unexpectedly raises its interest rates, that news (an external stimulus) will cause capital costs of all companies to rise (the response), regardless of variability in the quality of their reported information. Or, favorable news about inflation or unemployment may cause stock prices of most companies to go up, without any consideration of the quality of the information produced by each company. Again, the model, the mathematics, and the

FIGURE 9-4

The Basic Statistical Model

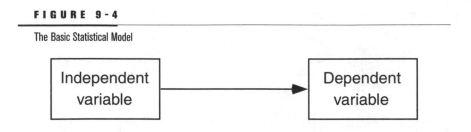

FIGURE 9-5

The Quality Financial Reporting Research Model

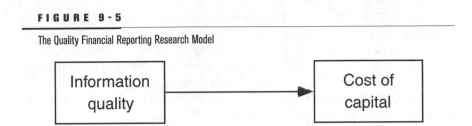

statistics provide ways to do this filtering, and that's about all we want to say at this point.

RESEARCH ON INFORMATION QUALITY

In light of their tendency to challenge self-evident axioms and other conventional wisdom, academics have not neglected the assertion that information quality affects capital costs. The recent progression has been gradual, working from simpler techniques to more complex ones.

As we suggested, one of the problems has been trying to find a useful way to describe quality that reliably reflects the real quality. While the quantity of disclosures is easy to measure (such as the number of words, sentences, or pages), the quality of the content is more elusive because it is all about using the right words and numbers and not simply more words and numbers. Also, narrative disclosures are often used in lieu of numbers in the financial statements, such that assessing the quality can only be accomplished subjectively. This subjectivity naturally injects bias, which reduces the reliability of the quality measures. Another problem is identifying which disclosure is the actual stimulus that produces the response. An obvious candidate is the annual report filed with the SEC, but its release date comes so far after the company's actual events that it takes a bit of faith to believe that its content drives the current stock price on or around its release date. This mix of problems, plus others, make it clear that the research findings are limited.

A second, entirely different set of problems concerns the cost of capital. While the concept is well understood, actually measuring this cost can be quite complex. The cost of debt capital can be measured several ways, including historical interest rates and GAAP book values; other measures are based on market rates and market values of debt securities. The historical measures generally describe what the cost of capital was, while the market measures reflect current reality. Unfortunately for those who want precision, measuring the cost of equity capital is a whole different ball game. In effect, the cost of capital is the rate of return for investors that is captured in the relationship between the market value of the stock and the expected future cash flows. The market value can be known, but there is no way to figure out the consensus expected future cash flows. As a result, measurement of the cost of capital has to take a different direction, typically by evaluating the risk-adjusted performance of stock prices but also by doing other things. The models used to measure stock performance and the cost of capital are not perfect and often involve complex methodological issues and statistical analyses.

This sort of complexity is like ice cream and cake to academic researchers. To them, the payoff of being the first to verify (or debunk) a popular proposition is so great that the work is well worth it. The following discussions summarize the findings of several recent studies that have focused on the relationship between information quality and capital costs.

WELKER

Michael Welker, the author of the first paper, used published evaluation results to find a measure of the reported information's quality. In particular, he tapped into a quality survey produced by the Association for Investment Management and Research, the same AIMR that produced the monograph described in Chapter 7. Welker's study was published under the title "Disclosure Policy, Information Asymmetry and Liquidity in Equity Markets" in the Spring 1995 issue of the academic journal *Contemporary Accounting Research.*

The AIMR publication that Welker used is called *An Annual Review of Corporate Reporting Practices.* These reports, which used to be published annually until their unfortunate discontinuance in 1996, were prepared by industry subcommittees of leading financial analysts for the purpose of evaluating the effectiveness of selected companies' actual corporate disclosures. The evaluations were compiled by looking at information from three sources: (1) annual reports, (2) quarterly reports and other published information, and (3) management's responsiveness to analysts' inquiries and other investor relations activities. Thus, the subject matter encompasses the kinds of activities included in QFR. The analysts prepared their evaluations after considering the content of a company's communications and their timeliness. According to one summary, a typical report in the series described 460 companies in 27 industries; furthermore, an average of 13 analysts participated in each subcommittee that evaluated each industry.[2] Although not totally objective, the evaluations in the AIMR reports stood as fairly reliable measures of financial reporting quality.

With this measure of the stimulus in hand, Welker then had to select a response to measure. Building on prior research and keying on comments in the Jenkins Committee report, he chose to look at the bid/ask spread for a sample of the companies covered by the AIMR quality rankings. In general, it is believed that the wider the bid/ask spread, the greater the risk associated with the company's stock; thus, risk is a surrogate for capital costs. If risk is directly related to the spread, the spread could be used as a surrogate surrogate variable for the cost of capital, as shown in Figure 9-6.

As expected, Welker's results show that higher quality rankings (the surrogate for more informative disclosures) are associated with narrower bid/ask spreads (the surrogate surrogate for cost of capital). Specifically, he summarized his findings with these words:

> Relative bid/ask spreads for firms with disclosure rankings in the bottom third of the empirical distribution are approximately 50 percent higher than spreads for firms with disclosure rankings in the top third of the empirical distribution. (p. 801)

In other words, the stockholders of firms evaluated as having low-quality financial reports paid the price for management's failures by facing a higher cost at purchase and a lower selling price for their shares.

While this research suggests that the cost of capital is lower for companies with higher-quality disclosures, the evidence is not completely satisfactory because it assumes but does not test the double linkage between the bid-ask spread and the cost of capital.

FIGURE 9-6

The Welker Research Model

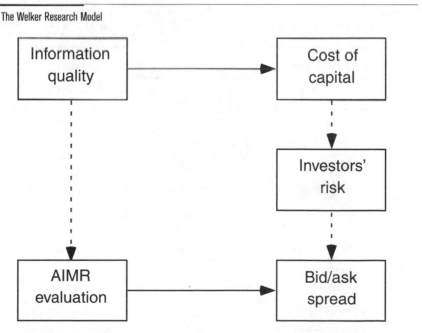

LANG AND LUNDHOLM

A similar study, entitled "Corporate Disclosure Policy and Analyst Behavior," was published by Mark Lang and Russell Lundholm in the October 1996 issue of *The Accounting Review*. In their research, the authors also used the AIMR rankings as a surrogate for quality. For assessing risk, they turned to published sources that report information about analysts' activity concerning a company's stock. Thus, they too used a surrogate surrogate dependent variable, as represented in Figure 9-7.

Lang and Lundholm summarized their findings by observing that:

> . . . [F]irms with more informative disclosure policies [actually, higher AIMR scores] have a larger analyst following, more accurate analysts' forecasts, less dispersion among individual analyst forecasts and less volatility in forecast revisions. (p. 467)

They then used this evidence to suggest that:

> . . . [T]he potential benefits to disclosure include increased investor following, reduced estimation risk and reduced information asymmetry, each of which have been shown to reduce a firm's cost of capital in theoretical research. (p. 467)

FIGURE 9-7

The Lang and Lundholm Research Model

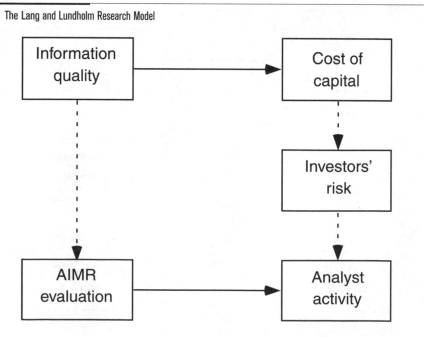

Like Welker's paper, this one cautiously suggests but does not prove that more informative disclosures are associated with lower capital costs.

Despite these limits, the fact that these two studies were published in leading journals and had what are called "robust" findings in turn stimulated other researchers to pursue inquiries that create more direct tests of the linkage between disclosure quality and the cost of capital.

BOTOSAN

The next significant study of this relationship was produced by Professor Christine Botosan and described in a paper called "Disclosure Level and the Cost of Equity Capital" that was published in the July 1997 issue of *The Accounting Review*.

Unlike the two preceding papers, this ambitious and award-winning[3] study does not rely on the AIMR rankings as a measure of quality. Instead, Botosan developed her own new measure of disclosure quality, called DSCORE, that is more encompassing because it does not reflect the potential bias inherent in the AIMR reports through their singular focus on larger companies. This approach allowed her to include smaller companies in her sample and reap two benefits. First, the theory could be tested for generality by applying it in a different arena. Second, smaller companies tend to have a wider range of capital costs, thus creating a wider range of observed values of the dependent variable (the response to the stimulus) and thereby providing a richer data set for analysis. Botosan also innovated by trying to get a direct measure of the companies' cost of equity capital using a proven method called the residual income model that relies on variables in GAAP financial statements. Her research can be described with the diagram in Figure 9-8.

FIGURE 9-8

The Botosan Research Model

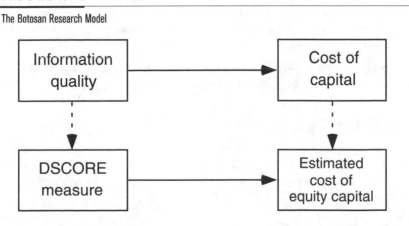

For clarity, the DSCORE measure evaluates a management's voluntary reporting practices using five separate dimensions identified in other studies as being useful to investors and financial analysts. The suitability of DSCORE as a surrogate for quality is limited by the fact that it was based solely on the sample companies' annual reports and did not embrace the broader range of management communications, including quarterly reports, press releases, and analyst conferences. It is also limited by the fact that it was developed and applied by Botosan herself instead of a disinterested third party.

To eliminate some of the extra stimuli, Botosan looked only at companies with similar operating and environmental risks, focusing on a sample of 122 companies in a single industry (machinery manufacturers) in the single year of 1990. She summarized her results as follows:

> This paper provides direct evidence on an association between cost of capital and disclosure level, and an indication of the magnitude of that effect. For a sample of firms with relatively low analyst following, the evidence suggests that greater disclosure is associated with a lower cost of capital . . . (p. 346)

These results do not hold for companies with high analyst following, a finding that Botosan suggests is due to the possibility that

> . . . the disclosure measure is limited to the annual report and accordingly may not provide a powerful proxy for overall disclosure level when analysts play a significant role in the communication process. (p. 323)

In addition to confirming this important linkage between disclosure and cost of capital, she also says that the article

> . . . provides some preliminary evidence on the type of disclosure that seem to play an important role in reducing the cost of capital. Specifically for firms with low analyst following, disclosure of forecast information and key nonfinancial statistics is particularly important while for firms with high analyst following, disclosure of historical summary information is beneficial. (p. 347)

Managers who choose to ignore these findings do so at their own risk. Unfortunately, they also do it at their stockholders' risk.

SENGUPTA

Apparently stimulated by the same precedents that Botosan followed and guided by her results, Partha Sengupta produced a study that was published in the October 1998 issue of *The Accounting Review* as a paper called "Corporate Disclosure Quality and the Cost of Debt."

Like the authors of the first two studies, Sengupta decided to use the AIMR's quality measures as his surrogate for quality. Unlike the authors of those studies that used surrogates for the cost of capital, and unlike Botosan, who tried to estimate the cost of equity capital, Sengupta chose to produce a direct measure of the cost of debt capital based on new issues of debt securities. A diagram of his research model appears in Figure 9-9.

In a sense, Sengupta's research was extraordinarily successful. Not only did he find a strong inverse correlation between the measure of quality and the cost of debt capital, he actually generated an equation that allowed him to predict a company's new debt capital cost given its AIMR score. He briefly summarized his findings with these words:

> . . . [F]irms that are rated favorably by financial analysts for the degree of detail, timeliness and clarity of their disclosures, are perceived to have a lower default risk and are rewarded with a lower cost of borrowing. Moreover, the results indicate that there is a greater reliance on disclosures when the market uncertainty surrounding the firm is high. (p. 473)

He also writes about the importance of his debt-based results:

> Although previous studies have not explored this relationship, the issue is important because debt financing is the predominant form of external financing for publicly traded firms in the U.S. For example, during 1992, publicly traded companies raised approximately $2,764 billion through investment grade debt in comparison to approximately $932 billion raised through common and nonconvertible preferred stock issues. (p. 460)

Again, preparers should not bury their heads in the sand when they read these words. It seems very clear that quality really counts.

FIGURE 9-9

The Sengupta Research Model

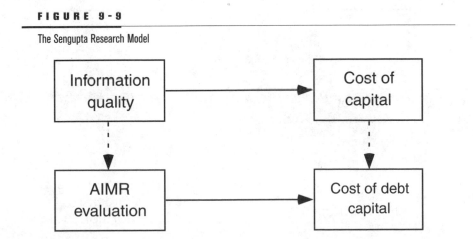

HEALY, HUTTON, AND PALEPU

A three-person team consisting of Paul Healy, Amy Hutton, and Krishna Palepu (who was mentioned in the prior chapter), published a paper on this same stimuli/response situation. The article is entitled "Stock Performance and Intermediation Changes Surrounding Sustained Increases in Disclosure" and appeared in the Fall 1999 issue of *Contemporary Accounting Research*. Their work epitomizes the evolutionary nature of research streams as they put a new twist on some of the work that had gone before.

Like others, Healy et al. used the AIMR quality reports to provide measures of their independent variable. Unlike the others, however, they focused only on those companies that experienced changes in their quality ratings between years to see whether the performance of their stock also changed. Their model can be represented by the diagram in Figure 9-10.

A key process in their research screened out changes in AIMR scores that seemed to have been caused by something other than changes in the companies' disclosure quality. In particular, they report that they found evidence of substantive change in the AIMR score when a company provided the following things:

> (a) improved segment disclosures; (b) more in-depth discussions of operations and financial performance, and more candid management discussion

FIGURE 9-10

The Healy et al. Research Model

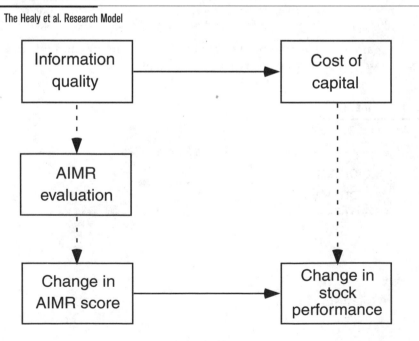

of company prospects in annual and quarterly reports; (c) publication of supplemental disclosures in fact books; and (d) improved investor relations through increased analyst access to top management, and additional company meetings and presentations for analysts. (p. 489)

To measure stock performance that might have resulted from the change in quality, they looked at recent stock returns, bid/ask spreads, and the degree of institutional ownership. (The institutional ownership percentage is considered to be indicative of inherent investment risk, such that lower risk would increase this proportion.) In the *FASB Status Report* (September 29, 2000) the FASB summarized the results with these words:

... [The] average sample firm showed a 7% improvement in stock performance in the year of the disclosure increase and 8% the following year. (p. 2)

They also found that the companies with higher quality scores experienced increases in institutional ownership in the 12 to 24 percent range three years after the higher scores were reported. Again, this empirical study confirms the axiom that better information reduces capital costs.

LANG AND LUNDHOLM, THE SEQUEL

Another study by the same Lang and Lundholm team cited earlier led to a paper called "Voluntary Disclosure and Equity Offerings: Reducing Information Asymmetry or Hyping the Stock?" that appeared in the Winter 2000 issue of *Contemporary Accounting Research*.

Like the Healy team, Lang and Lundholm looked this time at changes in the AIMR ratings to try to figure out what sort of motive might be behind the new, improved financial reporting policies. Among other things, they found that those companies that did experience improved ratings were much more likely to have issued new debt securities after the new reporting policies were put into effect than those companies that did not make any changes (or did not have a higher rating). They went on to suggest that this pattern might mean that the managers were simply using the improved disclosures to reap a lower cost of debt capital in the short run. They then expressed their doubts about whether the managers were really committed to their new policies as a long-term pattern.

One point that stands out about this particular project is that the authors were not really trying to test the stimulus/response phenomenon that was the central issue in the earlier studies. We interpret this point to mean that these experts now seem to consider that question resolved; that is, they believe the empirical evidence shows that higher quality does indeed produce lower capital costs. That conclusion, of course, is music to our ears because it removes one more obstacle to the implementation of Quality Financial Reporting.

BARTH, HALL, KURTZMAN, WEI, AND YAGO

A major study was conducted with funding and other support from the PricewaterhouseCoopers accounting firm by a five-person team consisting of Mary Barth (a member of the new International Accounting Standards Board), Thomas Hall, Joel Kurtzman, Shang-Jia Wei, and Glen Yago. This project is significant for the size of the undertaking and the fact that it went outside the United States capital markets to test the relationship between disclosure quality and capital costs. The outcome is a report called *The Opacity Index*.[4] For this study, the authors decided to pick up on the trendy use of the term *transparency* to describe high-quality accounting practice by examining a variable that they call *opacity*, which they defined as

> ... the lack of clear, accurate, formal, easily discernible and widely accepted practices in the broad arena where business, finance and government meet. (p. 3)

Their approach was to assess the impact of various economic factors, including the quality of public financial reporting, by identifying their combined impact on the cost of capital as measured by the cost incurred when a country's government borrows. In turn, they suggest that these same facts either create or remove obstacles to foreign direct investment. They developed a model that links the cost of capital to the governments in 35 countries with five key opacity factors. A diagram of their model appears in Figure 9-11.

The process for assigning an Opacity Index value to a country's economy involved assessing five different factors. Among them is one of interest to us, the quality of public financial reporting information. This factor was called simply *accounting/corporate governance*. The composite opacity score (called the *O-Factor*) equally weights all five components and has a scale ranging from 0 to 150, with the higher score indicating the greatest opacity.

The authors found that they could use the O-Factor score to explain differences in government bond yield rates in the 35 countries they studied. With some precision, they stated that a

> ... one point increase in O-Factor score leads to a 25.5 basis point increase in the interest rate that investors demand in order to purchase new-issue bonds originated in that country. (p. 11)

In other words, the greater the opacity, the higher the cost of capital. By extension, the same sort of risk penalty would be applied to securities issued by companies operating in the country.

Our readers might want to know that the O-Factor scores ranged from a low of 29 for Singapore to a high of 87 for China. The U.S. was relatively low, and tied Chile for second place with a score of 36. In the vari-

FIGURE 9-11

The Barth et al. Research Model

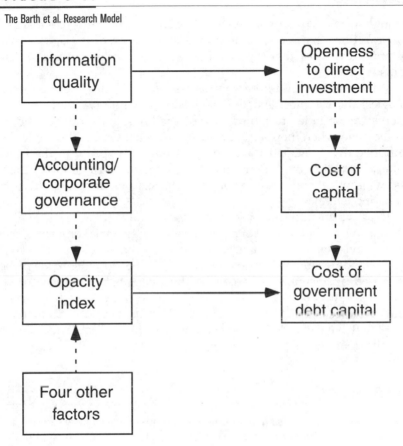

ous rankings, the U.S. scored better than Singapore on the accounting/ corporate governance factor but was worse on the other four. In fact, the U.S. had the best score for this factor of any of the 35 countries. While it might be tempting for Americans to take nationalistic pride in having this rating, they need to remember that the QFR goal is to be the very best that you can be, not just be the best among all the competitors. Previous chapters have shown that U.S. GAAP are really inadequate for providing the information that the capital markets want and need for them to be more effective at generating and distributing capital. In other words, there is much room for improvement. If U.S. managers don't improve their practices, it is possible that managers in other countries will overtake them. Furthermore, managers from any country will be better off when they outperform other managers in providing higher-quality reports.

SUMMARY

Although a half dozen or so research studies might seem like relatively few, we believe that the ones described in the preceding pages provide substantial evidence that the common sense underlying the four QFR axioms is valid.

While there is certainly room for discussing issues about the methodologies, the samples, and the statistical analyses, we think that our readers can continue on into the rest of the book with more confidence than they had when they started reading this chapter. Unlike the Jenkins Committee that lamented the absence of empirical proof of the fundamental assumption that higher-quality information brings lower capital costs, we think there is now enough empirical evidence to defuse that kind of opposition.

If, as we suspect, this objection was a smokescreen used by opponents of progress in the form of higher quality in financial reporting, these studies provide enough fresh air to blow away that smoke and leave the axioms standing and victorious. However, if the opponents keep their eyes closed against this research like they have when presented with sound logical arguments, they will continue to deny the advantages of Quality Financial Reporting. If so, those managers who do decide to pursue QFR will have that many fewer competitors for favorable treatment by the capital markets.

NOTES

1. As we said, researchers are not limited to looking at only one stimulus. Through the techniques of multiple regression, they can construct models that include many independent variables and one dependent variable. With enough observations, they can obtain measures of the impacts of each of the independent factors on the total response.

2. M. Lang and R. Lundholm, "Corporate Disclosure Policy and Analyst Behavior," *The Accounting Review,* October 1996. This paper is described in the next section.

3. As evidence of the academy's respect for this research, the American Accounting Association awarded Botosan its 1996 Competitive Manuscript Award and its 2001 Notable Contribution to the Accounting Literature Award.

4. Information about the index and its values for the rated countries can be found at www.opacityindex.com.

CHAPTER 10

State Your Objections!

As might be imagined, we have encountered a lot of questions when we have taken the Quality Financial Reporting concept around to different places. There is certainly no better way to polish your ideas than to take them on the road and present them to other people so that you can hear what's good and what isn't. In doing so, we have encountered a variety of objections, including the following:

- "You can't make me!"
- "That's proprietary information."
- "The markets aren't that efficient."
- "It's too expensive."
- "No one else is doing it."
- "I don't have the information handy."
- "I might get sued."
- "But what if I have to report bad news?"
- "It'll make us look volatile."
- "The users won't understand."
- "That's disclosure overload."

No doubt those who have read this far have raised at least some of these objections and maybe several others in their own minds as they have been reading along. Before going any further into the book, we want to use this chapter to address and eliminate those blockades so that the communication channels are open for the additional thoughts that we raise in coming chapters.

"YOU CAN'T MAKE ME!"

Perhaps this most common objection to QFR comes about because most members of the business world, including managers and their accountants, auditors, financial statement users, regulators, and educators, have grown accustomed to the present mandated reporting system. Under the status quo, basically nothing is reported in the statements that isn't mandatory.[1] Whenever the FASB or another authority proposes a new practice, it is always presented as a new requirement. Virtually without exception, managers object because they don't want to have another obligation imposed on them. That's understandable, of course.

But, our call for applying QFR is not a demand for new rules and regulations to force managers to do what we think makes sense. We're not trying to develop adequate political power to push through new rules that will make the capital markets more efficient. We don't even want to be in the position of telling people what they have to do.

Instead, QFR is totally voluntary. It is optional. It is up to management to decide whether to do it or not. It is up to management to decide how to do it. Indeed, QFR is as much an *attitude* as anything else. It is the attitude toward the capital markets that seeks to understand what the participants would benefit from knowing. Once that understanding is gained, management's efforts are then directed toward providing the information with reliability and timeliness in order to reduce the users' uncertainty and risk.

The bottom line is that we're not insisting that managers apply QFR or that they be somehow formally punished if they don't see it our way. What we *are* doing is encouraging them to acknowledge that by not applying QFR they are already being penalized by the markets through higher capital costs and lower security prices. Those who do apply QFR, on the other hand, will find that they can have lower capital costs and higher security prices, and no one is making them do anything against their will.

Keep this situation in mind as you consider the remaining objections. If you find our dismissal of a complaint to be inadequate, just remember that you get to make up your own mind about what you're going to do.

"THAT'S PROPRIETARY INFORMATION."

The first thing that comes to many managers' minds as an objection to disclosing more information is that doing so will create a disadvantage because the company's competitors will now have more information to use to win in the customer marketplace. This defensive attitude reached an extreme at Volkswagen under the management headed by Ferdinand Piëch, as described in *Fortune* in "Getting the Bugs Out at VW," in the

March 29, 1999, issue. This quote from that article summarizes his attitude:

> [Piëch] likes German accounting methods, which give companies great
> flexibility to understate profits, because they keep competitors from seeing
> exactly how VW invests its money. They also keep suppliers, unions, and
> the tax collector from demanding more. "I don't say shareholders don't
> count for Volkswagen, but they count on the same level as our customers
> and our employees," says Piëch. "This is very European. If I would need a
> lot of capital, we would have to adapt. But as long as I can build up
> enough trust through the German system for our shareholders, what I try
> to do doesn't show up to our competitors." (p. 102)

By keeping information from the capital markets, Piëch thought he was
building up trust? We don't think he was doing any of his constituents a
big favor. Why not?

> One thing Piëch hasn't overhauled is VW's backward relationship with its
> stockholders. Unlike [other CEOs in the German auto industry], Piëch
> spurns Wall Street and international accounting standards, preferring Ger-
> many's opaque methods. . . . The effects of that attitude are far-reaching. "It
> has definitely hurt their valuation and raised their cost of capital . . . ," says
> Greg Melich [a financial analyst] at Morgan Stanley. (p. 102)

The writer, Janet Guyon, then described a specific outcome of Piëch's attitude:

> The damage was most visible in 1997, when VW suddenly reversed course
> and said it wanted to raise $3.7 billion through a stock offering but didn't
> bother telling investors why. VW shares plummeted, and the company was
> forced to put off the offering until last year. In the end, VW raised half the
> original amount, belatedly saying it was for acquisitions. VW now admits
> it bungled its communications with investors. (p. 102)

We think this anecdote clearly explains why QFR makes sense, but
we need to dig into it further. First of all, let's consider that the domain of
financial reporting is, well, financial matters. We think this fact means that
it is a large leap from your providing enhanced financial statements to
revealing to your competitors your darkest industrial secrets about future
products and other plans.

Second, if your competitors are really competitive, they have surely
found other ways to get inside your laboratories, design centers, budget
offices, information system centers, and factories to uncover what you're
doing. Unless you incarcerate your former employees and throw away the
key, you can be fairly certain that their memories are being scrubbed by
your competitors. This debriefing even happens in the financial reporting
shop as accountants and others move to new jobs. In short, we think it is
naive to believe that a company's industrial security is so tight that finan-

cial reports will actually reveal something that its competitors don't already know.

Third, a company competes in at least two markets—the customer market and the capital market. This objection is really arguing (falsely, of course) that only the first one is important and that it must be protected at all costs, as Piëch seemed to be saying. This position blithely ignores the effect of the higher cost of capital that inevitably follows from not reporting financial information openly. Of course, it is possible that an advantage might be lost if proprietary information is revealed too early, but we return to our opening comments to the effect that the decision to report or not report the extra information is entirely up to the managers. All we really suggest is that they thoroughly consider their decision to withhold information before they make it.

As a fourth point, we draw an analogy to advertising. If you think about it, promotional campaigns are intended to reveal to potential customers the characteristics and capabilities of your products and services so that they can see how their lives would be enhanced by buying them. However, at the same time you advertise these qualities to customers, your competitors are also learning about what you're offering. We are hard-pressed to imagine that management would totally shut down all communication with customers in order to deprive its competitors of useful information. In the same way, why would it make sense to have poor communication with capital markets to protect against your marketplace competition? Your competitors have other means of discovering your product's capabilities, if only by buying it for themselves.

In summary, we think the proprietary information objection is almost entirely without substance. Of course, even if we don't see it as an effective argument against QFR, managers are certainly free to decide for themselves.

"THE MARKETS AREN'T THAT EFFICIENT."

Not long ago, one of us was trying to summarize QFR for an accountant who has been a leader in the profession for years. Early on, he sort of rolled his eyes and interjected, "You must believe in market efficiency." The tone and apparent dismissal made it clear that efficient capital markets rank in this guy's mind up there with Santa Claus, the Easter Bunny, and the Great Pumpkin. He seems to think that they are all fictitious concepts that must never be taken too seriously.

As we showed in Chapter 7, the sophisticated financial analysts who produced the AIMR monograph have no difficulty accepting the concept that the markets are efficient. They also are clear in attributing that efficiency to the free flow of information to market participants and to the activity of analysts trying to get their hands on more information. In short, there is plenty of evidence that the markets are efficient, with some evidence to the contrary. We think the main obstacle to acceptance of efficiency is a lack of understanding what it means and doesn't mean.

Efficiency does not mean that the markets are always right. Unexpected events occur all the time and cause adjustments. In fact, adjustments even occur when expected (but still tentative) events take place and reduce the uncertainty. Efficiency also does not mean total stability in stock prices; in fact, efficient markets can be quite volatile because the rapid distribution of news causes it to reach a great many buyers and sellers within a short period.

What efficiency does mean is that only brand spanking new and previously unknown information can allow its holder to deliberately achieve above-normal returns (of course, a person can get lucky at any time by owning virtually any company's stock when something unexpected and good happens). Conversely, efficiency also means that a person cannot pick up an annual report or a day-old press release and use the contents to make a killing. Today's markets (especially in the U.S. and increasingly in other places around the globe) are so well plugged into communication networks that even information as new as a press release has a very limited useful life, if any at all. Many capital market research studies actually show that stock prices move hours and even days *before* news is officially released.

Here's a true story in another setting that illustrates a kind of market efficiency: one night, one of us (who shall remain unidentified) was teaching an accounting theory seminar on his campus. It just so happened that the topic of discussion in the first half of the class was market efficiency, with a great deal of attention on the question of whether it is real or not. At the break, he went out to his car to retrieve some handouts that he had mistakenly left on the seat as he made his usual late dash to class from the parking lot. In fact, he had been so late that he ended up parking on the last row in the lot next to the classroom building. On the way out to the car, he passed a couple of closer in spaces that had just emptied, and decided to shorten his walk after class by moving his car to one of the more desirable spots. By the time he got to his car, started the engine, and moved to where the spaces had been, they were taken. Shrugging his shoulders, he put it in reverse to reclaim his old spot, only to find that another car was parked in it. He was tardy getting back to class after trudging in from an even more distant lot, but at least he had a great new illustration to share with his students about market efficiency. Here's the moral to this story: if the market for parking spaces is so efficient that information about empty ones is valuable for only about 30 seconds or so, why would financial information worth literally millions of dollars last for weeks, days, hours, or even minutes, for that matter?

Because of all the research, but maybe even more because of the common sense behind the idea of capital market efficiency, we are inclined to think that U.S. markets are highly efficient—so much so that it makes sense for everyone, especially managers, to act as if they are 99.9 percent efficient. If that measure is correct, it means that only one management in a thousand can get away with using manipulated or omitted information to prop up its stock price. Even though these odds are very long, they are even longer when you realize that the markets' efficiency would allow that false advantage to last for only a very short while. Once the deception is uncovered, the market will come back against the perpetrators with distrust, attribute more risk to the investment, and then pump up the risk premium portion of the company's cost of capital.

In light of all that, we think it makes sense for managers to just report as if the markets really are efficient. It seems to us to be the only rational way to approach financial reporting. We don't see how you can lose.

Of course, if the markets were inefficient, then one might think they could be fooled by carefully chosen reporting policies that make the company's prospects look better than they are. However, even if the markets were that inefficient, they would still know that managers would be trying to fool them with these kinds of tricks. Thus, the perceived risk would be increased, and the markets would discount all stocks to compensate. However, if a management were to declare itself to be honest and forthright, and then prove it by putting out really useful financial information, even inefficient markets would know it and reward the management with higher prices. Again, the strategy is the same—use QFR, and the markets will reward you, whether they're efficient or not.

"IT'S TOO EXPENSIVE."

We hear this objection a lot, usually with words like these: "It will cost too much to provide all that extra information." A lunch one of us had one day with the CFO of a growing private company included this exchange:

"We had to go to a different bank to get a loan big enough to support our expansion, but they insisted that we have the audit done by a Big Five firm instead of our regular auditors. I was upset by that because we had to train the new auditors on how our system works, they charged us a whole lot more, and when we were finished, I don't think we got anything extra for the cost."

"Did you get the loan you needed at a favorable rate?"

"Yeah, but what's your point?"

"Would you have gotten the loan without the Big Five audit?"

"No."

"Sounds to me like it was worth your while!"

FIGURE 10-1

Preparation Costs vs. Processing Costs (Part 1)

We also talked about this objection back in Chapter 2 when we addressed the deadly sin of focusing only on preparation costs.

The real cost function for financial reporting has two variables: preparation costs plus the cost of capital. The cost of capital reflects at least three things: the supply and demand for capital (future cash flows), the markets' processing costs (including financial analysis and the accumulation of supplemental data), and risk. It seems to us that managers focus way too much (perhaps even exclusively) on their own preparation costs and never look at the others. If you cut corners and don't give the markets what they want or need, they will respond by incurring additional information gathering and processing costs and thus put themselves in need of a higher return. Of course, another possibility is that they will just walk away from your company because the risk and the processing costs are too high.

To create a picture, let the lever in Figure 10-1 represent the balance between a company's information preparation costs and the financial statement users' costs of processing that information and the costs of gathering and processing other information.

In a situation in which the fulcrum is in the middle, a reduction in preparation costs will be matched by a roughly equal increase in the users' processing costs, as shown in Figure 10-2.

In this situation, a decision to save a little money by not reporting some useful information produces a similar increase in the users' costs and thus a higher cost of capital to the firm. In these hypothetical circumstances, cutting the preparation costs may not do much damage.

FIGURE 10-2

Preparation Costs vs. Processing Costs (Part 2)

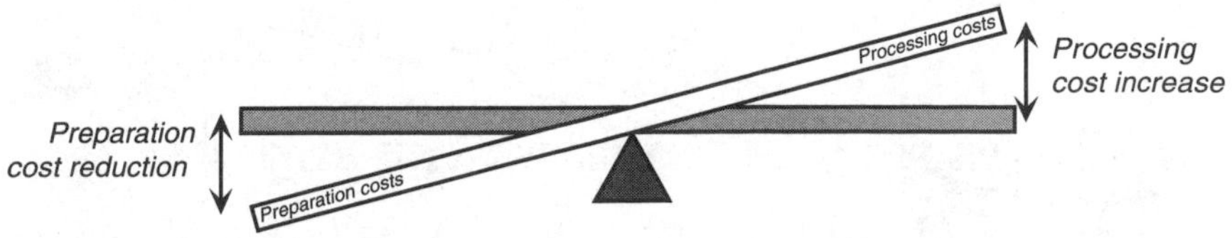

Preparation cost reduction

Processing cost increase

Processing costs

Preparation costs

FIGURE 10-3

Preparation Costs vs. Processing Costs (Part 3)

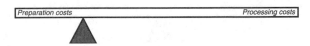

However, as we see it, the lever is not balanced equally in the capital markets because the preparers naturally have greater access to the useful information and can make it available without much effort. Symbolically, this condition of asymmetry would cause the fulcrum to be offset toward the preparers' end, as represented in Figure 10-3.

Under these circumstances, management's decision to save a little money by cutting back on the CFO's efforts will produce a substantially higher cost for the users, as represented by the diagram in Figure 10-4.

This leveraged effect happens for several reasons. One factor is the duplicative efforts of all the interested users that cause them to incur their own individual costs. Another is their need to search out secondary or tertiary sources of information. A third factor is their uncertainty because the information is not firsthand and has not been subjected to an auditor's scrutiny. The result is that a relatively small reduction in preparation costs greatly increases the users' processing costs. That increase, in turn, gets turned back against the stockholders because the company now faces a higher cost of capital, and their share prices will decline.

On the other hand, this leverage can work the other way if management decides to incur the additional preparation costs needed to engage in Quality Financial Reporting and provide greater quantities of more useful information. Consider the final version of the lever in Figure 10-5.

We are confident that management's willingness to spend these relatively few extra dollars to generate and audit really useful information that users demand will generate a much larger payback. That payback will happen because the users will incur much lower processing costs and,

FIGURE 10-4

Preparation Costs vs. Processing Costs (Part 4)

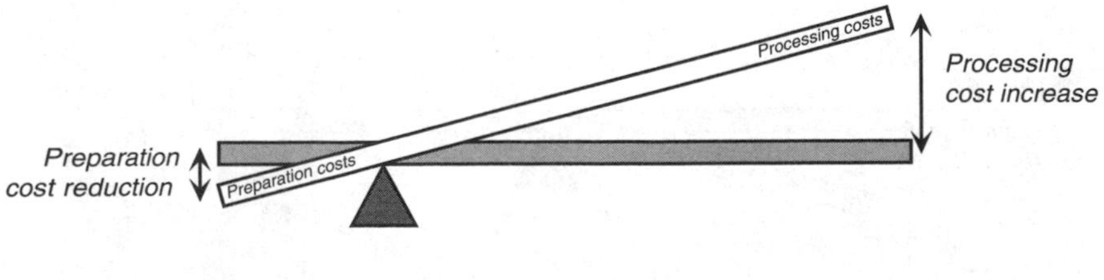

Processing costs

Processing
cost increase

*Preparation
cost reduction*   *Preparation costs*

FIGURE 10-5

Preparation Costs vs. Processing Costs (Part 5)

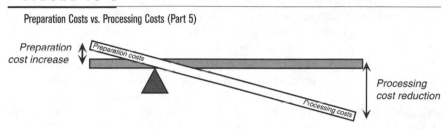

more importantly, will not have to rely as heavily on unaudited second-hand sources. Thus, their reduced uncertainty will enable them to be satisfied with a lower rate of return, which means the company will enjoy lower capital costs and higher security prices.

Because QFR is totally voluntary, it is entirely up to management to decide whether to incur the additional preparation costs. This analysis shows that they would be seriously mistaken in not deciding to do so if the only thing they looked at were their own out-of-pocket costs. However, that's exactly what happens when CFOs are put in charge of financial reporting under a system that evaluates their performance using only the costs they incur in complying with the rules. This compensation system just doesn't cut it because it motivates the accountants to constantly look for opportunities to reduce their preparation costs without ever considering what happens when the resulting bargain-basement-quality information goes out the door. The solution, of course, is to figure out how to factor in the cost of capital as one of the variables in the CFO's compensation.

Before moving on, we also want to ask whether the new financial information produced in pursuit of QFR would also be useful to managers for making their own internal decisions. Given all the various flaws in GAAP information and the lack of relevance of essentially any information based on historical costs, we are hard-pressed to see how any decisions can be supported by the inadequate information that is routinely produced for public financial statements.[2] Thus, we would hold out another benefit to put into the cost/benefit analysis in the form of more rational and otherwise effective internal decisions.

"NO ONE ELSE IS DOING IT."

We can't begin to count the number of times people have responded to our descriptions of QFR with questions like, "Who's doing it?" or, "If it's so good, why isn't everyone doing it?" We can remember one student in an MBA class who was livid at the suggestion that a mere accounting professor could come up with an idea that had escaped the imaginations of everyone else (it turned out she was a practicing CPA, if that explains anything). These questions have come from reporters, editors, managers, other professors—even our parents. We don't resent these questions. In fact, they are good ones. Furthermore, there is a certain prudence in not being the first one to try something new that you're unfamiliar with.

We have already speculated in earlier discussions as to how the four axioms and the QFR concept may have escaped everyone's attention. We think the main reasons are lack of appreciation for the market's efficiency, reliance on bureaucratic systems to do one's thinking, and inappropriate education for managers and accountants. Add to that mix a large dose of complacency and a dependency on lawyers to establish reporting policies, and the result is likely to be a focus on maintaining the status quo instead of embracing new reporting practices. By analogy, some critic could have asked Edison as he came out of the lab holding his first working light bulb, "Oh yeah? If those things are so great, why isn't everybody using them?" It took a while, of course, but eventually the whole world was filled with light fixtures of all descriptions.

We have found that there is a major difference between questions asked out of prudence and questions asked merely to impede progress. After all, the question "Why isn't everybody doing it?" is basically unanswerable. If it is asked out of curiosity and a desire to really understand, then we're happy to proceed with the inquirer on the journey toward answers. On the other hand, many ask the question as a disguised dismissal of the QFR idea. All we can do for these people is to ask them to start rereading this book from the title page.

To return to our point, consider again what it must have been like for the people who developed word processing. Until the new technology was envisioned, explored, made workable, and demonstrated, all people really wanted was cheaper typewriters and slicker ways to correct their typographical errors. We cannot imagine anyone actually using a typewriter anymore. Until someone gets a vision for a change and articulates it, the status quo will stay dominant, with relatively minor improvements but no dramatic change that might be called a huge leap forward.

Furthermore, when new opportunities are presented, there are always some risks, and many people just don't care to take them. QFR seems risky because it is different from what most people are doing. We understand that point, maybe better than anyone else. However, the evidence and the reasoning behind QFR suggest to us that it is a no-brainer to decide to use it.

Some managers have responded to our personal urging by saying that they will use QFR when everyone else is doing it. That sounds to us like a perfect recipe for missing out on the advantages. Those who go first will reap rewards, maybe even the biggest rewards. Those who come along later will just be mimicking the pioneers, and they will not see as big a benefit. The holdouts who refuse to try it after it has worked for others will find themselves in the same condition as Ferdinand Piëch of Volkswagen—facing even higher capital costs than they had before. The penalty will be especially heavy on them because the mere decision to hold out will convey the impression that they are trying to hide something. That aggravated lack of trust will multiply the discount applied to their companies' securities.

Before moving on, we urge you to remember Warren Buffett and his success when you're wondering what straightforward reporting will do for you.

"I DON'T HAVE THE INFORMATION HANDY."

As a variation on the preparation cost objection, some are sure to object about reporting, say, market value-based information because they don't have it on hand. We're reminded of testimony that the FASB received on the use of the direct method of reporting operating cash flows: several preparers stated that they literally did not know how to prepare that kind of schedule and that they did not know how much cash was actually coming in and going out of their companies. We have said to each other that if we had been on the board, we would have used that testimony to require the direct method just to spur the management on to do a better job of informing itself, not to mention the company's stockholders and creditors or the capital markets in general.

Market Value Information

Given the effects of inflation, changes in exchange rates, and the rapid introduction of new technologies and economic upheavals, we simply cannot fathom how any management worth its salt can try to make decisions about its assets and liabilities without monitoring their market values. If only for setting amounts of insurance coverage, managers have to know what their assets are really worth. In an age of shifting interest and exchange rates, how can an intelligent and otherwise competent CFO not be monitoring the market value of the company's liabilities? If you don't have quality market value information handy, then you need to change your systems, as well as your management style. Furthermore, if the capital markets are trying to guess what your assets and liabilities are worth, why would you encourage their inefficiency by withholding information that they want and need and that you have? If, for example, they're trying to guess the values of your assets, what makes you think that they will systematically *over*estimate them? Or that they will systematically *under*-estimate the market value of your debts? Indeed, we think the markets will underestimate the assets and overestimate the debts to protect themselves. Perhaps the worst case occurs when you report your tangible assets at their woefully understated book values and the capital markets actually believe and act on those numbers.

Another facet is that withholding this known market value information greatly multiplies the users' processing costs. In *Financial Reporting in the 1990s and Beyond,* the AIMR committee commented on this point, and its words are worth repeating:

> In particular, it is the providers of financial statements from whom the claim of excessive cost is heard. We can respond by asserting that the cost to them, high as it may seem, is still less than the benefit to financial statement users of (1) minimizing the cost of providing the data by having the firm do it once and provide it to multitudes of users who otherwise would individually have to replicate the firm's effort; (2) having the firm as the source of information thus obviating the need for analysts to scavenge for less reliable data from secondary sources . . . (p. 81)

So, if you don't already have quality information on hand, go out and get it. If you do have it, go ahead and make it public. The markets will reward you for doing something worthwhile. Chapter 15 explains a great deal more about the relevance and reliability of market value information, as well as the demand for it.

"I MIGHT GET SUED."

This objection about lawsuits is tough to overcome. In a litigious age, stepping outside the boundaries of the norms seems to invite legal action. We cannot argue too strongly against the prudence of avoiding litigation. It's very expensive, even if you don't go to court and even if you are innocent.

As we have suggested, however, lawyers are trained and immersed in a carefully constructed and highly artificial legal environment. They live in a world in which decisions are verdicts that occur after carefully constructed and constrained legal procedures are completed. A judge or a jury must reach a verdict only on the basis of information that is presented in the courtroom in accordance with strict rules of evidence. Thus, lawyers tend to reveal information only when it makes their clients' cases look better or when a higher authority demands disclosure. Judges also exclude evidence that is tainted in one way or another, most often by the manner in which it was obtained.

It is a profound mistake to transfer that kind of thinking to the process for financial reporting to the capital markets. The market participants are not limited to data that the company spoon-feeds them in audited financial statements. They cannot be instructed like a jury to disregard a confession from the defendant or to ignore a witness's outburst in the courtroom. If they can find helpful information anywhere, they will go for it and use it. And there is nothing that anyone can do to force them to rely on what they consider to be useless information, even if it is presented in GAAP financial statements.

One more point is worth making in this section. Despite its foibles, the U.S. legal system is still organized and managed to punish wrongdoing and to not punish sound behavior. An old adage says that the best defense against being sued for libel is to tell the truth. In the same way, the best way to avoid litigation for faulty financial reporting is to ensure that everything you report has a factual and truthful basis. We admit a lack of knowledge of all the precedents, but we have never heard of anyone being successfully sued for fraud when they had made their best efforts to tell the truth. We also think that carefully worded disclaimers and caveats will alleviate the risk of successful litigation.

One area of reporting that is particularly vulnerable to litigation risk is predictions of future events. In our view, and as confirmed by others, predictions are in the realm of financial analysis and should be made by analysts, using information provided by managers and accountants. Consider these words from the Jenkins Committee report described in Chapter 8:

> Despite the relevance of forecasted data, . . . users generally do not need forecasted data from management in business reporting, for the following reasons:
>
> - Users generally prefer to make their own forecasts. Many users consider themselves experts in forecasting, valuing companies, or assessing credit risk and consider forecasting as an integral part of their role. Further, users believe they are more objective.
> - Point estimates of future financial performance are inherently imprecise. Further, users' experience with those forecasts leads them to believe that management forecasts tend to be overly optimistic.
> - Forecasts would increase litigation against the company. Forecasts that, with the benefit of hindsight, failed to foretell the future accurately would be easy targets for lawsuits filed routinely against companies whose stock prices have fallen. (p. 30)

It takes a careful management to tread the line of providing forward-looking information without crossing over into predictions. One technique is to explain what you intend to do if certain scenarios play out. This practice will help analysts make their predictions without exposing you to the risks of making precise forecasts.

There are some litigation landmines in financial reporting, that's for sure. But, we think a careful and complete focus on telling the truth and telling it plainly will be like legal Teflon. Of course, it makes sense to check with your attorneys, but be sure they understand the capital markets and what you're trying to accomplish. Don't let them get you to act as if the markets are courtrooms and that investment decisions can be managed like jury verdicts.

"BUT WHAT IF I HAVE TO REPORT BAD NEWS?"

This objection strikes at the heart of the usual preparers' financial reporting strategic objective of using their financial statements to look good. They prefer to commit the sin of hype and spin instead of coming to grips with negative results they have encountered.

The regulatory system has long been aware of this objection and has carefully constructed rules and regulations to accelerate the reporting of bad news. For example, the practice of reporting the lower of cost or market measure of assets makes managers report losses as soon as they're known to occur. The FASB issued SFAS 5 on contingencies to force managers to report contingent losses (or disclose information about them) while limiting the reporting of contingent gains. Both the SEC and the FASB have generally required managers to report asset impairments but have disallowed recognizing most gains from asset enhancements. The SEC has a special form, the 8-K, for reporting nonroutine events (such as losses) within days of when they occur, all to help ensure that bad news gets reported promptly.

Despite these requirements, managers are still reluctant to report bad news until forced to at the last possible moment. Far more earnings adjustments are reported, for example, in the fourth quarter of companies' fiscal years than in the other three quarters. Presumably, the auditors have compelled the managers to come to grips with the inevitable bad news that they have postponed acknowledging.

If we go back to what the AIMR committee report said about surprises, we can learn something about "bad news":

> When a financial statement contains a "surprise" or two that causes a market price to change, one usually may conclude either that the analyst lacked perspicacity or that the company engaged in duplicity. (pp. 12–13)

We interpret this comment to mean that the only bad news in financial reporting is any message that arrives unexpectedly, not just information that reflects poorly on management. Under this interpretation, a surprise in a delayed report that sales had doubled or that valuable new patents were acquired at a fraction of their value can be considered to be a kind of bad news because the act of withholding the information allowed stock trades and other transactions to occur under conditions in which the two parties did not really know what they were buying or selling. This situation surrounds the management with a cloud of uncertainty that will be hard to dispel.

In the same vein, good news is any information that reveals promptly and clearly what has happened, what is about to happen, or even what might happen. By being released without delay, this news allows the markets to adjust their expectations quickly and with less uncertainty. If management shows a pattern of prompt and clear release of all pertinent information, the markets know that they are less likely to be blindsided, and will reward this risk-reducing behavior.

This is the kind of information that QFR encourages managers to report. We think that establishing a pattern and reputation for being forthcoming, honest, and timely will boost stock prices and cut capital costs, simply because these actions will reduce uncertainty and risk for capital market participants.

In contrast, think what happens when managers hold onto news until they are forced to report it, either by mandate or by the existence of other information sources that have already revealed what happened. Even though there is less surprise when management finally reports the information, there is likely to be a negative effect due to the fact that management was foolish enough to think that it could string the markets along and avoid a drop in price. The resulting lack of trust will create uncertainty, promote risk, pump up the demanded rate of return and cost of capital, and inevitably lead to discounted security prices—certainly more discounted than they would have been if management had opened up and revealed what was happening.

Incidentally, we think the same phenomenon exists for sell-side analysts who continue to forecast higher stock prices and issue positive recommendations even when the company's situation is in the dumper and going lower. (Such recommendations continued for Enron's stock, for example, even as its price was screaming down in the fall of 2001.) These people cannot expect to have their opinions respected, or, more importantly, paid for, when they are found to have compromised their judgment for some other purpose, *even in only one instance.*

Of course, QFR is not mandatory, and managers can decide for themselves what to do about proclaiming or hiding information about events and conditions. Sooner or later, the truth will become known, and the full impact will be felt. In the meantime, the absence of information makes capital market participants wonder what's going on, and they will compensate by demanding a higher return.[3] As confirmation of our assertions, consider this quote from the Eccles team in *The ValueReporting Revolution:*

> . . . [W]hen management delays or stops reporting information that the
> market sees as important, the market will assume the worst: that manage-
> ment has something to hide—probably because it does. (p. 193)

There should be little remaining doubt that silence raises stock prices.

"IT'LL MAKE US LOOK VOLATILE."

We wrote earlier about the sin of smoothing, which is usually committed when managers and their accountants and auditors try to use accounting techniques to cover up unanticipated or unwanted volatility. The most dreaded form of volatility occurs in reported earnings because variation there suggests that the managers are not in control of the situation. It also creates a greater potential for surprises, and, as we just described, surprises are bad news.

There are, of course, two ways to deal with real volatility. One is to report it when it happens as faithfully as possible, but then try to do something to keep it from happening again by managing the economics of the situation, at least by planning more carefully. For example, before you invest in marketable securities as a way to increase earnings, you should realize that they change in value unpredictably, which means that you are about to create real volatility. You can act to eliminate that variability by not buying the investments or to mitigate it by building a diversified or otherwise hedged portfolio.

The other way to deal with real volatility is to produce financial statements that simply hide it from the users' view. You can do that by lying, but that strategy tends to be unsuitable for most situations. Another similar technique is to account for the investments using GAAP. If you can manage to classify the securities as "available for sale," you don't have to report any volatile gains or losses on your income statement until you sell the investments. Other examples abound, but depreciation is about the best (or worst). Instead of accounting for the changes in the asset's actual value, managers simply decide ahead of time how much expense will occur in each year of the asset's life, and the volatility just vanishes from sight. Interest income and expense are also smoothed out by GAAP, and so are income tax and pension expenses.

To summarize the second method, managers can often get rid of the *appearance* of volatility merely by implementing GAAP. If they do, the real economic volatility is still there, of course; it's just that no one can easily see it. The real risk of this "lookin' good" strategy is that management might actually come to believe that there really is no volatility and go on to make less than optimal decisions. In his *Owner's Manual*, Warren Buffett comments sagely on the risk that top managers face when they set out to deceive financial statement readers:

> We also believe candor benefits us as managers: The CEO who misleads others in public may eventually mislead himself in private.

Another negative side effect is that artificial smoothing filters out the real economic messages that the capital market participants know they need and know they aren't getting. Therefore, they will tend to increase their expected rate of return and discount the company's own security prices if they know that management is massaging the numbers.

With this background in mind, we can see why some managers would resist practicing QFR because telling the truth in a volatile situation will let statement users know that volatility exists and how bad it is. Thus, some managers will not want to use QFR for fear the reported numbers will cause stock prices to drop.

On the other hand, if the financial statement users know that the published data does not faithfully represent the real situation, they will discount the stock even more because of both the real volatility and the lack of useful information about it. Therefore, it makes sense to confess the real volatility to eliminate the discount imposed for not telling the whole truth.

Also, as we have seen before, making the commitment to report the truth about the volatility is more likely to make management actually deal with it by doing something other than covering it up, with or without GAAP. If so, and if management creates an effective economic strategy instead of a policy of managing the reported numbers, the consequence is likely to be a lower cost of capital because the real risk has been reduced.

"THE USERS WON'T UNDERSTAND."

Back in Chapter 3, we described the confusion that seems to exist between the politically expedient assumption that individual investors are the primary target for public financial reports and the realistic observations that the main users are sophisticated company, industry, and institutional financial analysts while individual investors depend on financial advisers, not periodic financial statements.

If managers make the mistake of believing that individual investors are the main users, then they would be right to raise an objection to QFR— or GAAP, for that matter—on the basis that the resulting information is too complicated for these people to understand.

On the other hand, if managers were to realize that the primary users are actually highly trained and experienced analysts, then they would no longer see complexity as an obstacle to putting out greater amounts of more detailed information. Of course, this more realistic assumption would never justify making the reports unnecessarily difficult to read and understand.

However, we have been around the block a few times, and we have heard a great many preparers object to FASB proposals by alluding vaguely to a concern that the resulting financial statements will be too hard for users to comprehend. When we listen between the lines, we actually hear a different story. Namely, we think that they are mostly trying to find some suitable way to stop whatever the board is trying to do.

Of course, if the financial reports really cannot be understood by users, sophisticated or otherwise, it seems to us that managers who elect to pursue Quality Financial Reporting will be attuned to that possibility and will focus on getting relevant and reliable information into their reports. In other words, they will be highly motivated to make the reports comprehensible and otherwise easy to use.

"THAT'S DISCLOSURE OVERLOAD."

The complaint of "disclosure overload" is very similar to the objection that users won't understand. The gist of it is the proposition that decision makers can process only so much information before they get overloaded, like a robot that sparks, smokes, and then freezes in some cheesy science fiction movie. There are two responses that can defuse this argument.

First, it is obviously management's responsibility to ensure that the information it publishes is understandable and accessible. Yet, when we look at annual reports and SEC filings, we find an incredible mélange of legal terms, technical discussions, and jumbled-up footnotes that do not contain all of the information on the same topic. The bottom line is that if there is overload, or if there could be overload, most of the blame has to fall on those who produce the reports.

Second, we again point to the fact that financial reports are used primarily, even exclusively, by highly trained and experienced professionals, not run-of-the-mill individual investors. Further, these sophisticated users are in a position to invest (or disinvest) millions and millions of dollars. While individuals can be overcome by too much information, we cannot in our wildest imaginations come up with a scenario where specialized analysts would cry out to a management, "Stop! Stop! We already know too much! We don't want to know anything else. Just take our money and leave us alone!"

As nonsensical as that seems, it is the mental picture harbored by all who raise the disclosure overload objection. Just like all the other objections, it is a smokescreen intended to hide the fact that some managers just don't want to tell the truth because they know it will hurt them. Of course, QFR reveals that they're wrong on that point, too.

ONE MORE TIME

As we said at the beginning of this chapter, the overarching point about all these objections is that no one really has to believe anything we have said in these pages, nor do they have to dispute our arguments to keep doing what they have always done. In fact, the last thing that we would ever agitate for would be to make QFR mandatory because that idea is in direct contradiction with the QFR attitude that we are trying to get people to adopt.

Furthermore, we are confident that huge amounts of potential innovation and improvement are currently locked up and unused because the
dominant worldview in financial reporting is that preparers should report
only what they are required to report and nothing more. When this
untapped potential flood of useful information is released, we think
accountants and analysts will be thoroughly amazed at what will happen
once visionary managers go to work to outdo one another by providing
information that is even more useful than that provided by their capital
market competitors. We are convinced that no management will ever
achieve that wonderful result by perfunctory compliance with politically
expedient accounting standards.

In closing, if you don't like QFR, you simply don't have to do it. Of
course, if you don't do it, you need to be prepared to be saddled with
unnecessarily higher capital costs and deeply discounted securities.

NOTES

1. As a reminder of what we explained in Chapter 8, Baruch Lev states: "A
   study on the disclosure activities of 100 of the largest U.S. public companies
   revealed that 55 companies made fewer than four voluntary disclosures
   during the seven years 1981–1987, and only 16 companies made at least one
   voluntary disclosure a year." ("Information Disclosure Strategy," *California
   Management Review,* 1992, p. 9.) Apparently very few managers feel they can
   beneficially take the initiative to report useful information on their own. We
   hope the thoughts in this book will inspire them to do so.

2. A decade or so ago, the world of managerial accounting was electrified by
   the introduction and then widespread adoption of Activity-Based Costing
   (ABC). We certainly were, and still are, in favor of the sort of careful analysis
   that underlies ABC, to the extent that it reveals opportunities to improve
   processes. However, we blanch at the thought that the eventual outcome is
   product or service unit costs based on allocated average historical costs,
   including depreciation, for example. No matter how the data is sliced and
   diced, the output can be no better than the input, and ABC systems that
   assign historical and average costs to products and services are less than
   fully useful for either internal or external decisions.

3. After hearing a presentation on QFR, a gentleman from Germany raised this
   objection somewhat obliquely by asserting that, as a shareholder, he
   assumed that the absence of information from the company's management
   meant that nothing bad was happening. When he answered "yes" to the
   question of whether he had small children at home, he was then asked what
   he assumed if they were playing together in another room and absolutely no
   noise was being made. He smiled broadly and said, "I see your point more
   clearly now!"

How Close Are You to QFR?

This section of the book is designed to take the reader down below the level of generalities to do a gut check. It's time to move beyond the intellectual stimulation of understanding that things might be wrong with practice and that things might be better under another paradigm.

These chapters contain three short questionnaires designed to assess your attitudes toward the capital markets and financial reporting, your past decisions in selecting accounting and reporting polices, and your relationship with your auditors. In the course of discussing those questions and analyzing possible answers, we also present more evidence of the shortcomings of the current supply-driven paradigm and the promised advantages of the QFR paradigm that can be achieved by voluntarily going beyond the minimum levels established by GAAP and other regulations. If minimum compliance does indeed create uncertainty, the consequence has to be a higher cost of capital compared to what is experienced when managers willfully provide more information aimed at meeting the currently unserved demands.

We know that it is never easy to let go of something you have held on to for a long time, especially in exchange for something unfamiliar. However, when the time comes, that change must be made. This section is intended to help you see whether that time has arrived for you.

CHAPTER 11

It's Time for an Attitude Check

This chapter represents a turning point in the sense that the theory behind Quality Financial Reporting has been presented, explained, justified, defended, and translated into a broad reporting strategy. We think we have done enough on the conceptual side and believe that it is now time to tackle QFR-related issues on a more specific and personal level.

At countless points in earlier chapters, we have stated that QFR is much more an attitude than a set of specific practices. When managers adopt this attitude, they are reaching out to the capital markets to bring them into the firm as partners, with the goal of building mutually beneficial relationships. One basis for a successful relationship is full disclosure with integrity, which, in turn, leads to trust and respect. The ultimate outcome is a rate of return for the investors and a cost of capital for the company that appropriately reflect the underlying operating risk.

An attitude check at this stage will allow you to judge for yourself whether you and others at your company have been practicing QFR on your own or if you have just been going with the GAAP flow like everyone else. If you are in this latter non-QFR mode, you are associated with people who choose to report as little as possible while trying to bias the reports to look good, all while neglecting to tell the whole truth. Of course, if this checkup reveals that you have not previously embraced QFR, you may decide that your next step will be an attitude adjustment to replace your old thought patterns with new ones.

THIS IS A TEST

Table 11-1 contains our first list of 10 questions (others will follow in the next two chapters). We invite you to take the time now to answer these

TABLE 11-1

Attitude Check	Yes	No
1. Do you think the capital markets react automatically to increases and decreases in reported earnings without carefully considering how those results were achieved?		
2. Have you ever tried to keep the price of your company's stock high by inhibiting the flow of information about it to the capital markets?		
3. Have you ever delayed reporting bad financial news until the last possible minute?		
4. Have you ever chosen an accounting policy with the objective of helping your company meet an expected earnings result?		
5. Do the financial analysts who follow your company encourage you to meet targets by choosing accounting policies instead of changing strategies and tactics?		
6. When contemplating the use of a new accounting policy, have you ever stopped after considering the costs of producing the information without determining whether it would reduce uncertainty and the cost of capital?		
7. Has anyone ever left your financial reporting shop because of unresolved ethical misgivings over accounting policies and implementations?		
8. Do you worry that your financial statements will give away operational information to your customer market competitors?		
9. Do you provide only summary financial statements in your annual report?		
10. Do you publish pro forma income statements that always produce higher measures of earnings?		

questions with a simple yes or no. Of course, you won't learn anything if you don't provide answers that reflect your actual attitude and history, so we suggest that you face up to the challenge of learning more about yourself by putting down your most honest answers. The questions are designed to be answered by top managers or financial reporting executives, such as finance vice presidents, CFOs, or controllers; if you are not currently in one of these positions, answer as if you are filling in for one of those people in your company.

Now that you have completed the quiz, it's time to interpret your answers. Unless you were really thinking about something else, you probably noticed that we designed the questions to cause "yes" to signal that you (and others in your company) are apparently not presently practicing QFR. In fact, we think that even a score as low as only one yes out of the 10 answers indicates that you have some room to grow before you can start claiming to be a Quality Financial Reporting practitioner and begin to enjoy its full benefits. Let's look at each question more closely and the possible meanings of your answers.

Question 1

Here is the first question:

> Do you think the capital markets react automatically to increases and decreases in reported earnings without considering how those results were achieved?

A "yes" answer suggests that you are committing the number one financial reporting sin, which is failing to appreciate how well the capital markets actually work. Life is more complicated than many managers seem to think when they believe that the markets do anything automatically. In fact, if the markets were to react automatically to public stimuli, like GAAP earnings announcements, by moving in a predictable direction by a predictable amount, they would indeed be inefficient, even terribly inefficient. Clearly, U.S. capital markets are not in that category. It's probably true that virtually all markets in the world are more efficient than that.

Perhaps a more important point is that management's financial messages sent through GAAP financial statements are obviously woefully incomplete and otherwise less than fully informative. And, as we have explained, GAAP are full of all sorts of discretionary choices, which means (among other things) that there is a nearly endless variety of ways of "acceptably" describing the same events and conditions. Thus, if you were to believe that the only thing the markets look at is reported earnings per share, you would be missing the point that management has many different ways to compute earnings in a year, all of which are generally accepted. The ultimate consequence of this fact is that financial analysts must spend a lot of time and effort taking apart a set of public financial statements to comprehend which choices the management made and how they affected the reported earnings numbers. Table 11-2 shows examples of alternatives that management has the discretion to choose from. In addition to the listed items, managers have always had substantial leeway in dealing with routine accruals and deferrals, especially bad debts.

TABLE 11-2

Effects of GAAP Alternatives on Reported Earnings

Area	Generally Accepted Alternatives	Effect on Reported Earnings
Inventory	FIFO, LIFO, average	This choice impacts the cost of goods sold. FIFO includes in gross profit the increase in value of items that were owned and sold during the year. LIFO, on the other hand, excludes that gain from earnings. Neither method, nor the average method, even tries to describe the real gains or losses on the *unsold* items that have occurred through value-adding activities or other changes in value.
Investments	Portfolios for trading, available for sale, and held-to-maturity securities (according to management intent)	If management classifies investments as belonging in the trading portfolio, changes in their market values during the year are included in earnings, even if they are not sold. If they are classified into the available-for-sale portfolio, the income statement reports only gains and losses on securities that were sold during the year, and the recognized amounts equal the full gains or losses accumulated since the securities were first acquired, thus contradicting the idea that an income statement should describe only what happened in a specific reporting year. If management classifies the investments as held to maturity, the balance sheet does not report current market value, and the income statement does not report a gain or loss until the securities are sold.
Depreciation	Straight-line and accelerated methods; different service lives can be used	By its name, depreciation is fundamentally an effort to include declines in the value of tangible assets as expenses on the income statement. For the convenience of accountants (but not users), depreciation is calculated (not observed) using predictions and assumptions, and amounts are assigned to income statements in accordance with management's expectations and desires, not according to what really happened to the assets' values. Obviously, this situation produces a lot of wishful thinking, and management can pretty well destroy much, if not all, of the usefulness of the information.

TABLE 11-2

Effects of GAAP Alternatives on Reported Earnings (*Continued*)

Area	Generally Accepted Alternatives	Effect on Reported Earnings
Amortization	Various capitalization rules	Amortization is the same as depreciation applied to intangible assets instead of tangible ones. However, it's even worse because GAAP require different treatments for different kinds of intangibles. For research and development, management reports no asset and no amortization because the year's full cost is reported as expense on the income statement. Costs incurred in applying for, acquiring, and defending copyrights and patents are added to an asset account balance that has no correlation with the asset's real value. However, some software development costs are capitalized and others are expensed, hinging on management's discretionary choices. Goodwill is recorded as the excess of the full cost of an acquired company over the sum of the market values assigned by management to its assets and liabilities. This amount only accidentally represents a market value of anything, and certainly cannot be equal to the value of the real goodwill. Nor is amortization useful since it occurs over an arbitrary period chosen by management. Under SFAS 142, management decides whether to carry that original cost forward or write it down but never ever up. (In the transition period, comparisons between years will be tenuous because early years will include goodwill amortization while later years won't.) In summary, no one should believe that the total reported amortization expense has any connection to real events. The same can be said for the amounts shown on the balance sheets for intangible assets. If the authors of GAAP for intangibles were eligible, we would nominate them for a Pulitzer Prize in fiction.
Business combinations	Pooling and purchase	A pooling treatment of a merger combines the irrelevant GAAP book values of the acquired company's assets and liabilities with the irrelevant GAAP book values of the acquirer's assets and liabilities on the consoli-

TABLE 11-2

Effects of GAAP Alternatives on Reported Earnings (*Continued*)

Area	Generally Accepted Alternatives	Effect on Reported Earnings
		dated balance sheet. These useless amounts are then used by accountants to compute reported earnings in the future. In contrast, the purchase treatment causes the market values of the acquired company's assets and liabilities to be presented on the combined balance sheet, added to the acquiring company's irrelevant GAAP book values to still produce a big mess on the income statement. As a consequence, no combination is ever accounted for in a way that is complete or otherwise rational, with the ultimate result that no informed capital market participant would ever believe or act on the numbers provided in consolidated GAAP financial statements. Even though SFAS 141 eliminated pooling, it did not require retroactive restatement to remove old pooling numbers from the accounts; thus GAAP financial statements that report previously pooled combinations will be thoroughly contaminated (should we say "pool-luted"?) for years to come.
Stock options	Recognition or disclosure	As mentioned several times, GAAP allow management to put option-based compensation expense in the footnotes instead of the income statement, which means reported earnings are incomplete and unreliable.
Pensions and post-employment medical benefits	Choices of discount rates, expected return rates, and actuarial predictions	By offering to pay these benefits, managers have taken a great risk by entering into irrational transactions because they are committed to pay unknown amounts to unknown individuals for an unknown period of time. As a result of this irrationality, there is no rational way to measure the real annual expense associated with offering these benefits to employees. Because the methods applied in SFAS 87 and SFAS 106 require major management discretion, and because the FASB was politically boxed in, the end results are reported expense numbers based literally on what was *expected* to happen instead of what *did* happen. Who can believe those numbers by the time they enter into the earnings calculation?

With all this background, you can now see the kind of trouble the world's various economies would be in if their capital markets really did react automatically to reported earnings numbers without digging into the calculations behind them. There is also every reason to believe that analysts have differing assessments of risk, so that it is impossible to determine ahead of time how the markets will actually react to any particular earnings number and totally pointless to try to trigger a specific stock price reaction by playing some sort of accounting game.

Thus, a "yes" answer to this first question clearly identifies a need to think more deeply about the markets and how QFR would help reduce uncertainty and create even more market efficiency.

Question 2

The second question asks:

> Have you ever tried to keep the price of your company's stock high by inhibiting the flow of information about it to the capital markets?

The root cause of this behavior is again the attitude that the markets can be fooled by keeping information out of public reports and thus out of their hands. Managers try this trick by simply leaving out useful but negative information, ignoring requirements that auditors don't enforce, and by complying with requirements in such a way that they produce confusing disclosures.[1]

The net result of this kind of behavior is a relationship with the capital markets that is rooted in deception and mistrust. There is absolutely no reason to go there when it is possible to do things differently by letting the markets know exactly what is happening in no uncertain terms. We would also ask managers why they would choose to live a professional lifestyle that carries the risk of getting caught.[2]

This QFR strategy is, of course, exactly what Warren Buffett works overtime to accomplish, and he seems like a good model to emulate.

Question 3

The next question asks:

> Have you ever delayed reporting bad financial news until the last possible minute?

In fact, this item is not much different from question 2, except that it acknowledges the need to actually disclose the bad news as soon as it's known. The typical negative management behavior is to hold on to that information until it has to be reported, either by mandate or by the fact that the word has already gotten out through other communication channels.

If particular managers have displayed this attitude in the past, the markets will remember and penalize them with a higher discount on their securities' prices because they cannot be trusted to release relevant information on a timely basis. On the other hand, the markets will reward managers once they get the reputation for candidly saying "Oops" every time it needs to be said. The mistakes have consequences, of course, but only for their immediate operational impact. When the QFR attitude is brought to bear on these situations, the markets will not apply additional penalties because you tried to keep them in the dark.

Question 4

The fourth question asks:

> Have you ever chosen an accounting policy with the objective of helping your company meet an expected earnings result?

By bringing in the concept of expected earnings, this question touches on a really strange situation in today's capital markets. Specifically, we find huge irony, even disgust, in the fact that the major currency in investing is what analysts *think* management will report instead of what management actually reports. This situation speaks volumes about the lack of timeliness in quarterly reports.

Beyond that point, this question also probes the practice of earnings management in order to reach a desired number instead of pursuing some sort of protocol to produce a number that gets reported without regard to what some analysts predict that you will report.[3]

This targeting practice, however widespread it might be, is destructive every time it happens. If market participants know that you're playing games to meet targets, then they will play games in setting those targets, which you will then play more games yet again to reach, ad infinitum, ad nauseam, and ad discountium. The consequence has to be a total disconnect between what is reported and what needs to be reported in order to put really useful information into the markets.

Despite the popularity of earnings management, we are totally convinced that it is a pointless game in which everyone loses, even those who aren't playing, because it causes the markets to swim in unnecessarily high and rough seas of uncertainty.

The Eccles team from PricewaterhouseCoopers addressed an entire chapter of their *ValueReporting* book to the "earnings game" and made an excellent case against playing it. For example, they said:

> From a negative point of view, [managers] may make decisions that deliver short-term results and sacrifice the longer-term benefits. Classic examples

include delaying maintenance on plant and equipment or cutting prices to generate sales before the period closes. Coupled with perfectly legitimate accounting "judgment calls," such decisions are designed to cast the most favorable light possible on the numbers. In some cases, exercising so much discretion pushes the allowable limits. When it exceeds the limits, it becomes accounting fraud. Any way you slice it, it's earnings management, a subject of great interest to companies, investors, regulators, and academics alike. (p. 76)

They also observed:

> . . . [R]eported earnings has become the end game itself. And companies work very hard to make sure the number comes out a certain way. They're not using earnings to manage the business; they're using earnings to manage the market. (p. 90)

Here is another sobering thought:

> If nothing else, [earnings manipulation] all adds up to a lot of management time, energy, and creativity spent in a completely unproductive pursuit because the rules of The Earnings Game require it. And it's big-ticket management time, energy and creativity that are being squandered.
>
> [A] *CFO Magazine* survey found that three out of five CFOs spend more than 10 percent of their time dealing with analysts and two out of five give analysts more than 20 percent of their time. . . . [This] time spent with analysts is most definitely time not spent managing the business and creating value. (p. 83)

For more detail, we recommend Chapter 4 of the Eccles team's book in its entirety.

Question 5

The fifth question probes the same issue from a different angle:

> Do the financial analysts who follow your company encourage you to meet targets by choosing accounting policies instead of changing strategies and tactics?

The real problem revealed by a "yes" answer to this question is management's dysfunctional codependent relationship with the kind of financial analysts who are playing the markets as suckers instead of trying to find the intrinsic values of securities and make a profit when they're out of equilibrium. In order to treat the markets that way, these sleazy analysts have to find sleazy (or gullible) managers who want to play the same game either for the same reasons or because they just don't know any better. If you answered yes, you need to do two things: (1) change your attitude and (2) change your analysts.

Using QFR, managers should see the game for what it is: a short-sighted, high-risk effort to pull off a kind of accounting fraud that will ultimately end in disaster. The game gets even more complicated when the auditors are dragged in to approve the policy choices. We also know from experience that sometimes it's the auditors who do the suggesting and then the pulling. In either case, these watchdogs are not doing any good for the managers, the stockholders, and especially the markets.

Notice that we haven't yet raised any ethical issues in analyzing this situation. QFR shows us that trying to deceive the markets brings its own economic punishments in its own way. To us and many others, however, playing any kind of financial reporting game is unethical.[4]

Question 6

The next question asks:

> When contemplating the use of a new accounting policy, have you ever stopped after considering the costs of producing the information without determining whether it would reduce uncertainty and the cost of capital?

This query obviously deals with the financial reporting sin of focusing on the preparation costs to the exclusion of the benefits the information produces. We are convinced that the financial managers of every company will have to respond to this question with a "yes" answer.

QFR thinking, in contrast, could still lead to rejecting a new method as too expensive, but the cost/benefit analysis would include the savings in lower capital costs. In effect, this decision needs to move out of the CFO's shop into the realm of top management, which must try to determine whether that new accounting policy might actually create new shareholder value in excess of its implementation costs. Managers also need to consider whether the new information might allow them to make better internal decisions than the reports they and their staffs are relying on. Admittedly, the cost/benefit analysis is much more complex than just the cost analysis. That complexity doesn't excuse anyone from doing it, though, does it?

In the Enron case, the management seems to have made another kind of preparation cost mistake in spending virtually unlimited amounts of money just to look good in the financial statements. In fact, they made the stockholders doubly worse off by spending the cash and producing misleading financial reports.

Question 7

The seventh question gets fairly personal:

> Has anyone ever left your financial reporting shop because of unresolved ethical misgivings over accounting policies and implementations?

As we just mentioned, there are some pretty close similarities between reporting decisions that are made using QFR and those that come out of adhering to ethical frameworks that value truth telling. The similarities are mostly coincidental because the two systems value telling the truth for two different reasons. QFR says that telling the truth brings economic rewards, while ethical systems generally assert that telling the truth ought to be done simply because it is the right thing to do.

So what is this question getting at? It's simple. If an employee doing financial accounting and reporting has grown sufficiently concerned to quit over an ethical issue, then someone has probably created a situation in which the truth is not being respected or told. If so, then the financial statements are not as useful as they could be, and it is time to bring about improved disclosure to avoid new discount penalties or eliminate existing ones.

Another dimension to this situation is that few employees actually ever take the extreme action of quitting their professional level jobs for ethical reasons. If someone has quit, or even threatened to quit, that means many others probably feel the same way but just haven't had the courage or the financial stamina to bail out. It also means that the office culture might be veering into unethical waters in other areas, such as internal reporting for budgeting and other kinds of cost controls.

In any case, even a hint that ethics are a problem in the financial reporting area is a bright red flag that needs top management attention, and quickly.[5] More to the point of this book, the existence of ethical problems related to truth telling almost certainly means that the best and most useful financial information is not flowing into the capital markets. Of course, the consequence is lower stock prices.

Question 8

The eighth question presents this challenge:

> Do you worry that your financial statements will give away operational information to your customer market competitors?

Previous discussions should have made it clear that there is little substance to the fear that full disclosure of financial affairs will reveal anything to competitors that they don't already know about your company, your products, and your plans. There are just too many alternative means for them to gather that kind of data to elevate this concern to the point that you decide to refuse to completely inform the capital markets about your company's future cash flow prospects.

The real risk is that intentionally withholding useful information from those markets will create higher capital costs that will actually overwhelm any of the alleged operating benefits of keeping information from competitors. Of course, practicing QFR means you can make this decision to hold back information without direct penalty if that's what you want to do, but you still need to be ready to pay the price in the capital market, just like CEO Piëch of Volkswagen had to when he decided to pursue this strategy. Don't even think about going there.

Question 9

This question is intended to poke a hole in a growing practice:

> Do you provide only summary financial statements in your annual report?

There is clearly nothing wrong in trying to make your financial statements easier for unsophisticated readers to understand and maybe even use. The problem is that the quest for "simplification" may just be management's cover story to justify deception if their real objective is to keep useful information from getting to the stockholders.

The public rationale supporting this choice asserts that reducing the size and contents of the financial reports affects only relatively unsophisticated individual stockholders, not the high-powered financial analysts who prefer using the 10-K filed with the SEC. While that observation might be true, the mere act of providing only summary reports may create a stigma that reflects the possibility that the managers are really only trying to keep the stockholders in the dark. In our experience, for example, summary reports we have seen all somehow omit the footnote that describes the stock option compensation. It's possible that this omission follows from summarizing and condensing; it is also possible that the decision to summarize has been driven by the ability to leave information out of the report that might prove to be embarrassing to management.

If the managers really are summarizing to keep negative information under wraps, the market consequence has to be at least a smidgen of distrust (and probably more), with the ultimate result of discounted share prices and a higher cost of capital. It doesn't take much of a percentage increase in the capital costs to outweigh the relatively minor cost savings from printing and distributing thinner annual reports.

In other words, we think the practice of providing a summary report carries quite a risk of creating much more trouble than it's worth. QFR is definitely a better way to go.

Question 10

The final question in this chapter is:

> Do you publish pro forma income statements that always produce higher measures of earnings?

Up to this point we haven't really talked about the booming business of pro forma reporting. In the old days, preparing a pro forma set of statements meant providing predicted statements of earnings and balance sheets as a matter of showing management, creditors, or investors what future results should turn out to be like. Somewhere along the line in the last decade or so, some managers started to associate the term *pro forma* with income statements that have been modified to show what earnings would have been if the managers had not been constrained to comply with GAAP.

In a sense, QFR will lead to this sort of practice. Under QFR, managers will present the GAAP financial statements and then rearrange and remeasure the amounts to show what really happened in what we call enhanced GAAP financial statements and supplemental disclosures. So, what's the difference between QFR and the pro forma activities the question asks about? It's all in the attitude, because what's being done today in pro forma reporting is to somehow always boost revenues and gains while reducing expenses and losses. One of the favorite tricks is to show earnings before interest, taxes, depreciation and amortization, also known as EBITDA. The problem with this number is that some interest and taxes have been paid and more will be paid in the future. As readers can surely tell, we have deep concerns about depreciation and amortization as measured under GAAP. However, we would not argue that they should simply be left out of the earnings calculation. Rather, we recommend that they be calculated as the change in market value of the assets, an amount that might be more or less than the GAAP amount.

So, if you answered this question with a yes, you still have a long way to go until you reach QFR. To get there, you need to make up your mind to report what happened, not what you wish had happened or just that subset of information that makes your performance look good. The idea is to get right down to the truth, as best you can. Then you can let the markets do their own analyses to predict the future, using whatever help you can give them to decipher your reports, and go from there.

HOW DID YOU DO?

As we said at the beginning, with one point for each "yes" answer, any total score greater than zero indicates that you are still short of being a QFR manager.

Anything up in the range of 4 to 7 shows that you didn't have much of a clue in the past as to how the markets work or the kind of information that they need. You also did not have a full appreciation of the markets' power to penetrate your financial reports and figure out what happened. If you want to overcome the possibility that you already have gained a capital market reputation for being somewhat devious, if not downright deceitful, then a full-scale adoption of QFR could produce a big bump in your stock price as you begin to eliminate a lot of uncertainty. You will also get rid of all those "yes" answers.

On the other hand, if you're in the 8 to 10 range, you may be an inveterate manipulator, nearly beyond restoration in the markets' eyes. It is likely that sophisticated financial statement users will be on to anyone who would commit that many reporting sins. While a switch to QFR might bring some sort of recovery, it will take time, and lots of it, to overcome an entrenched reputation for deceptive reporting, even if you stay firmly within GAAP's loose guidelines.

On still another hand, if you did manage to score a zero on this test, we applaud you for a deep grasp of the real purpose of financial reporting. It's possible that you're the Easter Bunny or Santa Claus, though, because we have yet to meet or read about anyone who gets all of it right. It certainly ought to be everyone's aiming point, we think. Even if you did score a zero, there is always room for improvement. Also, we would like to hear from you.

NOTES

1. The managers of Enron tried to pull off this kind of scheme by producing deliberately obfuscated financial reporting information. It also appears that they committed a series of deliberate violations of GAAP aimed at producing fraudulent information.

2. Our colleague Professor Ron Mano of Weber State University once said that he has a life ambition to never be afraid to pick up the phone because it might be the SEC calling.

3. Of course, an internal earnings target might just as easily be established for a CFO by the CEO or someone else. Even though the target isn't public information, the CFO faces very real pressure to deliver the expected number just the same.

4. Based on what we know about GAAP, we have decided for ourselves that complying with those principles produces misleading information; therefore, we are up against the logical brick wall that it is unethical to comply with them, while the accounting profession and the SEC assert that it is unethical to not comply with them. If you want to put your auditors through some mental loops, ask them what they think about this impasse: "Should we comply with GAAP or tell the truth?" Although they won't like it, they probably will understand this dilemma in their heart of hearts. At the very least, the question will show how much the psychological defense called denial has permeated the typical thought patterns used by accountants.

5. One of the early stories to emerge concerning Enron involved an anonymous letter received by returning CEO Kenneth Lay from Vice President Sherron Watkins. The letter warned Lay about the accounting frauds and deceptions that were taking place and the threats that they created for the company, its employees, and its stockholders. For all intents and purposes, the CEO ignored the letter and did nothing to assess whether this red flag was legitimate. By doing nothing, he subjected himself to a great deal more recrimination than he might have if he had investigated right away.

CHAPTER 12

It's Time to Check Your Choices

This chapter takes up where the previous one left off. While those questions tried to get you to check your personal attitudes toward financial reporting and the capital markets, the questions in this chapter get you to examine your specific past actions to help you assess whether your choices have contributed to inadequate communication with the markets.

ANOTHER TEST

As in the prior chapter, the questions in Table 12-1 are directed toward individuals who are in higher management levels, such as the CEO or the CFO, or whoever has the authority to choose and implement financial reporting policies. If you are not presently in one of these positions, then answer according to what you have observed in your present company.

As before, these questions are designed to solicit "yes" answers if your choices are contrary to Quality Financial Reporting. At one point per "yes," any score higher than zero suggests that you are a candidate for change because you have something to gain from implementing the QFR paradigm in your financial reports.

Let's look at each question in turn.

Question 11

The first question in this list asks:

> Have you ever timed or structured your company's transactions simply to produce positive impacts on the financial statements or to avoid negative impacts on the financial statements?

TABLE 12-1

Checking Your Choices	Yes	No
11. Have you ever timed or structured your company's trans- actions simply to produce positive impacts on the financial statements or to avoid negative impacts on the financial statements?		
12. Have you ever turned down an economically sound deal for your company simply because of how it would be reported on the financial statements?		
13. Do you select accounting policies that reduce reported volatility without affecting the underlying causes of the fluctuations?		
14. Does your statement of cash flows use the indirect method of reporting cash provided by operations?		
15. Do you report compensation expense paid with stock options in a footnote?		
16. Have you ever spent money to qualify a merger to be accounted for as a pooling?		
17. Have you ever entered into lease arrangements specifically because they produced off balance sheet liabilities?		
18. Have you chosen to use FIFO Inventory accounting In order to avoid reporting lower earnings?		
19. Have you classified your company's investments in securities as available for sale in order to avoid reporting market value changes in income?		
20. Have you established your company's policies on depreciation lives in order to manage the reported earnings?		

One objective of this question is to emphasize that the purpose of providing financial statements to the capital markets is to reflect the economic realities of business transactions and events. Nonetheless, a lot of managers get it backward. Being so worried about the image created in the financial statements, they design their transactions and events to produce good-looking *reported* results, even if the *real* economic results are not good for the company or the stockholders.[1]

One example—structuring business combinations so that they were accounted for as poolings of interest—is described in the discussion of Question 16 on page 199. Another example involves timing the sale of certain assets to happen just before or after the fiscal year end in order to put the reported gain or loss in the desired income statement instead of just doing what is needed to manage the stockholders' wealth. Still another example is the "in-substance debt defeasance" that many companies went through in the 1980s to report gains on their income statements.

These kinds of decisions are so common as to be ordinary; after all, we're accustomed to doing similar things to avoid or defer personal income taxes. However, the goal in financial reporting is to help the capital markets assess the future cash flows and arrive at a rate of return appropriate for the risk. Managing transactions to manipulate the information interrupts that communication and scrambles decisions about the cost of capital. Introducing more uncertainty makes that cost go up, not down.

Another commentator expressed his own frustrations in an article in the *Wall Street Journal* (online version, January 8, 2001) entitled, "Why Pay People to Lie?" Michael Jensen suggests that two problems exist. The first is gaming by managers in setting their incentive targets. Jensen says that managers who toil under a reward system tied to budgeted numbers "have no interest in seeing such information accurately portrayed. Indeed, it is in their best interest to underestimate what they can accomplish." The second is gaming in the realization of targets. He observes, "A manager who is in danger of just missing [a] target will accelerate shipments and revenues for next year into this year and move expenses from this year to next year even though by doing so overall profits are reduced two years running." Jensen's proposed solution is simply "eliminating the use of budget targets in compensation formulas. Only then can we be sure that we are paying people to perform, not to lie."

Some recent proof of the markets' reaction to this kind of behavior was reported by Geoffrey Colvin in the September 17, 2001, issue of *Fortune*. His column, entitled, "Earnings Aren't Everything," reports the results of an extensive survey by the Stern Stewart consulting firm that categorized the respondent companies into two categories: aligned and nonaligned. The aligned group is described as having managers who "are pulling for the same thing as their shareholders." The analysis of the performances of paired aligned and unaligned companies in the same industry showed that "in less than four years the aligned company's shares would be worth twice as much as the nonaligned company's." In other words, the markets perceived that something entirely different was going on in the two kinds of companies. Colvin reported two examples involving financial accounting:

> How do the groups behave differently? Look how they answered this question from the survey: Your company has a hot new product or service opportunity. Accelerating development will depress earnings for the next few quarters. Do you go after it? Most companies in the aligned group say they would. Most in the nonaligned group say they wouldn't.
>
> Another illustration: You're starting a new venture, and you can either capitalize the startup costs or expense them, which will reduce reported

earnings but will also reduce taxes and actually increase cash flow. What do you do? Most of the aligned companies say they'd expense the startup costs. Most of the nonaligned say they'd capitalize them.

The pattern is clear. The poor-performing companies worry about reported profit and admit they'll even destroy shareholder wealth to get it. The top-performing companies know that what really counts is not reported earnings but something else. It's what finance types call economic profit . . . —after-tax operating profit minus the real cost of the capital used in the business. (p. 58)

All of these points demonstrate that superior financial reporting will reduce uncertainty and the cost of capital, thus bringing about an increase in the economic profit.

We're pleased, of course, to find this recent evidence that QFR is already being practiced by some managers. It will be a different world when more and more managements see the advantages and get "aligned" by modifying their incentive plans to provide rewards for improving their financial reporting practices. We just ask, what's the point in waiting any longer?

Question 12

The next question asks:

Have you ever turned down an economically sound deal for your company simply because of how it would be reported on the financial statements?

This item goes hand in hand with question 11, which deals with doing bad things to look good. Specifically, it asks whether you have avoided doing good things to keep from looking bad. The previous quote from Geoffrey Colvin's *Fortune* article certainly applies here as well, in that nonaligned managers will do most anything to keep up appearances.

For example, suppose you have arrived at a call date for some debt securities you've issued. They're being carried on the books as a $100 million liability because that's the amount you borrowed when you issued them 10 years ago at 12 percent annual interest. Since then, interest rates have declined and the theoretical market value of your bonds is now $120 million. That amount is only theoretical because your debt covenant allows you to call the bonds by paying out $106 million. Clearly, the call is advantageous because you can retire debt with an intrinsic value of $120 million by paying out only $106 million, thereby increasing the stockholders' real wealth by $14 million. However, the catch is that GAAP would require you to report a $6 million loss because you would be paying out more than the severely understated book value of the debt. Thus, doing what is better for the stockholders makes you look bad; doing what's bad for the stockholders makes you look better.

Similar situations involve selling assets; for example, by putting only realized gains and losses from investment disposals on the income statement, GAAP actually encourage managers to "cherry pick" by selling their winners so they can look good and holding onto their losers so they don't look bad. This behavior seems backward, to say the least.

We think that you are a candidate for a change to QFR if you would even hesitate to do a good deal because it would make you look bad in the GAAP statements. If you would take the plunge, you may already be part of the small but QFR crowd.

Question 13

This question attacks a common vulnerability:

> Do you select accounting policies that reduce reported volatility without affecting the underlying causes of the fluctuations?

There is probably nothing in financial reporting that managers fear quite as much as volatility, especially in reported earnings. If the amounts bounce around from quarter to quarter or year to year, two negative images are created. First, the perceived risk of investing in the company is higher because of unpredictability. Second, this bouncing suggests strongly that management is not really in control of the situation, thus putting their jobs at risk.

As described in Chapter 10, there are two ways to deal with volatility—you can either tackle its real roots and change the way you do business or you can resort to smoothing with GAAP. In the first case, you really change the risk but all you do in the second is paper it over, hoping that no one will ever figure out what is going on.

If you routinely run to the latter strategy and cover up the volatility, you are clearly a candidate for conversion to QFR. This artificial smoothing behavior (some call it "accounting arbitrage") does nothing but compromise the quality of the communication with the capital markets about what is really going on. Since the markets have issues with real volatility, they won't reward your behavior if you simply don't tell them enough to let them know what is going on.

Don't be fooled yourself, by the way. It turns out that GAAP is full of institutionalized methods for smoothing out the mountains and canyons in earnings. Consider, for example, such things as straight-line depreciation and amortization, income tax deferral, reporting unrealized gains and losses in the equity section, and deferrals of all kinds of gains and losses associated with defined benefit pension plans. In these situations and others, all you have to do is comply with GAAP and the rough places are made plain. And you don't have to do anything to change the way you do business. What could be easier? Nothing, probably, but the real issue concerns what the capital markets do with this prechewed and predigested financial food. Not being born in the last week or so, sophisticated financial analysts know that the messages they receive aren't complete; in light of that incompleteness, they face more uncertainty, risk, and processing costs, and thus demand a higher rate of return.

Others have stretched GAAP to produce smoothness where it doesn't exist. In the 1990s, a lot of software firms found a disturbing pattern in their income statements. They would bring out a new version of a program and sell a ton all at once. Then, as they worked on the next version for a couple of years, they had high expenses and low revenues because not many new units were being sold. When the next version was released, another huge hump in revenue and income would occur. One way to deal with that volatility would be to explain carefully in the report what is happening so that the users know that management recognizes the problem and has everything under control; in effect, the reported volatility would be seen as benign because it is really only the consequence of an annual reporting cycle that is out of sync with the multiyear product cycle. Another way would be to develop a countercyclical strategy that would involve producing and selling other products in between the main product's release dates, thus actually getting rid of some of the year-to-year fluctuations. However, these solutions involve real changes in strategy and complete communication. Isn't there something easier?

Of course there is, and some big companies latched onto it. An old doctrine in GAAP is that sellers cannot report all revenue from their sales if they still face the possibility of having to make good in one way or another. For example, under conditions in which the sellers send out lots more product than can be expected to be sold (such as paperback books or sound recordings), they must allow for the likely returns and reduce the revenue at the time of recording the sales. In the software business, the developers saw that they often had to keep performing by releasing upgrades and fixes for bugs buried in the code in order to keep their customers happy and productive. Seizing this opportunity, they began to create really significant "reserves" against their sales revenue in those big years and then dripped this deferred revenue into the lean years. Voilà! The volatility vanished (from obvious view, anyway). At least, it vanished until the SEC got wind of what was going on, investigated, and forced the managers to restate their previously filed financial statements and to abstain from doing this smoothing again. We have no trouble believing that the capital markets had already dealt with the crime before the SEC arrived with flashing lights and sirens.[2]

In conclusion, if you have tried to cover up volatility, or you've been content to let the FASB take care of it for you, then you're in a position to reduce your capital costs and reap the other benefits of QFR by changing your approach.

Question 14

The next question is much more specific:

> Does your statement of cash flows use the indirect method of reporting cash provided by operations?

Under SFAS 95, the FASB recommended that management report their operating cash flows under the direct method that shows the gross amounts of cash received less the gross amounts spent; however, in light of complaints from preparers, the board compromised and allowed the indirect method that reconciles net income with the net operating cash flow without describing the gross amounts. As quoted in Chapter 7, the AIMR committee of analysts had specific advice for managers who elect this inferior alternative:

> A reasonable solution to this apparent impasse is not unattainable. Although the FASB has not seen fit to mandate the direct method, and neither has the IASC, both endorse it as the preferable method. Nothing other than inertia prevents progressive business enterprises that seek favor with analysts from adopting the direct method. (p. 67)

As proof of the inertia, the AICPA's 2000 version of the *Accounting Trends and Techniques* annual survey of 600 companies' financial statements shows that only 7 actually used the direct method. (Our correspondence with one of those firms revealed that it changed to the indirect method in 2001.)

As one consequence, we think most every manager reading this book will answer this particular question with a yes. As another, we also see a ready-made way for them to make a move toward QFR by doing something better than and before everyone else.

An added advantage of the direct method is that the managers who use it externally have also found that it helps them manage their cash internally a lot better than the indirect method.[3] We have more to say about reporting cash flows in Chapter 17.

Question 15

The next question asks:

> Do you report compensation expense paid with stock options in a footnote?

Gotcha! We anticipate a "yes" answer from virtually everyone reading this book who works for a company that issues compensatory options. According to what we hear, the only big companies that follow the FASB's recommended treatment are Boeing and Winn-Dixie. So, if you work for someone else, you're now clearly labeled as a non-QFR manager.

How can we be so swift and sure in our judgment? It's really simple. The only difference between the recommended approach of income statement recognition and footnote disclosure is where the information appears. The expense is computed the same way under both reporting methods, so there is really no issue related to the cost of compliance. Management's decision on where to place the expense is purely one of choosing to look better, and essentially everyone thinks they look better if their reported earnings are higher.

In contrast, we suggest that the footnote approach actually makes them look worse in the eyes of the capital markets because that decision reveals that the managers think they can deceive the markets into believing that earnings are higher than they actually are. If the markets can't trust managers to be forthcoming, uncertainty and risk are boosted, as well as the cost of capital. After all, here is what the AIMR committee said:

> . . . [W]e strongly believe that stock options have value, that they are used to compensate managers, and that they should be recognized and measured as compensation expense in the financial statements. (p. 47)

So, if you want to join the QFR movement, options are a place to start. Go ahead, be the first on the block to reach out to the capital markets where they are and on their own terms. Leave the old thought pattern behind. Chapter 17 contains more detailed suggestions on what you can do to provide additional useful information about options.

Question 16

This question gets into another discretionary choice:

> Have you ever spent money to qualify a merger to be accounted for as a pooling?

The difference between this question and question 15 is a matter of cost. In the case of accounting for options, there is no additional out-of-pocket cost in choosing one policy or another. However, in the case of accounting for a business combination as a purchase or a pooling, there are (or were, now that SFAS 141 has been issued) huge costs to be incurred to qualify the transaction as a pooling. Why? Because the old standard that governed combinations (APBO 16) established 12 specific criteria that had to be met to pool. They involved a number of points concerned with creating an appearance that the stockholders of both entities survived the merger as owners of the new entity. Thus, there were requirements involving past treasury stock transactions and restrictions on future deals.[4]

The outcome of this regulatory situation was that managers who wanted to do a pooling had to spend a lot of the stockholders' money on lawyers and accountants, and on a higher purchase price to compensate the sellers for their restricted ability to dispose of their shares in the new company. The irony is that the whole reason for these expenditures was to be able to produce incomplete financial statements with the ultimate goal of putting higher reported earnings on the income statement. Thus, the managers were paying out lots of the stockholders' money to cause them to be less informed, all while creating a lower stock price by giving inferior information to the capital markets. The ultimate puzzle for us is that it's clear that the only difference between a purchase and a pooling is the journal entries recorded in the new entity's books. So, think of the thousands, even millions, of dollars being spent to change the keys struck on the bookkeeper's keyboard.

Our ultimate point is that you are not a QFR person if you spent some money to do a pooling. You can achieve QFR status if you have never done a pooling, but only if you overcome being contented with accounting for a combination as a purchase. You need to be ready to go to the next level of reporting what really happened and what really exists. You can find more thoughts on business combinations in Chapter 16.

Question 17

This next question gets even more to the heart of managers' attitudes toward reporting the whole truth:

> Have you ever entered into lease arrangements specifically because they produced off-balance-sheet liabilities?

Certainly everyone reading this book has entered into one kind of a lease or another as a matter of convenience or some other economic advantage of paying to borrow someone else's property for a while. However, egregious leasing behavior happens whenever managers enter into leases only to manipulate the company's financial image, specifically by borrowing money while choosing to leave that fact off the balance sheet. The whole intent is to deceive the capital markets into thinking that the debt/equity structure is different from what it really is. As we look at it, not telling the truth when you know the truth is lying. And, lying when you intend to cause people to make decisions they wouldn't make if they knew the truth is fraud. As we look at the world through our QFR lens, we see that fraud (or attempted fraud) is greeted with discounted stock prices and higher capital costs, even if the financial statements are prepared in accordance with GAAP and audited in accordance with GAAS.[5]

Regardless of the fact that it is legal to enter into lease contracts that allow lessees to avoid capitalization, the capital market is not a sequestered jury that has to reach a verdict on stock prices using only the published financial statements. Besides, SFAS 13 requires managers to disclose plenty of information about operating leases that are not capitalized. Sophisticated financial analysts surely know what those footnotes reveal about the economic impact on the company and, more importantly, the kind of people the managers are because they endeavor to deceive. Harsh words, perhaps, but we think they are aimed right to the point that QFR addresses. It isn't just the ethics behind deception, it is the lack of wisdom in pursuing an empty strategy that wastes money and leaves the stockholders worse off.

We call on managers who aspire to practice QFR to get beyond the paltry politics that forced the FASB to allow off-balance-sheet financing to occur. Rise above the simple-minded deception and embrace the economic incentives that encourage truth telling.

Two other points before moving on. First, we have learned that some managers are now selling their existing office furniture and equipment in place to a leasing company, which then turns around and leases it back under an operating lease. Presto—overnight, without the employees knowing it, their stuff has disappeared from the balance sheet. What an abomination that flies in the face of common sense! Second, the FASB and other standard-setting bodies have been researching and talking about leasing for years and years. They have now published a couple of research reports in which the representatives acknowledge the deficiencies in existing GAAP and look forward to the day when the standards call for capitalizing all leases.[6] Now, wouldn't it be interesting if that new standard had to be applied retroactively? All that disappearing leased stuff would just come flying right back onto the balance sheet, along with the debt! Chapter 16 describes how applying QFR will alter reporting of lease-related information.

There is no reason for any management to make this mistake any more. QFR will eliminate this longstanding deception, even if the FASB and IASB don't act. Make the move toward quality and reap the benefits.

Question 18

The next question asks:

> Have you chosen to use FIFO inventory accounting in order to avoid reporting lower earnings?

The inventory accounting policy decision puts a dilemma before managers: they can choose LIFO and produce real tax savings and higher real income, or they can choose FIFO and pay more taxes and achieve lower real income. The bewildering catch is that under the intricacies of GAAP, using LIFO and actually doing good requires managers to look bad by reporting lower earnings on the income statement while using FIFO makes them look better by reporting higher earnings.

We figure that any managers who choose FIFO are obsessed with their financial image and don't care what happens to the stockholders' wealth. They are clearly not practicing QFR and might want to consider changing.

But, not so fast! Just because you have chosen to use LIFO does not make you a QFR practitioner. After all, LIFO produces tax savings by omitting information from the income statement (namely, holding gains on inventory that increases in value prior to its sale). Omitting information about these gains means that the financial statements are incomplete, which means that capital costs are boosted, despite the tax savings. To achieve QFR for inventory, more information needs to be disclosed than is required by GAAP. Chapter 16 provides suggestions on what to do.

Question 19

The next-to-last question asks:

> Have you classified your company's investments in securities as available
> for sale in order to avoid reporting market value changes in income?

In producing the relatively recent SFAS 115, the FASB compromised away reality-based financial reporting by allowing managers to classify their investments in marketable securities into one of three possible portfolios. It then produced different standards for determining the reported amounts of the investments and the income effects of changes in their market values. Because the treatment for "trading" securities reports all changes in value as gains and losses when they occur, the real volatility produced by investing is revealed on the income statement for all to see and judge. However, if the same securities are classified as available for sale, those gains and losses are not reported on the income statement but are herded together onto the equity section of the balance sheet, huddled out of obvious view and certainly not allowed to stray into earnings.[7] The main determinant of which portfolio the investments belong to is management's intent for disposing of them. Mind you, there is no difference in the fundamental realities: the company owns the securities, their values change, and the stockholders' equity is increased or decreased, all without regard for what the managers intended to happen. Despite these facts, the choice of which portfolio the investments fall into changes the representation of truth in the financial statements.

Thus, some managers, even those reading this book, might think they have reaped lower capital costs by making it harder for the capital markets to decipher their financial statements while looking good in them. By now, we all know what QFR tells us: don't count on ever fooling the markets.

Question 20

The final question says:

> Have you established your company's policies on depreciation lives in order to manage the reported earnings?

We anticipate that close to 100 percent of the honest answers to this question will be "yes." After all, what can anyone expect when there is such a direct connection between looking good and the kind of discretion inherent in predicting totally unverifiable[8] accounting variables? The mistake managers make is thinking that their choices of depreciation lives (and other related policies) are simply accepted by the capital markets without question or doubt of any kind. We hope that all readers of this book will no longer feel this way.

As long as cost-based, prediction-based depreciation is part of the GAAP reporting world, these sorts of policy decisions will have to be made and implemented. The QFR solution involves three things. First, never, ever believe that the resulting depreciation numbers have any connection with reality, and therefore don't use them internally and don't expect people outside the firm to believe them either. Second, fully disclose everything about your depreciation policies and even go on to provide pro forma descriptions of what amounts would be reported for income under different ones. Third, provide additional information about the real market values of the assets, including changes in them, because those facts contain the information that the capital markets really want and need. We have more to say about depreciation and QFR in Chapter 16.

THE BIG PICTURE

Now that we have gone through each question, we believe that you will have a good idea of how close you have been coming to displaying QFR behavior in your financial reporting practices. If we believed all the self-directed praise that U.S. accountants utter about the GAAP system, we would come to think that there is no way for that system to get any better. In fact, these questions should reveal plenty of opportunities for providing greater quantities of information that is more useful for the capital markets. The time for this institutionalized self-deception is past.

NOTES

1. As a reminder of what Warren Buffett says on this point, we repeat this quote from Chapter 8: "Accounting consequences do not influence our operating or capital-allocation decisions. When acquisition costs are similar, we much prefer to purchase $2 of earnings that is not reportable by us under standard accounting principles than to purchase $1 of earnings that is reportable."

2. One of the toughest actions the SEC can take against miscreants is to get them to enter into a consent decree in which they first deny that they have ever done anything wrong and then promise never to do it again. A real head scratcher is the even stronger step in which the SEC staff gets a court injunction that orders people to obey the securities laws. (Doesn't everyone have to do that?) In light of these weaknesses and the general consensus that the U.S. has about the best securities regulation in the world, one could wonder how anything works at all anywhere.

3. For example, this point was made by Kevin Trout, Margaret Tanner, and Lee Nicholas in their article, "On Track with Direct Cash Flows" (*Management Accounting*, July 1993, pp. 23–27).

4. We can't avoid observing that this huge focus on ownership was totally misdirected in terms of future cash flows. What matters to the capital markets is what will happen in the future with the assets and liabilities (which have the ability to impact future cash flows), not who does or does not own the stock (a condition that has no impact on future cash flows).

5. A number of years ago, Paul Miller had an occasion to ask a partner in a big CPA firm whether he was faced with audit clients who were entering into lease contracts that duck the capitalization criteria in SFAS 13. He smiled and said, "Paul, we help them do it!" A young professor learned a life-changing lesson that day on the real practice of public accounting and the ease with which at least some auditors denigrate their professional and social responsibilities to ensure that truth is revealed.

6. Warren McGregor, *Accounting for Leases: A New Approach—Recognition by Lessees of Assets and Liabilities Arising under Lease Contracts*, FASB, July 1996; Hans Nailor and Andrew Lennard, *Leases: Implementation of a New Approach*, FASB, February 2000.

7. Paul Miller and Ed Ketz wrote a column for *Accounting Today* (May 20/June 2, 1996) called "Hairsplitting and Nitpicking—Is There No Limit?". They reported how the management of NationsBank reclassified an investment out of trading into available for sale on the day it was purchased in order to avoid reporting a $7 million loss that occurred on an intraday market decline. What fools the managers must have been to display this kind of denial, and then to defend it when they were challenged in litigation

initiated by one of their own employees! The loss occurred, it was real, and they were accountable for it. They had no good reason to believe that taking it off the income statement would change these truths. In fact, their denial and cover-up only increased the perceived probability that they would do it again if they had the chance.

8. Although it might be true that, say, 90 percent of accountants would predict a 10-year life for an asset, this consensus does not verify that that life will actually be 10 years. That fact cannot be verified until 10 years pass or until the asset is retired, whichever comes first. Thus, if the predicted life is not verifiable, it is not reliable. And, if it is not reliable, any information produced with it is also unreliable and not useful.

CHAPTER 13

How Are Things Between You and Your Auditor?

This third chapter in the series of three asks 10 more questions. This time, the subject matter is the relationship between auditors and auditees and its impact on the quality of the auditees' relationships with the capital markets. According to a saying attributed to Ronald Reagan, it's fine to have a working relationship with someone, but it is always a good idea to "trust and verify."

The purpose of an independent financial statement audit is straightforward: knowing that managers are subject to temptations to look good by taking liberties in their financial reports, the capital markets attribute more credibility to those reports if they are examined by a third party trusted by both the managers and the markets. The purpose for adding this credibility is to reduce uncertainty about the reliability of the information in the statements, which, in turn, is a key step for reducing risk and the cost of capital.

According to this QFR view, an independent audit should be a value-adding activity. By reducing risk, the company and its stockholders should recoup the audit fees through lower capital costs and higher stock prices. Thus, the audit has value only if the auditors' processes and reports really do reduce uncertainty. Achieving that result depends on the auditors' perceived technical competence and ability to actually remove doubt. As with everything involving communication, appearance means a great deal, if not everything.

This potential value of the audit was so apparent in the 1930s that the SEC acted to make it a requirement for all public companies. Somewhere in the ensuing years, this perception has been lost, with the consequence that audits are now routinely considered by auditees to be not much more than mundane exercises in compliance, sort of like renewing your driver's license or paying your property taxes. Some auditors seem to feel the same way, with the additional thought that they can use audits as loss leaders that open up opportunities to sell nonaudit services to their clients. More is said on this relationship later in the chapter.

We believe that managers can discover much about their attitudes toward financial reporting by taking a fresh look at their relationship with their independent auditors and considering how they can tap into more of that latent value. That goal is what this chapter aims to achieve with its questions.

THE FINAL TEST

As in the prior chapters, the questions in Table 13-1 are directed toward individuals in higher management levels, such as the CEO or the CFO, or whoever has the authority for choosing and implementing financial reporting policies. If you are not currently in one of these positions, then answer according to what you have observed in your present company.

TABLE 13-1

Checking Your Audit Relationship	Yes	No
21. Have you selected your auditors because they offered the lowest bid?		
22. Does your engagement letter establish a fixed audit fee, regardless of the hours to be actually worked by the auditors?		
23. Does your engagement letter put any constraints on the tests to be performed by the auditors?		
24. Do the nonaudit fees you pay to your auditing firm exceed 25 percent of the audit fee?		
25. Have you ever stonewalled against your auditors' proposed adjustments?		
26. Have you ever changed auditors after a disagreement over an accounting policy or a proposed adjustment?		
27. Have your auditors ever recommended an accounting policy simply because it would make your financial statements present a more attractive image?		
28. Do you still have the same auditors after many years?		
29. Is your accounting department staffed with a large number of alumni from your auditing firm?		
30. Do you view the audit as a perfunctory process required by the law?		

As before, these questions were designed to solicit "yes" answers if your choices are contrary to Quality Financial Reporting. Let's look at how you did and what those answers mean. Remember, even a single "yes" means that you have substantial room for improvement.

Question 21

The first question in this list asks:

Have you selected your auditors because they offered the lowest bid?

Prior to 1972, the ethics rules for CPAs actually forbade their entering into competitive bidding processes to obtain audit clients. On one level, bidding was deemed to be unseemly for professionals. On another, the auditors saw that competitive bidding worked against the audit's objective of reducing uncertainty. If the auditors were known to have lowballed a bid, what would that say about the quality of their work?

The march of progress was inevitable, however, and the AICPA entered into a settlement with the Federal Trade Commission to do away with the stricture against bidding on the basis that it was anticompetitive. Of course, it *was* anticompetitive, and it was supposed to be.

Over the ensuing years, this seemingly small modification led to a bigger change in that clients found they could save a lot of audit fees if they used the bidding process to put the squeeze on their auditors to get the job done in less time at less cost.[1] What they seem to have missed (and so have you, if you answered this question with a yes) is that a low bid connotes low quality and a diminished ability to increase the reports' credibility. This outcome is similar to what we have talked about before. Because a great many preparers tend to think of financial reporting as a compliance exercise with no redeeming value, they often choose to go with the low-cost audit option. Unfortunately for them, and for their stockholders, they fail to factor into their decision the impact of the low credibility on the company's cost of capital and its stock prices. By putting out statements that are less than believable, the managers increase uncertainty and risk while producing greater discounts for their stock.

The next question on some lips has to be, "But how will the markets ever find out about the low bid?" One response holds that if the markets are efficient and if something affects the credibility of the public reports, they will find out. A second, entirely different response asks what this question says about managers who adopt significant policies hoping that no one, least of all their stockholders, will ever know what they did. An old ethical adage says: "Don't ever do anything that you wouldn't want to see on the front page of the paper." In the same sense, why would management take the extra risk of being found to have covered up a poor decision to take the low-budget route? Just because you're *allowed* to do something doesn't mean that you *should* go out and do it.

All of this discussion is separate from the issue of what kind of services clients can expect when they buy their audits at bargain-basement prices. Not that it doesn't make sense to find ways to save money, but you need to realize that there will be other economic consequences.

With regard to QFR, we think it's clear that managers should hire reputable auditors, pay them what they deserve, and empower them to do the work that will lead to a report that reduces uncertainty and the cost of capital. Beyond that, there isn't much more to say.

On the other hand, we would like to unleash minds more fertile than ours on the question of how to avoid fee-based independence issues by having the auditors hired and paid by someone other than the managers they're supposed to audit. It seems possible to us, for example, that intermediary organizations could be created to stand between managers and auditors to insulate them from fee-related pressures. If anyone reading this page gets a better idea, go for it. The necessary result will be lower capital costs due to eliminating the uncertainty created by the ambiguity of having the auditee pay the auditor.

Question 22

This question asks:

> Does your engagement letter establish a fixed audit fee, regardless of the hours to be actually worked by the auditors?

This item probes a point similar to the matters addressed by question 21. Specifically, does your audit arrangement impose any constraints on the auditors that will keep them from increasing your credibility and reducing uncertainty about the information in your financial statements?

A fixed fee is almost as bad as a low bid because it has the same effect of creating negative incentives for your auditors. In both situations, they are encouraged to get by with as little work as possible. The problem with this situation is that doing little produces little in the way of credibility and certainty. Imagine that a preliminary audit test shows that there might be a problem in accounts receivable, but dealing with it will cause the auditors to put more people and more hours into the job. Given that they have a fixed fee, they may be inclined to skip the work and cross their fingers when the report is signed. The client has perhaps saved some money, but only by missing an opportunity to fix what could be a major problem. In addition, if and when the market discovers this fee arrangement, the consequence will be more uncertainty about the financial statements and lower stock prices.

The trade-off in going without a fixed fee is the risk of turning the auditors loose to waste all the time they'd like because they're getting paid for it. This, of course, is where personal relationships and integrity come in. If you can't trust your auditors to be professional, then how will the capital markets ever perceive them to be professional?

So, you can see that a positive answer to either question 21 or 22 suggests that you are a long way from adopting QFR.

Question 23

This question attacks a similar vulnerability:

> Does your engagement letter put any constraints on the tests to be performed by the auditors?

In some rare occasions, clients engage their auditors to add credibility to their financial statements, but then turn around and put figurative blinders on them to keep them from "wasting time" pursuing matters of little or no interest to the stockholders. The trick, of course, is that the auditor does not have any idea as to what has been going on in the "off limits" areas, and should feel so uncomfortable as to either reject the engagement or take out extra professional liability insurance. If the restrictions are material, the auditors' report describes them and the capital markets know about the limits and act accordingly by not trusting either the financial statements or the managers who produced them.

In short, there is nothing worthwhile to be gained by putting limits on the auditor.

Question 24

The next question goes in another direction:

> Do the nonaudit fees you pay to your auditing firm exceed 25 percent of the audit fee?

In the summer of 2000, almost as a swan song (a duet, actually), then-SEC chairman Arthur Levitt and chief accountant Lynn Turner unleashed a proposal that rocked the public accounting profession at the highest levels. They proposed a change in the SEC rules such that the commission would consider auditors to not be independent from their audit clients if they provided them with certain kinds of nonaudit services, specifically those that would put the auditors' firm into a position of acting as management or of having to attest to the quality of its own work. (The SEC did not try to prevent auditing firms from providing nonaudit services to companies that are not their audit clients.) A lot of opposition was unleashed, much of it political. It was also irrelevant because it did not address the central issue of whether auditors can produce credible reports attesting to the reliability of the client's financial statements when they are deeply involved in a nonaudit business relationship.

As QFR advocates (and optimists) of the first order, we thought the debate would be healthy if it would somehow make preparers more conscious of the potential deleterious effects of having their auditors do nonaudit work. We also thought it would make auditors more sensitive to the possibility that their pursuit of profits from nonaudit services would diminish the power of their less independent audits to add value to their clients' financial statements.

The resulting political responses showed that our hopes were in vain. Three of the five largest audit firms strongly resisted the move,[2] as did the people occupying leadership positions in the AICPA, perhaps to an extreme. The opponents also persuaded several members of Congress (probably not by appealing to their patriotic pride) to enter the discussion, which they did, uttering threats of one kind or another. Completely missing from the mainstream discussion was any substantive acknowledgment that compromising independence diminishes or even destroys the credibility and usefulness of financial statements. Among the opponents' arguments was an assertion that the commission was acting precipitously by moving ahead without "empirical" research showing that providing nonaudit services compromised independence.

Given the harsh complaints and the time frame (according to traditional protocol, Levitt had only six more months to serve as SEC chairman because he would not be reappointed in 2001 by the incoming president, regardless of the victorious party), Levitt and Turner basically gave up and fell back to the safer zone of merely requiring management to provide disclosure of the amounts of nonaudit and audit fees paid to the auditing firm by the client in the preceding year. The opponents were somewhat satisfied that they had won a victory, but, alas, they missed the point. While auditors still have the freedom under the rules to go ahead and diminish the value of their audit opinions by performing nonaudit services that compromise at least their perceived independence, they have no assurance that they are actually providing any valuable services to their audit clients. In our opinion, they face the real possibility that their current GAAS audits add little or no value to the financial statements.[3] If so, they are being paid only to sign their name to a piece of paper that perhaps will be filed with a government agency, and that's it. QFR suggests that auditors could make a whole lot more money if they really added value to the financial statements by making them more credible and useful by staying scrupulously independent.

Subsequently, at least one team (Richard Frankel, Marilyn Johnson, and Karen Nelson) decided to do some empirical research on the issue. Their paper is called "The Relation Between Auditors, Fees for Non-Audit

Services and Earnings Management."[4] Ironically, these researchers used the newly required disclosures of nonaudit fees to produce a measure of the lack of independence (the stimulus) and then looked at several response variables. One of their tests showed that the disclosure of nonaudit fees produced significant declines in stock prices for the one-fourth of the 2450 companies in their sample that had the largest amounts of these fees (as a proportion of total fees). They also found evidence that nonindependent auditors (those who received larger proportions of nonaudit fees) were more compliant in going along with management's efforts to manipulate their reported earnings. Again, academicians tested some logical arguments and found them to be true, but too late (in this case) to help Levitt and Turner respond to their critics.

Putting all this together with question 24, we think that managers ought to consider the whole picture before they start signing contracts for other services to be provided by their audit firms. Of course, the 25 percent level in the question is arbitrary because the compromising effect can occur at higher or lower percentages. Incidentally, the sample in the Frankel research project had an average level of nonaudit fees of just less than 100 percent of audit fees. Enron's nonaudit fees were 108 percent of the audit fee in the year before its collapse.

It seems clear that QFR managers would simply choose to not engage their auditors to perform nonaudit services, just as they would not go for the low bidder or set a fixed price. The certain consequence of this higher road will be a reduced level of uncertainty and a lower cost of capital.[5]

Question 25

The next question asks:

Have you ever stonewalled against your auditors' proposed adjustments?

The next-to-final stage in an audit is the auditors' presentation to management of the adjustments that they think need to be entered in order to bring the financial statements into compliance with GAAP. It is usually a tense time that requires careful communication and sensitivity on both sides. In some cases, the adjustments are no-brainers for the managers because they increase reported earnings or otherwise make the financial statements prettier. The really tough ones are those that reduce earnings, reduce assets, or increase liabilities (or all three). The tendency of non-QFR managers is to resist these changes because they think they will look bad in their financial reports and automatically experience lower stock prices.

We're confident that this knee-jerk response is fundamentally mistaken. It isn't enough to just look good; you have to be good, and your reports have to be trustworthy. If the audit adjustments will toughen up your statements and communicate more useful information, you will be rewarded by the markets for your forthrightness. If you fight against your auditors, the word will get out and your credibility will be diminished, if not lost.

Sure, it's fine to discuss the issues with your auditors. After all, they might be wrong. Then again, so might you, but your defensiveness may make it difficult for you to see how you have failed or how you might improve. Even QFR managers will discuss proposed amendments with the auditors, but they won't resist blindly. In our dreams, perhaps, they would even send the auditors back into the records to see if there was anything else that ought to be adjusted.

Question 26

This question extends the preceding one:

> Have you ever changed auditors after a disagreement over an accounting policy or a proposed adjustment?

Going beyond stonewalling is the step of firing the auditor and hiring a new one who sees things your way. If you have ever gone this route, don't expect the capital markets to embrace your financial statements without question anytime soon. Just the opposite—expect them to disbelieve virtually everything you say for a long time. They will feel this way because you have shown that you are both biased and closed-minded when it comes to accepting criticism. Not only that, you have shown that you don't mind spending extra amounts of the stockholders' money to send them biased and useless messages.

For these reasons, and others, the SEC requires managers to file statements with the commission explaining why they changed auditors. (The former auditors have the opportunity and obligation to file their own statement if they believe the management's statement is not complete or accurate.) This extreme event is pregnant with possibilities, not many of which suggest that the financial statements will be more reliable after the new auditors finish their work.

Before they change auditors, some managers actually engage other auditors to look at the disputed situation and produce a recommendation for approval or disapproval of the management's controversial accounting treatment. Disparagingly called *opinion shopping,* this practice indicates to the capital markets that the financial statements are going to be somewhat funky and otherwise suspect, and the level of trust in management is cranked down. Regardless of how much better the messages in the statements might appear to be with a shopped-around opinion, the markets will stamp them as flawed. Under these circumstances, we cannot imagine how this practice would do anything other than deepen the discount in the price of the company' stock.

Obviously, QFR practitioners would not choose to do either of these things because they understand that the goal of financial reporting is to provide the markets with useful information, not to present them with transparently doctored images attested to by new auditors engaged under suspicious circumstances.

Question 27

This next question probes the auditors' behavior:

> Have your auditors ever recommended an accounting policy simply because it would make your financial statements present a more attractive image?

When you engage competent auditors, you should be getting more than the services of automatons that simply verify that your policies and decisions comply with GAAP. They also can suggest ways to improve your accounting system and, more importantly, the quality of your financial statements. This question probes whether your auditors are just as much in the dark as you are when you think it is good enough to present pretty pictures in the statements instead of getting them to describe the truth more usefully.

It is one thing for management to try to persuade the auditor to approve an accounting policy that just happens to make the company look better, but an entirely different matter for the auditors to propose the same sort of change. First, this situation suggests that the auditors are primarily loyal to the management, not the stockholders or the capital markets.[6] Second, it shows that they are inadequately educated in the way the markets work. Third, it shows that they don't understand how much value they can contribute to their clients and the capital markets, and how much society depends on a presumption that the auditors do not have either of the first two weaknesses.

The bottom line: if you have auditors who want to introduce you to new ways to play games with your financial statements, run like heck in the opposite direction. Fire them, and explain why in your annual report. Can you imagine how analysts will respond when you state that you've changed auditors because the previous ones were too loose in their standards and wanted you to put out misleading financial statements, even though they complied with GAAP? Besides providing front page news (sort of like "Man Bites Dog!"), your action will cause the market participants to look at your statements with renewed and upgraded credibility. That means less uncertainty, less risk, and lower capital costs. Again, it looks to us like QFR is a sure thing.

Question 28

The next question asks:

> Do you still have the same auditors after many years?

In most societies, a high value is placed on long-term loyal relationships. There is no friend like an old friend, perhaps. However, this idea turns a little sour in the audit arena. Specifically, we think, as do others, that it is possible to use the same auditors for too long. At some stage, the capital markets will look askance at the financial statements when they are reviewed every year by the same sets of eyes. For one thing, we all develop blind spots. For another, the longer the relationship, the less objective friends become about each others' flaws and weaknesses. For yet another, pressure mounts each year on the audit partners and managers to not be responsible for losing long-standing clients by being too tough on them. Thus, it is only rational for the markets to begin to feel uncomfortable unless some steps are taken to renew that independence and freshen up that objectivity.

For these reasons, many audit firms require partner rotation, even though this practice has never been mandated by SEC regulations. Client managers are wise to not resist these changes, but they often do because breaking in a new partner brings about additional costs and may stir up renewed controversies over accounting policies. However, the QFR perspective adds the consideration that the change should increase credibility, reduce uncertainty, and lead to lower capital costs. We think this savings will far exceed the expense and inconvenience.

Without wishing to be extreme, we think the same positive effect will happen with magnified effects if the client will go so far as to simply replace the auditors every four years or so with a new firm and make it clear that the change is happening in order to dispel any perception that objectivity had been lost. We're not sure, of course, and we would never argue that managers ought to be required to make such a change. Doing so voluntarily will have much greater impact anyway.

Question 29

The next-to-last question asks:

> Is your accounting department staffed with a large number of alumni from your auditing firm?

According to conventional wisdom, one of the advantages of a career in public accounting is that people build up networks of contacts for later employment among the clients they serve. Another bit of conventional wisdom is that it makes sense for a client to hire its financial accounting staff from its audit firm because these people are a known commodity and they are already trained in the system. We've both heard public accountants try to recruit our students by boasting about the large number of "alumni" they have placed with clients.

All that is well and good on one level, and we have no difficulty acknowledging that individuals should have the right to work anywhere they want and that managers should have the right to hire whomever they want (consistent with civil rights, of course). What we do have a problem with is that hiring former auditors can destroy independence, if not in fact then at least in appearance. And, after all, appearances do matter when the capital markets are assessing the credibility and reliability of a company's financial statements. Thus, like almost any good thing, hiring former auditors carries with it a risk that doing too much of it can turn back against you and do harm.

Perhaps as an extreme, there is the case of Waste Management. Specifically, its managers committed a multiyear financial reporting fraud in which they stretched the limits of GAAP but were never called down by its auditors (Arthur Andersen). Eventually, the truth came out that they extended assets' depreciable lives well beyond industry norms in order to greatly boost the reported earnings. When the dust finally settled, it turned out that an extraordinarily large proportion of the Waste Management financial managers were Andersen alumni. Eventually, the audit firm went on to pay a large multimillion-dollar settlement to get out from under an SEC action. Something similar happened at Cendant (an even bigger and more outright financial reporting fraud) in that four top financial managers at that company were alumni of its audit firm (Ernst & Young).

As we all know, two anecdotes are not enough to make a case that will be convincing in court. However, the venue for this trial is the capital markets, and, as we have said, the jury doesn't face any limits on the kind of information it can use to make investment decisions. It is possible that incestuous hiring is a red flag to the market participants, with the consequence that the audit doesn't build confidence the way it would under other circumstances.

Are you a bad person for hiring former audit personnel? Of course not! Are they automatically bad because of their background? Of course not! So what's the risk? It's the possibility that the capital markets will perceive that your staff is too familiar with the auditors and that the job isn't being done in a way that will reduce uncertainty as much as it would under other circumstances.

One way to handle the situation is to at least disclose the existence of this possible taint. After all, if you "confess," the news is less shocking than if it is discovered through some other means. You might also describe the responsibilities of the alumni and explain what controls are in place to ensure that independence and objectivity aren't compromised. Another way has already been mentioned—rotate audit firms occasionally, and there won't be any sort of buildup of alums from one firm or another. Perhaps the most stringent is to just refuse to hire former auditors, but you need to disclose this policy for it to produce any change in public perception.

Do we know that these QFR practices will bring higher stock prices? No, we don't, but we do think that they will never pull your price down. The nature of QFR is that the call is yours, not a regulator's, and certainly not ours.

Question 30

The final question says:

> Do you view the audit as a perfunctory process required by the law?

We have to admit that we loaded it with a fighting word when we used *perfunctory*, but we wanted to be really clear.

What we have observed in practice is a general belief among auditors, clients, regulators, and just about everyone else that an independent audit is nothing more than a simple exercise in compliance with securities laws (or contracts, for private companies). Some of the evidence has been described already in this chapter: low-bid contracts, fixed-fee contracts, limited-scope audits, burgeoning nonaudit services, resistance to adjustments, opinion shopping, and auditor changes. People in leadership positions in the audit profession routinely state that audits are simple commodities with nothing to distinguish one from another. For example, Robert Elliott, a former AICPA chairman, offered up these resigned words in an article entitled "The Future of Assurance Services: Implications for Academia" that appeared in the December 1995 issue of *Accounting Horizons:*

> The market [for audits] seems saturated; there is over capacity and price competition. . . . The audit service is generalized—a one-size-fits-all product. (p. 118)

When looked at from this perspective, it sort of makes sense to answer question 30 with a "yes," doesn't it? However, the nature of Quality Financial Reporting is to question the status quo at all times.[7] Just because audits have become commodity compliance exercises doesn't mean that they should be, or that they can't be something else.

As we have described, audits are an essential component of the financial reporting process for both private and public companies. Without an audit, financial statement users have nothing to fall back on other than their trust that managers are doing the right things when they prepare reports. With some history in mind, and some natural skepticism, it's understandable that the capital markets would have trouble considering all financial reports to be equally trustworthy, if trustworthy at all.

Thus, we dispute those who have declared that audits are necessarily without value by making our own assertion that they can add tremendous value to financial reports and provide economic returns well in excess of their out-of-pocket costs, even high out-of-pocket costs. The keys are for audits to be treated that way by both the client and the auditor, and for the facts about them to be revealed publicly in the client's disclosures. After all, what would bring more credibility to the financial statements— a standard audit opinion with silence about the engagement on any point not governed by mandatory disclosure or a special opinion backed up by solid disclosures of the reasons this audit can be trusted? Instead of hiring the most compliant auditors they can find, managers should find the roughest and toughest, and pay them well to pursue all reporting issues to their resolution. Clients should ask the auditors to test all their financial accounting and reporting policies to see if they are truly communicative, not merely in compliance with minimum government standards. And, as we shall see in the next few chapters, auditors should be engaged to advise on ways to enhance the GAAP financial statements and to attest to the credibility of supplemental disclosures in excess of GAAP requirements.

As described in Chapter 2, the typical question at the end of an audit asks whether the statements comply with GAAP. A much better pair of questions asks whether the statements contain useful information and what can be done to make them even more useful. This QFR attitude has the capacity to change everything, don't you think?

THE BIG BIG PICTURE

Now that we have gone through 30 questions in these three chapters, you should have a much better assessment of how close you come to being a QFR practitioner. You should also have some clues on what you can do differently to reach that level.

We have to warn you, though, that getting to QFR is a never-ending process. There is never a place for feeling like things are "good enough." The competition in the capital markets for lower capital costs and higher stock prices will always force quality-minded managers (and their auditors) to keep out in the lead in order to avoid being left in the dust by their competitors.

The following chapters address more of the specific actions that you can take to get and stay in Quality Financial Reporting.

NOTES

1. At the same time the ethics rules were changed to allow bidding, the AICPA also eliminated a prohibition against one auditor's "encroaching" on another auditor's practice by offering to a client to do a better job for less money. This rule was obviously anticompetitive, but it also gave auditors the confidence that they would not be undercut by their colleagues. In turn, this freedom from competition gave them a great deal of power over their clients to persuade them to improve their financial statements. The unintended consequence of eliminating the encroachment rule is obvious—audits are now commodities and auditors have become relatively less powerful.

2. The three were Andersen; Deloitte & Touche; and KPMG. The Levitt proposals were supported by the other two, Ernst & Young and PricewaterhouseCoopers.

3. Forgive us for repeating this observation, but if compliance with GAAP produces information that isn't useful, and if audits attest that the financial statements comply with GAAP, isn't it true that the only thing audits accomplish is to proclaim that the statements contain useless information? At least you ought to think about this possibility.

4. The paper is forthcoming in *Accounting Review*.

5. As this book was in the final production stages in June 2002, several pieces of proposed federal legislation contained prohibitions against nonaudit services by auditors. True to form, the proposals were being resisted by audit firms and the AICPA. They were also opposed by Harvey Pitt, the SEC chairman who succeeded Levitt.

6. We also look skeptically at suggestions from high-level commissions and task forces that it is sufficient protection for the public interest if auditors describe their conflicts with management by communicating with the client's audit committee. Because this committee is always composed of individuals who are elected to the board by shareholder proxy after being nominated by management, there is every reason to think their independence is impaired in fact, appearance, or both.

7. One of the joys of teaching is frequent encounters with the unexpected. One time in the midst of a passionate admonition to an accounting theory class that they needed to challenge the conclusions of authoritative bodies, a student raised his hand and asked Paul Miller, "Who are you to tell us to question authority?" Think about it.

Getting Started

Now that we're entering the last third of the book, we believe there is a pretty good chance that we have jarred your confidence in the GAAP paradigm while also drawing you more and more into accepting the idea that QFR offers significant advantages as the alternate paradigm.

The four chapters in this section are aimed at describing our suggestions about what managers can do to ensure that their financial reports provide much more complete information to the markets. In addition to describing how minimum compliance produces minimum financial statements, Chapter 14 also shows how managers can produce enhanced statements that still comply with GAAP but provide greater usefulness. We also show how greater quality can be obtained through large amounts of supplemental disclosures that are neither required by GAAP nor presently used in practice.

To go in this direction, you (whether manager or accountant) will need to confront what the status quo has characterized as the wrong direction. Specifically, you will need to tackle and then overcome your fear of market values. Chapter 15 is designed to be a nonthreatening but still unequivocal explanation of the obvious point that market values provide information that is not provided by historical costs. We refuse to be drawn into the ancient but irrelevant conflict about whether GAAP should be based on cost or market. The irrefutable facts are that (1) managers must comply with cost-based GAAP and (2) market value information reveals a great many useful facts that complying with GAAP does not.

Chapters 16 and 17 take you through 12 crucial financial reporting topics, showing how you can just get by with minimum GAAP statements, how to produce enhanced GAAP statements, and how to produce useful supplemental disclosures.

CHAPTER 14

Filling in the GAAP Gaps

Building on all that we have said up to this point, it's time for us to talk more directly about specific actions that managers can start taking to move closer to achieving Quality Financial Reporting. That will be our basic focus from here on until the end of the book.

Specifically, we hope that we have established that mere minimum compliance with generally accepted accounting principles is not anywhere close to good enough for providing the kind of useful information that the capital markets need to efficiently evaluate securities in terms of the amount, timing, and uncertainty of the future cash flows. The political system that establishes GAAP is just not up to the task of creating innovative methods that put the right kinds of information into the financial statements. The problem is compounded by the long-standing dominance of auditors and preparers over the standard-setting process, with the consequence that the issues are virtually always defined, discussed, and resolved from the supply point of view with little if any attention given to the demand for more informative financial reports.

Thus, if managers want to move toward QFR, we suggest that they have two primary strategic directions to pursue on their own, voluntarily, without coercion or mandate:

1. Comply scrupulously with GAAP by going beyond the minimum requirements to really provide useful information
2. Present large quantities of high-quality supplemental information that is complete, consumable, and credible

The objective of both strategies is to create capital markets that are fully informed about the managers' individual firms. The ultimate goal is for them to compete successfully in those markets with other managers to achieve lower capital costs and higher security prices.

We have put together some simple diagrams to help explain what we're suggesting.

FILLING IN THE GAAP

To start, consider Figure 14-1, where the smaller circle represents the information that must be provided under GAAP, while the much larger circle symbolizes the information that the capital markets need to make good decisions under conditions of reduced uncertainty.

As we see it, and as we have explained in mind-numbing detail, the information included in GAAP financial statements is just not good enough to meet the needs of the markets. There are at least two explanations for this situation. First, many managers choose to implement the least informative alternatives under GAAP by doing such things as using the indirect method of reporting cash flows, putting stock options expense in a footnote instead of the income statement, and creating off-balance-sheet liabilities. Second, the supply-driven standard-setting process has generated requirements for mandatory reporting of information that the markets don't demand.

We want to use these observations to make two specific points. The first is that very little of the information currently provided in GAAP financial reports actually addresses the markets' needs. The second is that there are a great many unaddressed needs. Both situations offer major opportunities for those managers who will seize them.

FIGURE 14-1

GAAP vs. Information Needed by Capital Markets

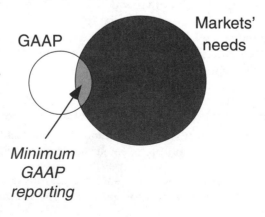

All through the preceding chapters, we have been describing and advocating the new Quality Financial Reporting strategy that aims to serve these vast unmet market needs for information. Without overt efforts by managers to provide the information, two things are happening. One is that market participants are paying a lot of money to intermediaries (such as analysts and financial advisers) to provide estimates and other guesses about the true conditions and results that managers are not describing. While this diverted capital is presently lost to managers, they could attract it to their companies by reducing the markets' dependence on the interme- diaries. Second, the quality of this externally generated information is in- ferior; it is inherently unreliable because it comes from secondary and tertiary sources and the analysts and advisers can do little to remove that uncertainty. As a result, the capital markets are deeply discounting stock prices and doing other things to boost rates of return, with the ultimate result that management is paying much more for its capital than it would if the perceived risk were not so high.

Under QFR, managers try to serve those market needs to reduce uncertainty and reap higher stock prices and a lower cost of capital. As Figure 14-2 shows, though, even a full-blown adoption of QFR still leaves the markets with needs for information from other sources, if only for the purpose of confirming the self-representations made by the managers of the reporting companies.

To return to the first of the two strategic initiatives stated at the beginning of this chapter, we believe that adopting QFR includes report- ing in accordance with GAAP. After all, GAAP financial statements are required by law for public companies and by contract for many private ones. If managers wanted to claim they provided high-quality reports without meeting the minimum mandatory levels of reporting, they would have to do so from their jail cells. However, when we talk about quality

FIGURE 14-2

QFR Meets More of the Markets' Needs

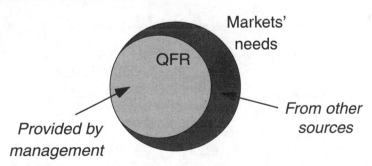

compliance with GAAP, we don't just mean perfunctory compliance. Instead, a full commitment to QFR causes management to aim for maximum compliance in terms of ensuring that the GAAP reports contain as much useful information as they can under the constraints and circumstances. The diagram in Figure 14-3 summarizes our points.

We have drawn this picture by moving the GAAP circle more toward the right to produce a larger overlap with the markets' needs. This movement reflects efforts by QFR managers to improve their GAAP reporting to meet more of those needs. To be perfectly clear, we are not proposing that these improvements would occur by making changes in GAAP through the political process. One point of our proposal is that managers who pursue QFR voluntarily (or as a result of new internal incentive systems) make different choices *within* GAAP to provide more of the information that the markets need instead of just doing the minimum. We call this practice *enhanced GAAP reporting.* For example, these managers will not engage in off-balance-sheet financing or report off-income-statement expenses. They will not spend money to be able to adopt accounting methods that obscure the facts, and they will compose footnotes that make sense. They certainly will not provide summary financial statements that gloss over or otherwise hide the truth or keep important facts from their stockholders and other capital market participants. As we said, this point is suggested by the larger overlap between GAAP and the markets' needs.

Although enhanced GAAP compliance will help produce quality, it will not be sufficient to produce the full impact of QFR. Specifically, there is a great deal more information that managers can reveal that presently

FIGURE 14-3

Enhanced GAAP Reporting as a Step Toward Achieving QFR

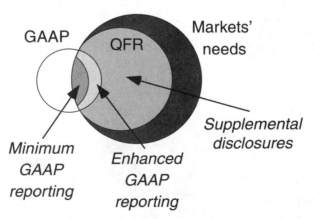

lies outside the domain of GAAP. Thus, fully adopting QFR also involves going way beyond those mandatory minimums by providing substantial quantities of high-quality information in *supplemental disclosures.*

The rest of this chapter, and essentially the rest of the book, elaborate on these two strategies and suggest specific actions that managers can take to implement them.

ENHANCED GAAP FINANCIAL STATEMENTS

If we've said it once, we've said it a half dozen times, but here it is anyway: QFR is a mental attitude, not a set of specific practices. This characterization applies thoroughly in the way QFR managers approach preparing their GAAP financial statements. Instead of painting pretty pictures that no one should believe (least of all the managers) and trying to make the statements as difficult to understand as possible, they aim at using the guidance in GAAP to describe their companies' present conditions, past performances, and future prospects. This attitude tries to maximize exposure, clarity, and trust while minimizing surprise, obfuscation, and suspicion. Enhanced GAAP reporting simply calls for accounting policies that boost communication without prevarication. Adopting this approach means no longer looking for silly games to play to create an appearance of being good. Instead, it is an intense search for new ways to reveal what has happened more reliably and more completely.

We think that managers who pursue enhanced financial statements will obviously provide more details instead of condensing the results down to meaningless totals. Taking into consideration new computer-based presentation formats, including HTML and XBRL, managers can publish condensed financial statements in electronic files that contain links that will allow users to drill down to the level of detail they would like to have. Clicking on the "Sales" item, for example, would let users access quarterly, monthly, or even weekly figures; results by segments or regions; trend lines for several years; the cash and credit mix; or any of a myriad of other details. Similar information could be provided for expenses, of course. For the balance sheet, a click on accounts receivable might show aging and maturity schedules, while a link from the property item might take the user to schedules showing different categories, locations, depreciation assumptions, or all sorts of other things. Rather than trying to get by with reporting as little as possible and thus creating uncertainty and risk, managers who facilitate these analyses will allow users to gain more certainty by helping them dig into the reports as far as they would like to go.

In previous chapters, we have already identified several places where GAAP allow managers to choose among alternatives. QFR-minded managers would make those choices with a view to providing more information, not less. Our favorite three examples are the direct method of cash flows, stock options expense, and supplemental information about market values, but there are many others. Under a QFR-based approach, managers would provide additional information explaining why they made their choices and describing the impacts of those policies compared to others. Some policies would just not be used, like off-balance-sheet financing and putting investments in the available-for-sale portfolio. We would go so far as to suggest that some conscientious managers would want to undo the financial statement effects of any past poolings they've done now that the FASB has officially declared them to be incomplete and unacceptable. Although that task would be huge, it would go a long way toward eliminating uncertainty, reducing the amount of guessing that financial analysts have to do, and building trust between management and the capital markets. The overall tone would be forthright and clear. The outcome would be more than just "user-friendly" financial statements: instead, the goal would be to make the users fully informed. If you want an example, we again refer you to Berkshire Hathaway and Warren Buffett, but even he can do a better job.

SUPPLEMENTAL DISCLOSURES

As reflected in Figure 14-3 on page 226, supplemental disclosures offer the greatest opportunities for going beyond the limits of GAAP. In effect, the sky is the limit—within the constraints of telling the truth, of course. The whole emphasis would be on uncovering what users consider to be useful and then giving it to them, although it might be possible that some managers would get some ideas on what to report on their own, generally based on their own internal decision-making processes.[1]

Beyond any doubt, we are convinced that information about the market values of companies' assets and liabilities is both relevant to users' decisions and more than sufficiently reliable to be reported publicly. Because this area has been so controversial in the past, and so frequently approached from the information suppliers' perspective, we have devoted all of Chapter 15 to explaining more about it. We think it is enough for now to say that management is in the position to provide this information to reduce the users' needs to guess and otherwise rely on unsubstantiated secondhand estimates that promote uncertainty and risk.

We also think that supplemental disclosures would be a good place for managers to provide useful sensitivity analyses that show different measures for financial statement items under different assumptions. One obvious place for this practice would be in the area of cost-based depreciation allocations. Because depreciation depends on predictions of future events and conditions, users would find a great deal of useful information in tables that would show possible ranges of results under different predictions, including the service lives and salvage values, as well as alternative allocation methods. Of course, market value information about these assets would enhance the usefulness even more.

Another significant area that is underdisclosed in GAAP concerns inventories. Companies that use LIFO could show results under FIFO, and vice versa, and both could show pro forma results for average and pure replacement cost. Although inventory accounting practice is traditionally limited by the "conformity rule" enforced by the federal Internal Revenue Service, there is still substantial flexibility and freedom to report this kind of information.

Some kind of forward-looking data would also be useful, although going into that area is pushing against the limits of the realm of facts that accounting should report and possibly straying into the domain of financial analysis that should belong to the users. Nonetheless, in *Financial Reporting in the 1990s and Beyond*, the AIMR had these pithy words that should challenge managers to get moving in this area:

> The financial reporting process is most useful when it goes beyond the past and present to include management's views of its future strategies, plans, and expectations. For example, management currently is required in the MD&A [Management Discussion and Analysis] section of its annual report to shareholders to report how the results of each of the past three years differ one from another. The SEC strongly encourages but does not require similar discussion of how management expects the results of future years to differ from those of the past. Why have managements been so slow to respond to this urging? We have seen some improvement recently, but the pace is glacial. (p. 21)

It makes sense to us that managers would want to provide users with a pleasant surprise by not meeting their expectations for paltry disclosures.

Our next recommendation may be a heart-stopper for most of today's CEOs. Nonetheless, their going into this territory would help defuse some very difficult reporting and governance issues that impact the basic question of whether stockholders can trust the managers. The specific point is management compensation from all sources, not just options. Is this area sensitive? Of course! That fact makes clearing the air even more important and beneficial. Is there a real problem? Anyone who reads proxy statements knows that compensation comes up often, and stockholder proposals never suggest that *less* information be reported. We have to ask what managers are thinking when they are not forthcoming about their compensation. From their actions, it looks like they're saying, "If we don't make the amounts clear, the stockholders will surely assume that we're not paying ourselves too much." If this was a vaudeville act, the hook would be out and around their necks.

This issue does not exist only in our imaginations. In 2001, we produced a column for *Accounting Today* that criticized the management of Consolidated Edison for ostentatiously proclaiming several times in the company's annual report that they were totally committed to serving the needs of their shareholders while, out of the other sides of their mouths, they published summary financial statements. Even more condemning was the managers' refusal to respond positively to a stockholder proposal calling for reporting more information about compensation paid to management. Here is what we said in the column:

> We believe the interesting question is whether management will voluntarily go beyond GAAP to promote shareholder value. In ConEd's case, the answer is not at all. How do we know? Because the proxy solicitation describes a stockholder proposal to create a policy to fully disclose compensation for all executives who receive more than $250,000 in order to boost stockholders' ability to "evaluate the soundness and efficacy of the overall management."
>
> So, how does the stockholder-oriented management deal with this suggestion? With these words: "Disclosure of executive compensations is governed by the Securities and Exchange Commission proxy solicitation rules. In accordance with those rules CEI currently provides information . . . for the five highest paid executive officers. The proposal would impose on CEI more stringent disclosure requirements than those imposed on other companies by the Commission's rules. The board believes that any changes in the disclosure requirements should emanate from the Commission and should be uniformly applicable to all companies subject to the proxy rules."
>
> In other words, "We won't go beyond the bare minimum and you can't make us!"[2]

This excerpt reveals that this management group has not only a haughtiness toward its shareholders but also a severe dysfunctional codependence with the SEC by allowing the bureaucratic regulatory system to be responsible for all innovations in reporting. The managers clearly have no idea that they are competing in the capital markets with other firms to win a lower cost of capital. We don't know, but we suspect that whoever produced this answer must have thought it was a clever way to put down the shareholder who was bold enough to speak out. In fact, what it tells us is that Con Ed's management doesn't have a clue about the relationship between information quality, trust, and the value of the company's stock. Surely other managers can adopt the QFR communication model and destroy these people in the capital market competition.

Another ripe area for supplemental reporting has been addressed by Professor Russell Lundholm, who suggested in the December 1999 issue of *Accounting Horizons* that managers should provide enough information to allow users to assess their credibility by evaluating their use of discretion in the past. Lundholm suggests, for example, that disclosures would facilitate comparing managers' predictions with actual outcomes. One specific point would be the allowance for uncollectible accounts, but there would be multitudes of other situations where management discretion affects reported earnings.

It goes without saying that QFR would lead managers to do more than just pour out huge volumes of data without organizing and indexing them. Again, computer technology that allows linking would be especially useful in helping users navigate through large volumes of additional financial data. The key would be to enable the users to access, understand, and apply the information so that it will actually reduce their uncertainty.

AUDITOR INVOLVEMENT

Consider this chain of logic:

- Financial statements are provided to reduce uncertainty about management performance and future cash flows.
- GAAP are created to reduce uncertainty by constraining the representations in the financial statements.
- Audits are performed to reduce uncertainty about management's claim that the financial statements were prepared in accordance with GAAP.
- Audits are performed in compliance with GAAS to reduce uncertainty about the quality of the assurance they provide.
- GAAS and other professional standards require auditors to be competent and independent to reduce uncertainty about their dependability.
- Professional bodies and government agencies enforce these professional standards to reduce uncertainty about compliance.

If all these procedures are implemented merely to reduce uncertainty about the low-quality information in GAAP financial statements, doesn't it make even more sense to submit the really useful information in these supplemental disclosures to the scrutiny of independent third-party experts? It would if you wanted the financial analysts and other users to have a greater degree of comfort in consuming and relying on this otherwise unregulated reporting. We think this conclusion is valid, even if a particular management group is already considered to be highly trustworthy.

We also see that extensive supplemental reporting offers a special opportunity to auditors to add much more value to their clients' total reporting packages than they can now add by only auditing minimally useful GAAP financial statements. We also foresee that auditing firms could become QFR consultants by helping their clients develop new topics to be reported and new ways to present them. PricewaterhouseCoopers has clearly led the way in this direction by promoting its ValueReporting framework.

REPORTING FREQUENCY

At various places in preceding chapters, we have criticized the continuing acceptance of quarterly reporting by managers, auditors, regulators, and even the AIMR financial analysts. As we suggested toward the end of Chapter 7, it is way past time for improving on a practice that was initiated two-thirds of a century ago when the Securities and Exchange Act of 1934 was passed. How, in today's world of instant communications in a literally networked world, can everyone be so complacent as to keep reporting at the same frequency that was established when databases were stored in leather-bound ledgers, when the main input devices were No. 2 pencils and fountain pens, and when the fastest method for output was typing multiple carbon copies? Please excuse our hyperbole, but we struggle to understand the lack of complaints from analysts who can pick up phones and instantly talk to colleagues in any place in the world, or consult any of a number of huge computerized data warehouses from anywhere. Why are they so content to wait 90 days for new financial information? We're reduced to head scratching on that one.[3]

Having been involved in regulation ourselves, we do understand how the SEC and FASB can focus so intently on the hot issues du jour and be oblivious to something like this anachronistic lack of timeliness; however, we do not excuse their oversight. We also understand that accruing and closing the books is a tedious process that involves a lot of judgment and access to data that is created only after the end of a reporting period. However, we also know how much computing power and data storage capacity that the two of us have sitting on each of our desktops. Our conclusion is that, once again, there has been a culturewide focus on the issue of how often financial reports can be supplied instead of how often they are demanded or would be demanded if only financial statement users could ever let themselves think that more frequent reporting might be possible.

So, one more time, we find that the QFR paradigm shines a bright light into a dark corner of the financial reporting world. The four axioms connect high capital costs and low stock prices with incomplete information. We are confident that reporting every 90 days or so creates at least a 60-day period that makes the markets live with grossly incomplete information, leading to the consequence that all stock prices are likely to be depressed because of the uncertainty. These facts provide a reasonable explanation of the bizarre truth that the hottest piece of information in today's capital markets is analysts' projected earnings numbers. The absence of timely facts from management makes these soft numbers immensely valuable. The absence of timely facts also makes the markets far less efficient than they would be if managers provided reports more frequently and more quickly after events happen.

In light of these observations, consider what the markets would do if a company's management started publishing credible financial information every six weeks, every month, every two weeks, once a week, or even on a real-time basis. In these circumstances, how much would analysts' forecasts be worth? Next to nothing, as near as we can tell. To address another point, what would happen to capital market volatility if credible financial information were available at these faster frequencies? We think it would virtually cease to exist, except as a reflection of external risk factors.

As a result of our contemplating along these lines, we have concluded that managers who would choose to report more often would see the value of their companies' securities go higher, their capital costs decline, and the volatility of their stock prices diminish. After all, the markets would only have to wait a short while until the latest reliable information was released to the public.

We again see a huge opportunity just waiting to be seized by visionary managers who want to build a QFR link to the capital markets. Even if the information were only partial and unaudited, like daily sales receipts or weekly cash flows, we believe that the markets would increase their demand for these companies' shares and bid their prices up. Asserting otherwise would be relying on assumptions that would surely prove to be false.

The technological solutions for more frequent reporting are also at hand through the Internet, primarily by public posting of the information on the companies' websites. Some might find this concept to be objectionable and nearly impossible to implement. Others, especially managers, will wait for regulators to take the lead and impose the change. Some will also wait for their competitors to go first and then play catch-up. Still others will object by saying that crooked managers will use this freedom to pump their stock prices. Regardless of the medium, the last time we looked into the securities law, it was still a major crime to present misleading information in a financial report. Why would fraud be any more heinous if it occurred over the Internet than if it was accomplished with printed pages?

As we have said, we see a huge opportunity just sitting in the laps of some risk-taking, profit-seeking management teams. All they have to do is seize that opportunity and sweep in the rewards. Their only cost will be setting up a server and ensuring that fresh data is supplied as often as possible.

SUMMARY

Once managers come to understand the deficiencies of existing financial reporting practices and get a glimpse of the advantages of QFR, we believe that they will want to change their patterns in two ways. First, they will want to step up to a higher level of reporting under GAAP, such that their financial statements are not just in minimum compliance but very consumable and useful. This step can be accomplished by changing attitudes without waiting for the FASB or SEC to force a change. Second, we also envision that QFR managers will work overtime to develop truly informative supplemental disclosures that will address at least some of the presently unanswered demands for more and more data about what has happened and what the current situation is. A third strategy is to report more often and more broadly to as many people as possible.

The next three chapters describe more detailed suggestions that can be followed to increase the usefulness of your financial reports.

NOTES

1. According to the ValueReporting strategy advocated by the Eccles foursome and PricewaterhouseCoopers (see Chapter 8), a prime area for innovation for managers would be reporting information about the internal performance indicators they use in their strategic planning and assessments. Unlike typical efforts to standardize and make everybody do the same things, ValueReporting recommends that managers report unique indicators that reflect their business models and management styles.

2. Paul Miller and Paul Bahnson, "Con Ed: 'Disclose Useful Information? We Won't and You Can't Make Us!'," *Accounting Today*, July 2/22, 2001, pp. 14, 17.

3. One hypothesis suggests that their silence arises from the fact that, prior to the SEC's Regulation FD, the analysts had ready access to managers for so-called "guidance" on what information would be released in the quarterlies. If managers react to this regulation by not providing more timely public disclosures, maybe there will be more complaints from analysts who have been forced out onto that level playing field with all other investors.

CHAPTER 15

Reporting Market Values

A warning, or at least a disclaimer, is perhaps in order at the beginning of this chapter because we are going to discuss the most controversial and long-lasting issue in financial accounting. Our warning is twofold: (1) we will articulate positions that are not popular among practitioners, and (2) when the last page is turned, we will not have resolved the issue in the traditional sense. In fact, we are not apologetic for ruffling any feathers or for leaving the question unanswered. Unlike others who have approached market value accounting, we are advocating Quality Financial Reporting and are not trying to create new mandatory requirements through GAAP. So, while it is possible that some of you reading this book will grow uncomfortable as we make our points, we want you to hold on until we're done, if you can, and see whether we have shed some new light on the situation.

THE OLD ISSUE

This long-lasting controversy surrounds the traditional question of whether public financial statements should be based on *historical cost* or *market value.* No other question has divided accountants or stirred their emotions quite like this one. But, we're not going to try to resolve it, and for a very good reason. Specifically, we won't answer this question because QFR makes it irrelevant.

Under the traditional financial accounting paradigm, especially as it has been applied in the political standard-setting process, the search has always been for the single best way to report all events and conditions. Therefore, the issue has been framed as "historical cost versus market value," with the emphasis on the *versus,* as if only one or the other ought to be used in every situation.

Several factors have framed the debate in this way. One is technological in that accounting systems were, and still are, costly to create and operate; as a result, most managers want to have only one. A second reason is psychological, in that some people did, and still do, believe that there is only one single best way to account, such that adopting historical cost would mean that market values couldn't be used, and vice versa. Yet a third reason is political. Specifically, GAAP have originated through the slow and steady accumulation of "accepted" practices, virtually all of which were rooted in historical numbers. Thus, practitioners have grown comfortable with that state. It's only natural that they would resist proposals for change, especially one as big as moving to market value accounting, because going in this direction repudiates all that has gone before. Therefore, when they frame the issue as historical cost vs. market value, what they really see in their minds is this question: "Should we stay with the status quo or should we change to something we don't understand?" As a result, it has been very difficult to get people to focus on the real question of how we can find a way to progress, and even more difficult to get them to consider the alternatives.

However, QFR shows that asking (and answering) the question this way will not lead to improvement. As a superficial analogy, we can't imagine that a group of fast food restaurant managers would sit around and debate for years and years whether it's better to serve only hamburgers to all customers or only cheeseburgers to all customers. Instead, they would quickly see that they can make more sales and profits if they sell both products. To put it another way, a decision to sell hamburgers to some customers does not keep them from also selling cheeseburgers to others. Furthermore, how foolish would it be if some managers refused to sell cheeseburgers simply because they personally don't like them? The overarching objective is to sell something that customers like and will pay for. The fundamental principle is to shape your strategies to meet the markets' needs by responding to demand instead of meeting your needs by managing the supply.

To get back to financial reporting, QFR shows it makes sense to find out what kind of information is or might be useful, and then provide it. It also shows that the decision on what to report would not simply be based on the costs of providing the information but would include the "hunting and gathering" costs incurred by the analysts if the management doesn't provide it. The equation also needs to include the benefits of lower capital costs resulting from more complete information.

These observations lead us to suggest that we can reframe this issue as three separate ones:

1. Are historical costs useful? If so, report them.

2. Are market values useful? If so, report them.

3. Are other kinds of information useful? If so, report them.

In other words, each measurement system must stand or fall on its own. If historical costs are useful and generate net benefits, then we ought to report them, without regard to what we decide about market values or some other kind of information. The same is true for market values. A decision to report one should not stop us from reporting the other, if they are both in demand.

In addition, the old framing of cost vs. value is irrelevant because companies have to provide reports based on GAAP. Even if we could prove that values are more useful, we know it would be impossible to wrest sufficient control of the standard-setting process to force wholesale change on all preparers, auditors, and users, so it makes little practical sense to advocate, say, that market values should be the sole basis for GAAP. It just isn't likely to happen that way in the lifetime of anyone reading or writing this book, although stranger things have happened.

Therefore, under QFR, there is no huge debate. Given that GAAP statements must be presented, the remaining question is whether users would face less uncertainty if managers voluntarily provided market value information. Thus, the issue is not whether the supplemental information is *more* useful than GAAP but whether it is a useful *addition* to GAAP. This framing changes the debate to a simpler search for a way to do things better.

SOME HISTORY

To show that it hasn't always been this way, we want to briefly describe a couple of periods in recent history in which there was a lot of debate over costs and market values. In the 1960s, academics wrote tons of articles and books arguing which system was better. Before long, proponents of market value also split over the second question of whether reported market values should be based on purchase or selling prices. While this literature is interesting (at least to us), our retrospective evaluation shows that it had little chance of shaping practice.

Next, the FASB was created in 1973 and charged with developing a "conceptual framework" to guide its standard-setting process. As described in Chapter 2, the first pronouncement in the framework (Statement of Financial Accounting Concepts 1) was published in 1978 and established that financial reporting should provide useful information.[1] It was followed by others identifying the qualities of useful information (SFAC 2) and the elements of the financial statements (SFAC 3), as well as the objectives of reporting by not-for-profit entities (SFAC 4). All of this effort led up to the next stage, which was supposed to settle the question of what kind of measurements should be reported. Given the dominance of the supply-driven paradigm of the 1980s and the legacy of the 1960s literature, the issue was framed for the FASB as historical costs vs. market values, and a line was drawn in the sand. The debates raged long and loud, and board members' tempers flared.[2] The stakes were very high, especially among those who feared that GAAP would be based on market values. True to form, the political process eventually did what it is supposed to do, which is slow down and otherwise resist change. The board was evenly divided, with the chairman somewhere in the middle trying to keep the board alive. SFAC 5 was issued in 1984 with virtually no new concepts included on any of its pages. With regard to the controversy, the board members merely observed that several different measures are used under GAAP, including costs and market values, in different situations, and said that they expected this mixed practice to continue in the future. After years of effort and rhetoric, everyone was back where they started, with an unresolved issue and a lot of bruised egos.

In addition, the board had been pressured by the SEC to require supplemental disclosure of market value information, which it did by issuing SFAS 33 in 1979. However, the FASB called this standard an experiment, made it applicable to only about the 1400 largest public companies, required less than comprehensive disclosures, provided wide latitude for calculations, and did not require the information to be audited. As Paul Bahnson observed when he was a FASB staff member evaluating the results of this experiment, there wasn't much else the board could have done to ensure that it would fail to produce results.

Once the conceptual framework effort fell apart, the board rescinded SFAS 33 in 1986 by issuing SFAS 89. Accidentally consistent with what we now recognize as the QFR paradigm, the standard recommends that managers voluntarily continue reporting market values and experiment with new ways of presenting them. But, consistent with their old supply-driven paradigm of minimum compliance, virtually no managers have done so, despite extensive and persuasive evidence that market value information is desired by statement users and is useful for both internal and external decisions.

In the following pages, we do not try to prove that market values are more useful than historical costs. However, we do show that GAAP information based on costs is incomplete and that market value information can overcome some of that incompleteness. Although we have given up on pleading with the FASB to change everything, even anything, we are firmly convinced that real progress will come when QFR-minded managers decide on their own to pursue the seemingly large and obvious economic rewards for providing more useful information to the capital markets.

IS THERE A DEMAND FOR MARKET VALUE INFORMATION?

In response to the question in the heading, we think the answer is a resounding yes. Our enthusiasm reflects our understanding and endorsement of the FASB's demand-driven wisdom in SFAC 1, namely that financial reporting has the objective of providing information that is useful for assessing the amount, timing, and uncertainty of the reporting entity's future cash flows. Furthermore, information about the reporting entity's resources and obligations is useful for making those assessments.

Without any doubt, market value information is useful because it reflects a current consensus among many buyers and sellers about the intrinsic value of the future cash flows inherent in an asset or liability. For example, if one asset is expected to produce a larger amount of cash than another, it will be worth more, all other things being equal. If one asset will produce the same amount of cash sooner than another, the market will also value it more highly, all other things being equal. And, if one asset is more likely to produce the same amount of cash at the same time as another asset, it will also be worth more, all other things being equal. Nothing contains as much information about these three cash flow dimensions of the asset as its market value.[1] Thus, if users want an idea about the intrinsic value of the entity's assets and liabilities, information about their market values will prove to be useful.

Beyond any rational dispute, then, market values provide useful information that old costs do not reveal. Specifically, a cost reflects the consensus between only two parties about the intrinsic value of the asset or liability at some point in the past when expectations about the amount, timing, and uncertainty of the cash flows were different. From another angle, creditors, especially those who are secured, want to have information about the market values of their debtors' assets so that they can assess how much cash would be available if liquidation had to occur. From still another perspective, market values are also useful for judging the adequacy of the return earned from assets; after all, an alternative strategy would be to sell them and earn a return elsewhere. Dividing the current return by an old cost is insufficient for supporting a decision to hold or dispose of the assets. Thus, supplemental facts about market values would give insights that cost does not.

In addition, any measure of return that fails to include the change in the asset's value has to be incomplete. The same can be said for any measure of a return based on a priori assumptions about changes in value. Therefore, a more complete description of the real profit is provided by information that includes actual holding gains and losses based on market values and excludes predetermined amounts of systematic depreciation or accretion.

Three Basic Ideas

We want to explain three basic ideas before going further. First, we acknowledge that an entity's market value is quite different from the sum of the market values of its assets and liabilities. Estimating the value of the firm is the business of financial analysts, not accountants. Nevertheless, information about the market values of the pieces has to be helpful to these analysts for estimating the market value of the whole.

Second, we are learning to think of market value as a distribution of amounts instead of a single amount. Because the value describes the prices incurred by a great many buyers and sellers in a period of time, it is more likely to be a bell-shaped curve of some kind rather than a single amount. This insight is proving helpful to us as we look afresh at the extreme hyperfocus among accountants on precise measurements. In particular, we are learning that approximations of relevant values are more useful for decisions than precise calculations of other irrelevant amounts.

Third, a market value is not a hypothetical number, like "what we would have to pay *if* we bought the asset today." Rather, it is a real number that equals "what other people *are* paying to buy the asset today." We find that this idea helps us understand the reliability of values and overcome our old conditioned responses to view market values as unreliable "what-if" numbers. They are, we have come to realize, just as real as costs.

THE USERS SPEAK

All this discussion is interesting, but what about financial statement users? What have they said? We certainly cannot speak for them, but we can provide some insight into their thinking by presenting several additional comments from the AIMR committee report that we quoted in Chapter 7.

Although there are disagreements among the financial analysts on whether values should replace historical costs (according to the old framing of the issue), it is clear that they strongly prefer having market value information available for their analyses. Consider these straightforward comments favoring market values from *Financial Reporting in the 1990s and Beyond:*

> It is axiomatic that it is better to know what something is worth now than what it was worth at some moment in the past. (p. 39)

> There is no financial analyst who would not want to know the market value of individual assets and liabilities. (p. 39)

This next comment shows the analysts' reluctance to throw out GAAP while proclaiming their strong demand for access to value information:

> Our position is that we would like current value reporting to be given a chance. We need to be able to assess the extent to which volatility really exists, even though the financial statements themselves may, as a political matter, need to be shielded from it. As long as current values are not seen, financial analysts cannot use them. The vehicle of disclosure, however, should be used so as to offer financial analysts the opportunity to use current values. (p. 87)

The same reluctance to substitute market values for costs appears in the following quote, but the analysts again described their demand for value information to help them do their work:

> The . . . major issue . . . is whether mark-to-market accounting is the remedy for the deficiencies of historic cost as applied to financial instruments. Some AIMR members support it wholeheartedly and believe that it should supplant historic cost on the financial statements. Others have reservations about or are opposed to market value accounting. None is opposed to disclosure of market values, and most believe that it is vital.
>
> . . . In sum, we are agreed that information about market values is important, but we differ on the degree of importance and the extent to which they should be incorporated in financial reports. (p. 31)

Two more comments describe these users' demands for market values. This first one laments the lost access to value information after the FASB's decision in SFAS 89 to make its disclosure voluntary and preparers' decisions to not provide it:

> In Financial Accounting Standard No. 33 (FAS 33), we were provided with information that, although imprecise, was a godsend to those financial analysts who understood it and were able to use it in their work. (pp. 86–87)

Notice two points in this sentence. First, they acknowledged that the information was imprecise but nonetheless useful. Second, by calling it a godsend, they proclaimed that it was needed but unavailable through any other means.

As to the desirability of actually replacing GAAP with market-based principles, the analysts revealed their own bell-shaped curve of diverse opinions:

> A few financial analysts and investment managers are unequivocally opposed to (and a few are unalterably in favor of) mark-to-market accounting. But most have adopted a wait-and-see-attitude. It is difficult to forsake historic cost when it is uncertain that its replacement will accomplish what its advocates promise. (p. 4)

From the QFR perspective, we see that the analysts are describing their demand for values; we hope that we are successfully passing this message to potential suppliers of that information. To reiterate, these expert users are plainly saying that they will use value information to make better decisions if managers will just provide it. They are also making it clear that the information can be useful without being included in GAAP financial statements.

Thus, we guarantee that the result of responding to this demand will be higher stock prices and lower capital costs. Why? Because we are certain that these proclamations about the usefulness of values mean that users are now making their decisions using their own biased and otherwise less reliable estimated market values. In turn, we are confident that their estimates are protective, in that they put a downward bias on asset values and an upward bias on liability values. If so, publishing managers' more reliable value estimates will have two effects. First, the removal of some of the uncertainty about the analysts' own crude estimates will reduce their risk and, in turn, capital costs. Second, it is likely that the unbiased management estimates will be new information to the capital markets that will support predictions of larger future cash flows. If so, it is reasonable to expect stock prices to go up in response to what is really new data, not just better-looking data.[4]

Far be it from us to impose our interpretation on anyone by trying to persuade the SEC or the FASB to require managers to report market value information. We're content to let potential suppliers see the unmet demand and react by supplying it on their own. Our patient confidence grows out of the simplicity of the QFR paradigm and its demand-driven focus.

RELIABILITY

Now that we have established (at least in our own minds) that there is a demand for market values because of their relevance, it's time to turn to the biggest, or at least the most frequent, complaint against value-based information, namely that it isn't reliable. Somewhere in this argument is an allusion to the factual nature of historical costs. We have a few things to say that might help some managers look beyond this superficial argument to focus on usefulness.

Our first step is to ask whose definition of reliability matters in deciding whether value information is reliable. To return to history, we point out that the U.S. standard-setting process has been influenced or controlled by auditors from the beginning. Furthermore, auditors' perceptions of reliability are clearly focused on the defensibility of the reported amounts, not their faithful representation of some relevant fact. Thus, they consider an invoice to be proof of reliability, when all it really does is corroborate the recorded amount without proving whether that number represents anything useful about the asset, especially at any later date. In particular, that single outdated fact cannot possibly be reliable for assessing future cash flows for more than a limited time after the cost is incurred. Therefore, one can hardly call historical cost reliable for helping financial statement users predict and assess the amount, timing, and uncertainty of future cash flows.

There certainly can be issues concerning the verifiability of market information, especially if the assets and liabilities are not traded frequently. However, in a growing number of situations, it is possible to access databases of transactions involving the same assets and gain confidence in the market value measures.[5] In these situations, market values are more verifiable than costs because they reflect a large number of recent transactions involving other buyers and sellers. In contrast, the owner's original cost lacks the same degree of verifiability because it emerges from a consensus of only two parties, including the reporting entity's managers, who can hardly be considered disinterested in what the statements report.

Being iconoclasts through and through, we have decided that most market value information is likely to be sufficiently reliable to be useful in supplemental disclosures, at the very least. We think others will come to the same conclusion once they get out of traditional supply-driven thought patterns and begin to think more about what the information is supposed to be used for. When they do, they will see the inadequacies of the status quo concepts of reliability and move on to something better.

Users and Reliability

Does the AIMR committee have anything to say on the reliability and decision usefulness of market values? The following quote from *Financial Reporting in the 1990s and Beyond* shows more than a little tinge of irony, perhaps to tweak accountants who insist that costs ought to be supplied and that users should be totally content and grateful to have them:

> Certainly financial analysts desire information that is both relevant and reliable, but their bias is towards relevance. In a phrase, analysts prefer information that is equivocally right rather than precisely wrong. Inexact measures of contemporaneous economic values generally are more useful than fastidious historic records of past exchanges. (p. 33)

In other words, it doesn't really matter to these sophisticated users how precisely managers and auditors tie a reported cost down to an invoice or a depreciation schedule—all that effort doesn't amount to beans because it won't make historic records more useful than reasonably good market value estimates.

Killing a Bad Stereotype

We think one more point needs to be made about the reliability of historical costs. Specifically, we find that most accountants justify their conclusion that cost measures are reliable by using the stereotypical and grossly
oversimplified example of a single tangible asset purchased in a cash
transaction. In fact, many other acquisition situations (such as asset exchanges, deferred payments, lump-sum purchases of multiple assets,
asset/stock exchanges, incidental expenditures, and business combinations) introduce factors that create significant uncertainty about the accuracy of original recorded costs of individual assets. Furthermore, any
reliability is fundamentally destroyed when the costs are depreciated or
amortized over a predicted and thus unverifiable future time period. In
short, we are dumbfounded by the large amount of unreliability actually
associated with cost measures used under GAAP, yet most managers and
accountants (and accounting teachers, for that matter) simply do not see it
or choose to look the other way in order to avoid confronting the need for
change.

AN IN-PROCESS SUMMARY

Again, we want to declare that we are not trying to reform GAAP, just to
show that there seems to be a significant demand from financial statement
users for information about market values because of their relevance and
reliability. All of this demand exists despite the discomfort auditors and
managers seem to feel in working with values because of their unfamiliarity and lack of precision. QFR, of course, reveals the potential rewards
from responding to this demand, so let's go on.

COMPARABILITY

Another quality of useful information is that it describes similar events
and conditions as similar while describing dissimilar events and conditions in a way that shows how they are different. This quality is called
comparability.

Perhaps the most common traditional apology for historical costs is
an assertion that goes something like this: "The information is comparable
because everybody is recording the same thing when they record their
cost." However, this reasoning is facile. If different costs occur at different
points in time, one can hardly conclude that everyone is recording information that allows them to make valid and useful comparisons forever.
Consider the cost of a factory bought in the early 1960s and the cost of the
essentially identical one next door bought in the early 1990s. Although
each would have a historical cost, those amounts (or their depreciated

book values) would never produce comparable descriptions of their ability to generate cash flows in 2002. A financial report would show a huge difference between their costs despite the similarity of their intrinsic values at the present date, which is when a decision has to be made. If, on the other hand, all companies describe all their assets and liabilities at their market values on the same date, the result is truly comparable depictions of their abilities to generate future cash flows.

The AIMR committee elaborated on this point in the following comment responding to criticisms of the comparability of market value data:

> Some argue that if we are to be presented with market values that are bound to be historic by the time they arrive, we are better off with older but transaction-based historic cost.

> The counter-arguments to that line of reasoning are two. First, many historic costs are seriously out of date. They may have little relation to the current market value of assets, whereas the balance sheet market values (which are only slightly out-of-date) still will have a good amount of relevance. Second, market value data are comparable. If all enterprises mark their balance sheets to market on the same date, they are all out-of-date by the same interval. Historic cost data are never comparable on a firm-to-firm basis because the costs were incurred at different dates by different firms (or even within a single firm). (p. 39)

If sophisticated analysts consider market values to be comparable but find historical costs to be noncomparable, and if they consider comparability to be important, then doesn't it make sense for management to provide value-based information to them?

INFLATION AND MEASUREMENT

In addition to denying the weaknesses of costs and the strengths of values, U.S. accountants have also pretended for decades, if not an entire century, that inflation does not cause the value of the dollar to decay as time passes. Because inflation changes the purchasing power of a currency, there is no usefulness in comparisons between nominal costs that are incurred at different points in time. Thus, there is no logical validity in adding up (or subtracting, averaging, or performing any other mathematical operation on) historical costs from different dates because the currency units used to describe those measures are not equal.[6] Thus, the historical cost and historical dollar data required for GAAP reporting seems to us to be woefully incomplete.

On the other hand, if all market values are measured on the same date, there is at least logical validity in the total or the results of some other arithmetic operation. Even though comparisons between total market values at different dates suffer from the same measuring unit inconsistency, it can be taken care of with price level adjustments through the processes that the FASB called *constant-dollar accounting*.

Again, we are persuaded that supplemental reporting of values will help QFR managers overcome the flaws of GAAP. Remember, we are not arguing that new standards are needed to make market value accounting mandatory, only that managers can report market values to overcome the incompleteness of GAAP and thereby reap lower capital costs and higher stock values.

THE REALIZATION ISSUE

Back in the 1960s, some academic accountants developed systems for transmuting historical cost statements to market value statements. Although they were in new territory, they continued using old paradigms and conventions.[7] In particular, they were handicapped by the old concept that unrealized gains and losses are significantly different from realized gains and losses. Just to be clear, unrealized gains and losses occur because of changes in an asset's value while it is still owned or a liability's value while it is still owed. In contrast, realized gains and losses occur on assets that are no longer owned or liabilities that are no longer owed. As near as we can tell, this difference does not reflect a real economic distinction. Nonetheless, it continues in practice, especially in accounting for investments held in the available-for-sale portfolio. Under SFAS 115, unrealized gains and losses on investments assigned to this portfolio are not reportable income; instead, they are accumulated since acquisition and added to or subtracted from the company's equity accounts on the balance sheet, while the annual change in the accumulated amount is reported as an item of "comprehensive" income.[8]

When the investments are sold, however, the realized gains and losses are reported as part of the year's earnings. The fatal flaw is that the entire amount of the gain or loss accumulated since acquisition is included in the income for the year of the sale instead of only the amount that actually occurred in that year. The result is reported income measures that are unreliable because they are not faithful representations of the increase or decrease in equity in either the year of the sale or each of the years in which the value changed.

Here is our point: the act of selling an asset (or paying off a liability) does not create or consume wealth. Before the sale, for example, you have an asset worth $100,000; after the sale, you have $100,000 of cash. The transaction merely transformed the asset to another form of asset, and no wealth was either created or consumed. In the same way, if you pay off $100,000 of debt with $100,000 of cash, you have not produced any change in net wealth. Although the sale of the asset changed cash, that result is reported on the cash flow statement and has no effect on income. And, although the event changed management's exposure to risk from later value changes, that result is reported on the balance sheet and has no place on the income statement. We are convinced that there is no good reason to bring the income statement into this team effort and use it to try to say something that is said more clearly elsewhere. To reiterate our conclusion: if an event does not create or consume wealth, then there is nothing to be usefully reported on the income statement as a result of that event.

To return to the example, assume the asset's book value at the sale date is $100,000. Thus, there is no gain or loss on the income statement. But what if the book value is different? Suppose the asset had been marked to the then market value of $90,000 a few weeks before at the end of the prior fiscal year. The sale would imply that the asset had increased in value by another $10,000 in the current year, and only that change can be considered to be a gain of the current year. Further, it arose from holding the asset while it went up in value, not from selling it.

To us, it makes little sense to compromise the income statement's usefulness by reporting a gain from a sale when a sale cannot produce a gain. It makes even less sense to report the entire gain accumulated over the life of the asset to the point in time at which the sale occurred. If, for example, this asset had been purchased for $5,000 ten years before, historical cost accounting would report a $95,000 gain in the year of the sale, when indeed only $10,000 was attributable to that year, and none of it was created by the sale. As we see it, the only thing accomplished by the traditional GAAP treatment is a cluttered income statement containing information that does not really help financial statement users to either judge the past or predict the future. At the risk of beating the same drum too often, this fixation in GAAP on realization reflects the information suppliers' concern with defensibility instead of the markets' demand for useful information.

Because we know that these "radical" ideas may be making some of you uncomfortable, let's get back to the point of where the practice came from.

Where Did Realization Come From?

We firmly believe that auditors have exercised control over GAAP, that GAAP have shaped the accounting culture and language, and that the culture and language shape thought processes. According to today's accounting culture, unrealized gains are somehow considered "unearned" or "unreal" because no transaction has occurred. But, who has to have a transaction? The clear answer is auditors, because they need an invoice, check, or cash receipt to file away as evidence. If they don't have these pieces of paper, they believe that they are at risk. Since they were put in charge of writing the rules, they were able to write them to meet their own needs, and produced the convention that unrealized gains are not part of earnings. There is no valid information-related reason for this treatment; rather, it comes about because auditors don't want to be sued. While we cannot blame them for pursuing what they think is their best interest, the fact remains that this supply-based approach keeps users from being fully informed.

On the other hand, how do auditors feel about unrealized losses? Of course, auditors (as a group) have been more than willing to create GAAP that force these losses to be recognized and reported as soon as possible after they're discovered. Evidence of this willingness abounds in the doctrine of "lower of cost or market" that permeates GAAP. Inventories, for example, are written down to market, but never above cost. Impaired property assets are written down but never up (this practice is governed by SFAS 144, issued in August 2001). Another recent endorsement of this bias is SFAS 142 concerning goodwill (also issued in 2001). The cost of this highly intangible asset is not to be amortized; rather, the management must periodically test its market value to see whether an impairment has occurred so that it can be written down. Again, it is never to be written up. The only excuse (but not a good reason) for this one-sided view of reality is to protect the information *suppliers* against recrimination. This view does not reflect information *consumers'* needs for useful information about both gains and losses.

Providing More Information

So, what should you do with holding gains and losses in a QFR financial report? Actually, you can do whatever you want, because that is the nature of QFR. To be more direct, however, we think that this major hole in current practice can be filled by enhanced information about unrealized and realized gains and losses. It seems to us that the GAAP income statement can be constructed to show how much of the realized gains and losses actually occurred in the current year and how much in prior years, perhaps with this sort of format for the example we have been using:

```
UNDER CURRENT PRACTICE:
   Realized gain from disposal ............................. $95,000
UNDER QFR-ENHANCED PRACTICE:
   Realized gain from disposal:
      From the current year ................................ $10,000
      From prior years ..................................... 85,000
      Total realized gain .................................. $95,000
```

While this presentation clarifies some facts about realized items, it does not address the unrealized gains and losses for the year. Under existing GAAP, information about only a few unrealized items for the year is reported, and even most of that is presented outside the income statement.[9]

Reporting Comprehensive Income

Speaking of unrealized gains and losses, another QFR-enhanced practice would be careful presentation of the components of comprehensive income for the year. SFAS 130 requires managers to report this item, which equals the reported net income plus and minus other changes in equity, such as unrealized gains and losses on investments and foreign currency gains and losses.

As we understand it, most managers are not putting this presentation on the income statement but hiding it in the statement of changes in stockholders' equity. All we can do is speculate that at least some managers want to make it harder for users to know what happened by making their statements as opaque as possible. QFR, of course, says just the opposite, and leads managers to report the comprehensive income clearly and completely.

MAKING THE MOVE TO MARKET VALUES

It's one thing for us to persuade managers to consider making the move toward higher quality by reporting market value–based information, but it is quite another for us to show them exactly how to do it.[10] Keeping in mind that there are no rules or regulations for pulling together market value financial statements, you can try whatever you want. However, it is clear that the initial route will involve disclosures that supplement the GAAP financial statements.

If we were doing it, we would start with a supplemental balance sheet that would put market values on everything we own, including assets that are not recognized under GAAP, such as research and development, intellectual capital, and other soft assets related to marketing and personnel. It seems to us that it would be important to carefully identify the softer assets in the balance sheet so that users can more easily do a "with and without" analysis. The softest assets probably wouldn't make it onto our balance sheet, nor would any other asset that did not have a reliably estimated market value.[11] We would also report market values for all liabilities, probably based on what other firms are having to pay to get out from under similar debts. As to stockholders' equity, it would merely be the difference between the total values of the assets and liabilities.

Our supplemental market value income statement would look pretty much the same, but would present substantially different numbers for many items. Under GAAP, several items (such as sales and current expenses) are already reported at the market value received or sacrificed. An exception for sales would be the realized portions of any deferred revenues, which we would pass through the income statement at their market value, not their book value. Another difference in the revenue category would be interest income, which we would measure as the change in the market value of the receivable instead of the result of multiplying the GAAP book value by the original historical rate. Another major innovation would be identifying the income from adding value to manufactured inventory; its amount would equal the difference between the wholesale value of all finished goods and the cost of the inputs consumed in producing them. This income would be reported even if the inventory had not been sold; we're really trying to liberate ourselves from the realization mind-set.

Among the expenses, we would have major differences for the cost of goods sold and depreciation expense. In fact, we would report the value of goods sold instead of the cost. (This practice is consistent with reporting income equal to the value added to the goods during production.) We would actually measure depreciation instead of calculating the amount. The amount of depreciation (or appreciation) would equal the change in the plant assets' market values over the year, taking into consideration additions and disposals. Intangibles would not be amortized; instead, the income statement would likewise report their change in value as a deduction from or increase in earnings.

Our expenses would include increases or decreases to reflect changes in the value of our liability to sell shares at a fixed price under compensatory options granted to employees (or anyone else). If the options' value increased, we would report an expense; if the value went down, we would report a negative expense.

We would put all unrealized holding gains and losses on the income statement, carefully described, and limited in amount to the changes in value that actually occurred during the year. The only realized gains and losses reported on the income statement would equal the change in the asset or liability value between the preceding balance sheet date and the disposal date.

With regard to income taxes, we would report an expense equal to the amount paid (or currently payable) and merely disclose the possible effect on future taxes of events that happened this year. We are troubled by the deferred tax liability because it has no readily determined market value, in which case we have to think it might not really exist.

Others, of course, could do any of these things differently if they think their way is more useful to the users than what we would do.

There would be a thousand specific issues to resolve, and we're not going to go into them here. Suffice it to say that each question would be resolved under QFR in accordance with the objective of providing full and complete reporting to reduce uncertainty for financial statement users. If you are thinking that this kind of freedom is a ready-made dream for letting you choose policies that make you look good, then either stop thinking that way or stop calling yourself a QFR manager. Remember, the goal is to help users understand what happened in the past and what exists today so that they can do their job of predicting what's going to happen in the future. The supplemental market value statements are neither the time nor the place for managers to perform financial facelifts.

ONE MORE TIME, THE USERS SPEAK

Before closing out this chapter, we want to put in one more quote from the AIMR on making the move to market values:

> AIMR members have different views on market values. Virtually all favor disclosure of market values, at least for financial instruments. No one seems to believe that disclosure alone could be detrimental to analysts' interests, and all but a few believe that disclosure would be beneficial. Most are opposed to *replacing* historic cost with market values, but a significant minority favors such a move. Most oppose extending mark-to-market accounting from financial assets to real assets, although a small number does not. Almost all agree that if mark-to-market accounting were to be mandated, it should be applied with equanimity to both the left-hand side and the right-hand side of the balance sheet. All agree that it is only specific identifiable assets and liabilities that should be marked to market; determination of the market values of entire firms is the business of financial analysis, not financial reporting. (pp. 38–39)

To return to our superficial analogy, this comment reminds us that some fast food customers will always prefer hamburgers to cheeseburgers, and some will always prefer cheeseburgers to hamburgers. In the same way, some financial analysts prefer to have the information provided under the status quo while others want something entirely different that they believe addresses their needs more usefully. Supplemental reporting of market values is a way to deal with this spectrum of demands, and it is generally accepted and encouraged under SFAS 89. Like the FASB, we recommend it, but we have no power to make it mandatory, and we harbor no desire to have that power.

How will users feel if they get this information? Here are some words from Peter Knutson, the lead writer of the AIMR monograph, taken from his article called "Criteria Employed by the AIMR Financial

Accounting Policy Committee in Evaluating Financial Accounting Standards," published in the June 1998 issue of *Accounting Horizons:*

> We lament the disappearance of FAS No. 33, *Financial Reporting and Changing Prices,* that provided data which many of us found informative and useful despite their approximation.

Here is a clear statement of what sophisticated analysts demand. We think it makes great sense to ensure that it is supplied, even if that means getting outside the very comfortable confines of GAAP. The choice is yours. What are you going to do?

NOTES

1. As strange as it might seem, this objective was actually controversial, being supported by only 37 percent of the comment letters sent to the board in response to the exposure draft. From today's perspective, this purpose seems nothing short of obvious. At the time, however, it was an unsettling new test that was going to be applied to proposals for replacing old practices with new ones. Most accountants were uncomfortable with this switch to a focus on the demand for information instead of its supply; for that matter, many still are.

2. Paul Miller had the good fortune to be a member of the FASB staff assigned to this project from 1982 through 1983; in that capacity, he was able to see nearly everything that happened, including a great deal that was out of the public's eye.

3. The same analysis also applies for liabilities; after all, every payable is someone else's receivable.

4. The estimated intrinsic value of a firm is the present value of its expected future cash flows discounted at the market rate for cash flows subject to the risk associated with the firm. Publishing reliable market values of assets and liabilities will reduce the discount rate (by reducing the risk) and increase the expected amount of the cash flows (by increasing the estimated inflows). The result is a double-whammy increase in the estimated intrinsic value. This increased estimate will then encourage the capital markets to push the firm's equilibrium market value to a higher level.

5. In response to objections that these databases are not readily available, we project that a shift to QFR will greatly boost the demand for them and increase the value of the service. Sooner, rather than later, that demand will be met by increased supply.

6. Note that this illogic also exists under the income tax law when a taxpayer computes a capital gain or loss as the difference between the sales proceeds measured in today's dollars and the asset's original cost in the more valuable dollars that existed at the purchase date. Despite the blatant inequity, Congress will never be strongly motivated to change this policy because

recognizing the effects of inflation would shrink the taxable amount of the gains, even to the point of revealing that they are actually losses.

7. A footnote in Chapter 8 described Copernicus and his paradigm-shattering book that proposed that the earth orbits the sun, not the other way around. Despite this visionary idea, Copernicus still held onto the old paradigm by believing the heavenly bodies are attached to crystal spheres and yet smaller spheres (called *epicycles*). Paradigm shifts are hard to go through, even for those who initiate them.

8. Managers are reporting these items in comprehensive income only because they were forced to when the FASB issued SFAS 130 in response to requests by users (especially the AIMR), and despite many preparers' unwillingness to present the information anywhere.

9. As an example of the stultifying twists and turns of GAAP, unrealized gains and losses on security investments in trading portfolios are reported on the income statement, while those related to investments in the available for sale and held to maturity portfolios are not.

10. We ask your forbearance in not reminding us of the old adage that states, "Those who can, do; those who can't, teach." Basically, we want to live out the QFR ideal of letting managers and accountants find their own ways to achieve quality without being slaves to what someone else has told them to do.

11. We're not as sure as Baruch Lev (see Chapter 8) about what we would do with goodwill because it is so intangible that it makes us uncomfortable when we look at it with the traditional mind-set of information suppliers. What really matters, of course, is what the financial statement users want to know about goodwill, not what we think ought to be reported, not what managers want to report, and certainly not what auditors are willing to audit. In Chapter 7, we quoted the AIMR committee's request that managers simply write off goodwill at the acquisition date. We wouldn't mind if that treatment were to be widely used.

CHAPTER 16

How to Do QFR—Part I

From the old days continuing on down to the present, hardly any kind of literature has sold as well as the "how to" line. There are magazines like *Popular Mechanics*, a gazillion do it yourself books, everything for dummies guides, countless websites, and numerous cable shows, all covering how to do everything from growing tomatoes without soil to building a birdhouse to making a car you can fly to work. Being aware of this phenomenon, we have been feeling a building pressure to become more concrete as we have proceeded through the first 15 chapters explaining concepts and arguing for the advantages of moving to the Quality Financial Reporting paradigm.

Therefore, in this chapter and the next, we are ready to segue from our theoretical discussions to a series of short how-to sections in which we share with you our basic ideas on bringing QFR concepts to bear on specific areas in the financial statements.[1] In this chapter we will discuss cost accounting; inventory flows; leases; property, plant, and equipment; intangible assets; business combinations; and receivables and payables. As we look at each topic, we present a brief background, describe how you can report about it under the traditional minimum approach to implementing GAAP, how you can comply with GAAP to produce enhanced financial statements, and how to provide supplemental disclosures that will get you closer to QFR results.

One last reminder before going through this list: Quality Financial Reporting is an attitude that leads to more productive communication. Those two things go together—you can't have the right attitude but fail to communicate openly and completely, and you can't communicate openly and completely if you don't have the right attitude. Therefore, just going through the motions and trying to implement the following how-to points will not make you a QFR manager.

COST ACCOUNTING

As our point of view has evolved, we (like Professors Tom Johnson and Bob Kaplan, authors of *Relevance Lost*, published in 1987 by the Harvard Business School) have concluded that cost accounting seldom if ever delivers the information that people expect it to provide. Most of its short-comings arise from its dependence on systematic allocations of overhead, usually on the basis of predictions or assumptions instead of direct observations. The result is the sum of average historical cost measures of the inputs, an amount that is seldom useful for anything. Another major flaw is its failure to acknowledge that the production process adds value to the products as they move through it. As a result, the GAAP balance sheet measure of the unsold inventory grossly understates its value while the GAAP income statement grossly overstates the accomplishments of sales efforts exerted in the reporting period. In particular, the income statement fails to recognize the value-added income until the sale occurs, thus understating the income earned from production and overstating the income from marketing. We attribute this ultracautious approach to the supply-based attitude of auditors who don't want to risk reporting income until the last possible minute. As always, they have ignored the demand for useful information, with the ultimate consequence that users are making decisions in an atmosphere of uncertainty that eventually leads to higher capital costs and lower stock prices.

Traditional GAAP

Under traditional GAAP practices, managers use various cost drivers to assign indirect costs to products and activities by pools. Activity-Based Costing expands the number of pools and makes driver selection more logical. However, the process is still cost allocation, not market valuation. Therefore, for their stockholders' sake, we hope managers don't use the GAAP information for managing their production lines or their inventories. These *average* numbers are merely the consequence of a set of highly structured allocation procedures and cannot be useful for internal or external decisions involving assessments of future cash flows. Nonetheless, you can get by if you do these things because you will be in perfect compliance with GAAP.

Enhanced GAAP

Is there anything management can do to enhance its presentation of cost accounting information about its inventories? As near as we can tell, not much within the GAAP financial statements themselves. Any further refinement of cost accounting will only produce a different set of allocated costs, and the problem will remain intact. The main thing is that management must not believe the numbers and must not expect users to do so either.

Supplemental Disclosures

We do believe that managers can supplement the GAAP financial statements with a great deal of additional information about their production processes. The most obvious is to describe the wholesale value of the in-process and finished goods inventories; they can also project their eventual selling prices, all with appropriate caveats to indicate that any future cash inflows depend on actually selling the items.

INVENTORY FLOWS

Perhaps no aspect of modern business practice has been as scrutinized and reformed over the last couple of decades as inventory management. Besides all their efforts to improve quality and extend product lines, most managers have figured out that inventory is capital that needs to be deployed efficiently and sparingly. Thus, a lot of successful attention has been given to managing its content, size, and location, especially with the expanded application of Just-in-Time techniques. Despite all this attention, GAAP are largely unchanged from the early post–World War II era. Furthermore, most people don't realize how much these accounting practices are still dominated by income tax considerations rather than the desire to get useful information to the capital markets. As we described in Chapters 5 and 12, GAAP for inventory flows still force management to live with the dilemma of looking bad for doing what is good for the stockholders or looking good while doing what is bad for the stockholders. The main victim in this situation is the truth, with the ultimate consequence that capital costs are higher than they ought to be.

Traditional GAAP

To produce minimum GAAP financial statements, you should just pick an assumed flow and apply it. If you use LIFO, you'll postpone some income taxes almost indefinitely but show a lower reported margin and net income. If you use FIFO, your income statement looks better, but you're paying out more of the stockholders' money to the IRS than you need to. Under traditional GAAP, you'll just pick the one that you (the supplier of the information) like best, use it, and hope that the information consumers like it too.

Enhanced GAAP

As we understand it, most managers who choose LIFO start with their FIFO numbers and convert them to LIFO by using dollar value LIFO techniques. As a result, they have both the FIFO and LIFO results on hand. It makes sense for them to openly share this information with the financial statement users so that they don't have to guess. The simplest way to make that revelation involves presenting the FIFO number on the balance sheet less a LIFO allowance (traditionally but inaccurately called a *LIFO reserve*). If you're still using FIFO without converting to LIFO, get someone to run the numbers on how much extra tax you're paying out that you shouldn't.

We have also looked into an approach called LIFO/FIFO that essentially uses LIFO to measure the cost of goods sold and the gross margin on the income statement while putting the FIFO number on the balance sheet as an approximation of the inventory's current replacement cost.[2] The difference between the two measures of the ending inventory is the unrecognized but fully realized holding gain. By omitting this gain from the tax return, management avoids paying some income tax. Unfortunately, omitting it from the GAAP income statement makes that report incomplete and otherwise inadequate for fully informing the capital markets about what's going on.

The challenge in improving inventory accounting is learning to operate within the tight control of the IRS over management's discretion. We find this bottleneck to be anachronistic because there are so many other situations in which the IRS and financial reporting regulators tolerate significant differences between tax and GAAP accounting. For what it's worth, we think the time is right to challenge the 60 plus-year-old LIFO conformity rule because it is contrary to the public policy goal of having fully informed capital markets.

Supplemental Disclosures

Apart from that call for a political campaign, we encourage managers to begin moving closer to QFR by providing all sorts of additional disclosures about the inventory, like those described in the prior section. A key point is the presentation of the wholesale and retail values of the inventory, assuming that it can be sold.

A recurring theme in all the topics in these two chapters concerns how to present information in a set of supplemental market value financial statements like those sketched out in Chapter 15. In this case, the market value income statement can show a deduction for the value of goods sold instead of the cost of goods sold, thereby putting into the reported income a measure of the margin earned from marketing the finished goods separate from the margin earned by producing them. Thus, there would be another line item showing the value added during the manufacturing process to reveal how much of the total profit came from there. Doing this will also associate the profit components with the time period in which the related value-adding activities actually occurred.

The market value balance sheet would obviously report the market value of the ending inventory. Other schedules could relate how the various measures of the inventory increased or decreased during the year, perhaps like this:

	Cost	Wholesale	Retail
Beginning inventory	$5,000	$8,000	$12,000
Purchases	20,000	22,000	33,000
Acquired through merger	7,000	7,000	13,000
Newly finished goods	23,000	40,000	50,000
Goods sold	(40,000)	(58,000)	(85,000)
Ending inventory	$15,000	$19,000	$23,000

INVESTMENTS

We have already written more than a little about accounting for investments in marketable securities, perhaps even more than the subject deserves because of the relatively low amounts involved in most situations. However, the topic is important because some companies—and entire industries—have very sizable investments. It is also significant because this situation involves few issues concerning the reliability of market value measures.

The background history is that GAAP started with cost, moved formally to lower-of-cost-or-market with SFAS 12 in the 1970s, and then evolved to the hodgepodge of methods now in place under SFAS 115. According to this standard, securities are classified and information is reported as shown in Table 16-1. The portfolio classification of an investment depends on whether management intends to sell it soon (trading), sell it later (available for sale), or hold it until it matures (hold to maturity).

Traditional GAAP

To attain minimum compliance with GAAP, you should classify your investments according to your goals of keeping useful information about real volatility out of your income statement. Thus, you should try to put every investment you own in the available for sale or held to maturity categories. When it comes time to manage reported earnings, you should decide which investments to sell from these two portfolios in order to

TABLE 16-1

SFAS 115 Methods of Classifying and Reporting Investment in Securities

Portfolio	Balance Sheet	Unrealized Gains/ Losses	Realized Gain/ Losses
Trading	Market value	Annual change in value reported on the income statement	Proceeds minus previous market value
Available for sale	Market value	Accumulated change in value since acquisition reported in the equity section of the balance sheet	Proceeds minus original cost
Held to maturity (debt only)	Cost ± amortization	None	Proceeds minus amortized book value

report realized gains or losses as you need. Never mind the unclear signals you send—you will be lookin' good!

Enhanced GAAP

To provide more information about what is happening, you can classify all your security holdings as trading and just let the financial statements reflect the underlying volatility you created by deciding to assume the risks inherent in investing.[3] When it comes time to decide to hold or sell, your decision will not affect the amount of reported income because the holding gains and losses will be reported on your income statement in either case. This treatment comes much closer to what the users demand than the smoothed results that traditional GAAP reporting supplies. This improved information will reduce the risk faced by your own stockholders. You will also make better investment decisions.

Supplemental Disclosures

Because enhanced compliance with GAAP is market value accounting, we don't think that there is much else you would need to disclose. In particular, the market value balance sheet and income statement would contain the same information as the enhanced GAAP financial statements. If there is sufficient activity, you could provide a summary like this one:

Beginning investments	$20,000,000
Acquisitions	65,000,000
Change in market value	(13,000,000)
Proceeds from disposal	(37,000,000)
Ending investments	$35,000,000

LEASES

Although there may be some financial or operating advantages to leasing property instead of owning it, there is little doubt that the majority of business leases are created to allow the lessee to evade the spirit of SFAS 13 and not put an asset and liability on the lessee's balance sheet, even though it controls the property and is in debt to the lessor. This off-balance-sheet financing also reduces the amount of interest expense that the lessee reports on the income statement, thereby producing misleading information for assessing the company's capacity for servicing its existing and future debt. Even if a management enters into off-balance-sheet leases without intending to escape the constraints of GAAP, the result is exactly the same—financial statement users are not fully informed in the most direct manner and end up either making uninformed decisions or spending money to figure out what is really going on. The eventual outcome is a higher cost of capital for the lessee, just the opposite of what its managers are trying to trick out of the capital markets.

Traditional GAAP

If all managers want to do is manage their financial image, they should engage their auditing firm to work with their leasing company to ensure that their lease agreements escape the four SFAS 13 criteria and thus qualify as operating leases. This outcome will increase the apparent return on assets by lowering the reported investment in assets and will decrease the apparent debt-to-equity ratio by leaving the lease liability off the balance sheet. (Mind you, the debt still exists, it just isn't reported.) To sustain this practice, the management must believe that the capital markets will either (1) not discover the ruse and be deceived into bidding up the stock price or (2) discover the ruse and bid stock prices up to reward management for its clever deception. We also think the problem is even worse because managers who are inclined to engage in this behavior probably won't mind spending more of the stockholders' money to pay the lessor a higher effective interest rate to avoid reporting the liability.

Enhanced GAAP

In contrast, we know that QFR managers will understand that some leases offer real economic advantages and enter into them to harvest those benefits. They will not manipulate their lease agreements to produce misleading financial statements, knowing that the capital markets will both penetrate the fog and discount their stock because of the lack of trustworthiness, the lack of useful information, and the fact that the financing cost of these leases is higher than other debt. Any footnote disclosures of operating leases will be complete in explaining why they are being used and in describing their terms.

Supplemental Disclosures

Like most of GAAP, SFAS 13 also misses the boat on providing useful information by not requiring the lessee's balance sheet to reveal the market values of the leased assets and the lease liabilities. Thus, managers in pursuit of QFR will put these items on their market value balance sheet at amounts that describe what they're worth on the reporting date, not just their depreciated and amortized book values. In addition, the market value income statement will reveal the market based depreciation cost and the interest expense based on real conditions, not historical ones.

We also suggest that any material leases classified as operating in the GAAP financial statements should be capitalized in the market value balance sheet. As mentioned in Chapter 12, the FASB and other countries' standard setters have suggested in research reports that all leases should be capitalized if the GAAP financial statements are to present useful information. We would go beyond this idea to report current market values of the leased assets and the lease liabilities.

PROPERTY, PLANT, AND EQUIPMENT

We have discussed accounting for property, plant, and equipment (PP&E) at great length in various places in previous chapters. The accepted treatment qualifies for all three variants of GAAP: PEAP (politically expedient accounting principles), WYWAP (whatever you want accounting principles), and POOP (pitifully old and obsolete principles). Despite the huge amounts invested in property, plant, and equipment, these assets continue to be reported on the balance sheet at their book values (original cost less accumulated depreciation) and depreciation continues to be measured by allocating the original cost over a predicted (and thus unverifiable) useful life. Perhaps you remember that the AIMR referred to SFAS 33 disclosures as a godsend. Included among these disclosures was the estimated market value of PP&E assets. Thus, there is a major disconnect between what GAAP reporting supplies to users and what they demand.

Traditional GAAP

Those managers who are content to keep reporting under the status quo can just keep buying these assets and capitalizing all possible related expenditures to keep reported expenses down. When it comes to depreciation, they should continue making their decisions on the basis of what makes them look good, generally by taking less annual depreciation rather than more. On the other hand, if they want, they can accelerate the depreciation, take a bath in the short run, and then look golden in the future as expenses fall and reported net income climbs higher and higher. Of course, to get to the point of actually believing that all this works to produce higher stock prices, the managers need to hold onto the fantasy that the capital markets are totally clueless about the limitations of GAAP and management's inclination to be manipulative.

Enhanced GAAP

To produce enhanced financial statements, managers can begin by at least ensuring that the initial recorded cost of assets equals a number relatively close to their market value on the purchase date. To reach this goal, they will need to expense some initial costs (like sales taxes) that don't increase the market value. Next, they should design and implement straightforward depreciation schedules, with careful warnings to financial statement users that the usefulness of the reported earnings numbers depends on the usefulness of the depreciation amounts. When the FASB issued SFAS 89 to rescind the SFAS 33 experiment, it also recommended that managers continue to report market value information and try new ways to generate and present it. Thus, managers can go well beyond the limits of current common practice and remain in compliance with GAAP.

Supplemental Disclosures

We think financial statement users would find a great deal of usefulness in having the results of sensitivity analyses generated by management that show amounts of depreciation that would be recognized under differing assumed useful lives or different methods. Management is in a far superior position to produce this information than users who really can't know enough to produce their own. Even more useful would be information about the market values of these assets that could be inserted on the supplemental market value balance sheet. This disclosure might even report a range of values around a mean or median so that the users will have a better idea of how much confidence to place in the disclosed numbers. And, as we have mentioned, we believe that the really useful description of depreciation expense is the change in the market value of the productive assets. In addition, we believe that users would find it useful to have reconciliations of the beginning and ending reported balances of the PP&E accounts, like the one described in Chapter 5.

In summary, pursuing QFR would lead to reporting a great deal more information about these large collections of assets than is currently presented under GAAP.

INTANGIBLE ASSETS

Much effort has been exerted by a lot of people trying to deal with the issues related to intangible assets, and much more will surely be accomplished in the future. Some of the most interesting work is being pursued by Professor Baruch Lev (see Chapter 8). The issues have been complex because of the perceived conflicting interests between the various financial reporting participants; they have also been complicated because of the many different situations. Nonetheless, we have observed that the difficulty has been greatly magnified by the lack of appreciation for the capital markets' ability to see through the smoke-and-mirror methods of making something unreal look real, or the forced reporting of nothing when something valuable clearly exists.

There are no easy solutions, in other words, and far be it from us to suggest that there are only a few simple steps to reporting useful information about intangibles. However, we are certain that adopting the QFR paradigm will help everyone move closer to providing more useful information than is now achieved under GAAP.

Traditional GAAP

Even though many managements are now practicing within the byzantine constraints of GAAP, surely no two treat their intangibles the same way. It is also true that not one of them treats all of its own intangibles the same way. The costs of some intangibles are capitalized and the costs of others are expensed. The sum of the capitalized costs surely doesn't equate to the value of the assets, and the past practice of amortization certainly created an even more mixed-up situation. Take research and development, for example. Under SFAS 2, these costs must be expensed right away, but under SFAS 86, some development costs associated with software are to be capitalized. Capitalization is required for costs incurred obtaining or defending a patent, although no one should equate that accumulated cost to the real value of the patent. Goodwill appears on the balance sheet when a business combination is accounted for as a purchase, but not as a pooling. Self-generated research and development assets and goodwill are not recognized, but if you buy someone else's research and development assets and goodwill, you do record an intangible. Don't ever think about capitalizing training, recruiting, or marketing costs, or recognizing intellectual capital and brand names under GAAP. Never mind that your company uses them to produce cash flows well in excess of what would be expected in light of your recognized tangible assets. Clearly, auditors rule. And, speaking of rules, the FASB issued SFAS 142 in 2001 that eliminates amortizing many intangibles and calls for submitting them to an impairment test. Of course, if the value increases, you won't get to report it. Auditors still rule.

Join us (and a great many others) if you think traditional GAAP treatments of intangibles are a mess.

Enhanced GAAP

The nature of intangibles is that information about them tends to be relevant but not very reliable, even in terms of reliability for financial statement users. In general, that condition suggests it is almost certain that your enhanced GAAP financial statements will be more useful if you just write off most intangibles and provide abundant disclosures to describe what you have done with the costs and why. We think this strategy treats capital market participants with great respect; it will also avoid the possibility of embarrassing yourself getting caught trying to fool them with meaningless accounting policy choices that put fluff in the financial statements.

Supplemental Disclosures

As we just said, the most likely route to producing QFR information lies in providing a great many supplemental disclosures that help users understand all recognized and unrecognized intangibles. You should use the disclosures to describe the origins of all your intangibles and what you think they're worth in terms of what they can contribute to future cash flows. If they can be separated from the firm, like patents or copyrights, describe that fact and their estimated market value. If they are wrapped up in the firm and cannot be sold separately, like intellectual capital and goodwill, say so. When valuing intangibles, don't try to put a single precise number in the schedules but describe a distribution of possible values (no one would trust the single number anyway). To the extent possible, get your auditors involved to lend credibility to these claims, but understand that they are not going to stick their necks out very far on these valuations. Some credibility is better than none, however.

Don't be reticent to describe what's going on, and don't be ultraconservative in your valuations. Just present what you consider to be facts and let the markets do their own analyses. If you want them to trust you, you will need to reciprocate.

BUSINESS COMBINATIONS

We have said a lot already about combinations, simply because existing practices, even the new ones, are so insufficient. In fact, combinations have been a playground for a great many managers with impaired reasoning abilities. In some cases, their mental mistakes come from thinking a particular merger will actually be worthwhile despite the clashing corporate cultures and high prices paid to make the acquisitions. Other bonehead decisions involve picking pooling of interests as the accounting policy to use to describe the merger and then structuring the transaction to permit that treatment when it was a bad way to do the deal. Until the summer of 2001, poolings enjoyed great popularity because they allowed management to (1) hide the true cost of the acquisition, (2) bring the acquired company's previous earnings straight onto the combined income statement, and (3) report (but not achieve) higher earnings in the future because of the lack of goodwill amortization on the combined income statement. As we have described, these thought processes are appallingly simplistic and would be laughable if they weren't so common in so many high-level corporate suites.

However, there are huge problems even in the FASB's new standard (SFAS 141) that requires managers to use the purchase method. In a nutshell, this approach records the acquired company's assets and liabilities at their market values and simply adds them to the book values of the acquiring company's assets and liabilities on the combined balance sheet. As the AIMR financial analysts are quoted in Chapter 7, "What a mélange!"

If the truth is to be usefully described, we think managers will get there only by restating all assets and liabilities to their market values, both before and after the acquisition takes place. In fact, under full market value accounting, dealing with combinations is only a matter of some fact gathering during the due diligence process because most of the time-honored accounting issues are virtually eliminated.

Traditional GAAP

If you want to be traditional, just pretend that it's good for you and your stockholders if you put out financial statements that don't say anything very close to the truth. The fact that you can report higher earnings and fewer assets can only be good because that means (you wish) that your stock prices will go higher and higher. (Not on your life, but don't let that hard fact stop you from enjoying your fantasy.)

Enhanced GAAP

If you acknowledge that GAAP are inadequate for producing useful information about combinations, then you will stop playing games to manage the financial statements. Instead, you will find a higher payoff in spending your efforts and time trying to manage the melding of two disparate cultures. Don't try any lame tricks with intangibles or the recorded values of the stock you issue to bring the other company into your fold. Just tell the truth in all that you do in faith that the markets will uncover it one way or the other, so they might as well hear it from you. We're confident that the markets will appreciate your candor and reward you with higher prices. Play games, though, and your goose is cooked.

Supplemental Disclosures

It seems to us that the supplemental market value balance sheet is ready made for usefully describing acquisitions of new companies. Don't just put the numbers together, though, and assume that these statements are self-explanatory. Show some appreciation for the hard work your staff went through by providing clear and thorough disclosures about the transaction in terms of its cost, the value received, and why the merger was a good idea. Don't do anything to leave the capital markets guessing because we all know that doing so brings about lower stock prices and a higher cost of capital. There is also no valid point in trying to look better off than you really are.

RECEIVABLES AND PAYABLES

It may be hard for some to accept the fact that GAAP for receivables and payables are deficient. After all, there haven't been any significant changes in those principles for three decades (APBO 21 was issued in 1971 and did little or nothing to deal with trade receivables and payables). Perhaps it's just us, then, but we find substantial shortcomings here as well. We trace most of them to a now vestigial link between GAAP and internal control issues. As we see it, the financial statement representation of these collective assets and liabilities is not much more than showing the balance of the subsidiary ledgers you use for managing your billing and cash disbursement processes. Apart from reducing the gross receivables for estimated uncollectible amounts, accountants consider the most useful information about them to be the sum of the amounts to be collected or paid.[4]

APBO 21 recommends excluding ordinary receivables and payables from discounting for time value from its scope in order to save some preparers' effort back in the Paleolithic days of computerized accounting systems. This labor-saving exclusion now seems quaint in light of today's technology and will look even more old-fashioned when the next generation of computers hits in another 18 months or so. (Of course, if you just bought a new machine, the next generation is only a few weeks away.)

Apart from that point, this particular component of GAAP does not put useful information in the financial statements because its application of present values to longer-term notes requires the original discount rate to be used until maturity, regardless of what happens to the market rate in the meantime. The FASB came back a couple of times to try to settle some resulting measurement issues with regard to troubled debt situations. The board missed badly when it issued SFAS 15 in 1977 because it basically ignored market rates. Then the FASB came back 16 years and 99 standards later on a long-delayed repair mission in SFAS 114; however, this effort was also botched because the creditor is allowed to minimize its reported losses by continuing to use the original market interest rate long after the troubled note is found to be definitely less marketable. We chalk this impoverished accounting up to poor finance education all the way around, from the board to the auditors and especially to the bank accountants, who keep insisting that principal cash flows are different from interest cash flows. Since they all spend the same way, we insist that cash flows are cash flows.

Still another set of unresolved issues involves hybrid securities, especially convertible debts and, by extension, convertible receivables. At present, GAAP reporting has the issuer account for them as if they are no different from regular payables and receivables. Surely no one thinks that financial analysts consider them to be the same, even though the politicized regulatory system hasn't been able to escape its supply-based paradigm or deviate from the easy route of reporting them as if they are nonconvertibles.

Traditional GAAP

To achieve minimum compliance with GAAP, you should just keep doing what you have been doing, which is ignoring market value changes in receivables and payables. Another part of the tradition is to play games with the allowance for uncollectible accounts, also called the *loan loss reserve* in the banking industry. By increasing or decreasing the allowance, year-to-year volatility can be smoothed out of the annual reports, even though the real story is something different. Another game that some have played, and that the FASB facilitated by issuing SFAS 76, is the in-substance defeasance that leads management to actually pay out large amounts of the stockholders' money as fees to a third-party trustee for the sole purpose of looking better in the financial statements.

Enhanced GAAP

The GAAP statements can be enhanced by providing more information about the populations of receivables and payables, specifically through schedules showing their age and the distribution of anticipated collection and payment dates. This information will help overcome the simplistic assumption that all receivables and payables due within a year are the same, and that all amounts due after one year are the same. We also interpret the language in APBO 21 as permitting managers to apply discounting to trade receivables and payables. This practice will improve the balance sheet description of the assets and liabilities while augmenting the quality of the information on the income statement about sales, expenses, and interest. When it comes to detail, we think that much more is needed to produce quality.

With regard to convertible debt, we think that more information will flow to the capital markets if the total is divided into its debt and equity portions on the enhanced GAAP balance sheet, perhaps like this:

```
Convertible bonds payable:
    Debt portion . . . . . . . . . . . . . . . . . . . . . . . . . . . . . . . . . . . . . . . . . $23,150,000
    Equity portion . . . . . . . . . . . . . . . . . . . . . . . . . . . . . . . . . . . . . . . .     1,850,000
        Total  . . . . . . . . . . . . . . . . . . . . . . . . . . . . . . . . . . . . . . . . . . . . . $25,000,000
```

There is no valid reason to force the capital markets to make their own estimates of these amounts just because the old APB did not have the political power to force managers to openly declare what everyone knew was true.[5]

Supplemental Disclosures

Receivables and payables clearly have a market value that is accessible to management through sales, assignments, factoring, and other arrangements. These values shift when economic conditions evolve and are reflected in interest rate changes. Thus, we believe that you can move closer to QFR by putting these items on your supplemental market value balance sheet at amounts that represent what they are worth, with suitable descriptions of their bell-shaped curves and their sensitivity to different assumptions.

Interest income and expense should be remeasured for the market value income statement to represent current conditions instead of continuing the blindfolded GAAP approach of applying the original outdated interest rate to the meaningless book value. We realize that this more complete treatment could make the reported interest volatile from year to year, but we keep thinking that useful information will follow if the reported amount behaves like the real economic amount. We are confident that sophisticated financial analysts apply concepts based on market values instead of the traditional assumption that market values don't change and don't matter. If so, it makes sense to help them produce the numbers they use.

If you are involved in a troubled debt situation from either side, don't stop your reporting effort when you comply with the official compromised rules. There is no need for you to stay at the lowest common denominator level; besides, the markets will penalize you for stopping short of telling the whole truth. Instead, just lay out the facts for everyone to see. They are guessing anyway, so you might as well give it to them straight and save them the effort while reducing their risk associated with their inability to get the facts. As we've said before, this kind of candor will knock your cost of capital down because it will increase the users' ability to rely on your numbers and build their trust while decreasing their uncertainty.

If you have issued convertible bonds, go ahead and distinguish between the debt and equity portions and mark them to their market values. It isn't hard, and you can certainly do it more easily and reliably than the financial statement users can.

NOTES

1. Because of the many revelations concerning accounting irregularities and other frauds associated with Enron, we added Chapter 19 to show how its managers created the perfect example of how *not* to do QFR.

2. To our knowledge, this method was first described by Mike Bohan and Steve Rubin in the September 1986 *Journal of Accountancy*. Apart from an *Accounting Today* column that we published in February 2001, we don't know of any other place it has been described.

3. One more time, here is what the AIMR committee said about smoothing: "We believe that financial analysis is best served by financial reporting that reports transactions as and when they occur. If there is smoothing to be done, it is the province of analysts to do it. If there are financial reporting anomalies that are attributable to seasonality, it is far better to report and explain them than to conceal them with undocumented smoothing." (*Financial Reporting in the 1990s and Beyond*, p. 58.)

4. We proceeded blithely through years of teaching about the allowance for uncollectible accounts receivable until one day it dawned on us that we had never taught anyone about an allowance for avoidable accounts payable. After all, shouldn't there be symmetry? More seriously, we have watched bank accountants struggle with what they call *core deposits,* which are the liabilities to depositors that will be left unpaid indefinitely. It seems to us that it would be helpful to deduct a core deposit contra-account balance from the deposit liability to show this effect, yet many have urged banks to report a debit balance among the assets as a "core deposit intangible."

5. In case there are any vestiges of doubt that the GAAP creation process is politically compromised, consider that the APB issued APBO 10 in 1966 to require separating out the equity portion. It was followed by APBO 12 in 1967, which recommended holding off on implementing APBO 10 until more process took place. Finally, APBO 14 came out in 1969, saying that accountants should not separate out the equity portion. Indecision is seldom a virtue, especially in those charged with making decisions in public.

CHAPTER 17

How to Do QFR–Part II

This chapter picks up where Chapter 16 left off. Before getting into the details, we want to state one more time that Quality Financial Reporting is an attitude, not a set of procedures. No rules can create that attitude, but the attitude can really shape what you do when you respond to the rules. If you stop when you reach the minimum requirements, you will not do enough to meet the markets' needs, and you will pay the price in higher capital costs.

This chapter covers cash flows, pensions and other benefits, stock options, earnings per share, reporting frequency, and a few miscellaneous other points. It follows the same pattern for each topic used in Chapter 16.

CASH FLOWS

In the 1980s, many managers began to transition voluntarily from the old working capital statement of changes in financial position to one based on cash. The FASB found itself in the virtually unprecedented situation of being positioned to assist a willing constituency that was asking for its help. In response, the board members set out to define a pure cash flow statement that would show the gross cash inflows and outflows, but it wasn't long until the politics took over.

The main issue involved reporting the cash provided by operations, presumably the most crucial information on the statement. Arrayed on one side were four board members who wanted to report gross operating cash inflows and outflows using what is called the *direct* method. Since this report is a statement of cash flows, they thought it would make sense to actually present cash flows on it. Aligned on the other side were three board members who preferred to think of the operating cash flow section as a supplement to the income statement and wanted to use the *indirect* method that turns net income into net cash flows by adding and deducting things that are not cash flows.

Another political factor that came into play was the testimony of several—even many—preparers who insisted that they did not know how to apply the direct method and that their existing systems were not up to the task. The fact that their thoughts on this point were even considered relevant by the board shows once again how the standard-setting process has been conducted under the influence of the supply-oriented paradigm instead of looking to the demand for information.

To shorten the story, one of the four board members who had been in favor of the direct method showed up one morning not long before the planned final vote with a changed mind. This shift caused the board to issue SFAS 95 with a half-hearted recommendation for the direct method while permitting the indirect method to be used. To make it worse, the board required managers who choose the preferred direct method to also incur the costs of providing the indirect reconciliation of net income to net cash flows. Being supply-oriented, virtually all preparers have chosen to save some preparation costs by publishing only the minimum indirect presentation, with no thought of doing what the board recommended in order to provide sophisticated users what they had asked for. They also seem oblivious to the fact that they are imposing on the users higher processing costs that are certainly greatly in excess of their own savings. The ultimate consequence is a higher cost of capital.

As to the desires of analysts, here again is what they said in the AIMR committee report (expanding on the quote in Chapter 12):

> A reasonable solution to this apparent impasse is not unattainable.
> Although the FASB has not seen fit to mandate the direct method, and neither has the IASC, both endorse it as the preferable method. Nothing other than inertia prevents progressive business enterprises that seek favor with analysts from adopting the direct method. We reiterate: not only is the direct method permitted, users of financial statements prefer it. (p. 67)

It seems that only totally oblivious suppliers would ignore this clearly articulated demand. It also seems that 99 percent of U.S. preparers are at least that oblivious.

In addition to this compromise, the FASB also acted to simplify preparing the statement in three other ways, even though users' processing costs are increased. First, interest payments are included in operating cash flows instead of financing flows. Second, interest and dividend receipts are included in operating cash flows instead of investing flows. Third, all income tax payments are included in operations, even those that arise from transactions included among the financing and investing activities. The supply-based rationalization for these requirements is that they make the indirect method easier for management to prepare.

So much for the board's ability to function in a supportive political environment. In tennis, we think SFAS 95 would be called an "unforced error."

Traditional GAAP

Minimum compliance involves presenting a brief indirect method schedule in the operating cash flows section that most managers prepare without asking whether it contains useful information.[1] If the changes in the working capital accounts on the cash flow statement don't match up with the changes indicated on two successive balance sheets, don't bother to explain why. If the users want to have the direct method, they can do it themselves.

Enhanced GAAP

The obvious place to start preparing an enhanced GAAP cash flow statement is to use the direct method. Furthermore, the presentation should clearly identify the amount of interest expense, interest and dividend income, and tax payments for operating, investing, and financing activities so that users can move them around according to their preferences.

Another enhancement would be to present the supplemental indirect reconciliation in a nontraditional reverse order that starts with operating cash flows and ends with net income. Consider this example of a typically formatted indirect method presentation:

Net income	$12,900
Plus: depreciation expense	600
Plus: increase in salaries payable	1,000
Plus: increase in accounts payable	23,000
Less: increase in inventory	(10,500)
Less: Increase in accounts receivable	(5,000)
Plus: increase in accrued revenue	6,000
Less: nonoperating gain	(15,000)
Plus: nonoperating loss	36,000
Cash from operations	$49,000

Only the most isolated and supply-centered accountant would consider the reporting task to be accomplished with this schedule.

On the other hand, consider this format for the reconciliation:

Cash from operations $49,000
Less cash inflows that did not create revenues
   Advances received from customers . . . . (6,000)
Plus outflows that did not create expenses
   Inventory expansion . . . . <u>10,500</u>
Net cash from income-producing events 32,500
Plus revenues that did not create cash
   Uncollected credit sales 5,000
Less expenses that did not use cash
   Depreciation . . . . (600)
   Accrued but unpaid salaries . . . . (1,000)
   Accrued but unpaid expenses . . . . (23,000)
Nonoperating gains and losses
   Gains 15,000
   Losses . . . . <u>(36,000)</u>
Net income . . . . <u>$12,900</u>

This format seems to us to be a lot easier to read because it does things in a more intuitive way, such as subtracting noncash expenses, adding gains, and subtracting losses. It also provides an intermediate subtotal that shows how much cash came from the regular income-producing events. We encourage our readers to take on the challenges of applying this enhanced format to their regular reconciliation to see how it turns out.

With regard to another common omission from the cash flow statement, we did some extensive research several years ago and discovered that changes in the working capital accounts shown in many published indirect reconciliations very frequently do not equal the difference between the amounts shown on two successive balance sheet dates.[2] This condition, which we have labeled *nonarticulation,* is caused by many different kinds of events (such as reclassifications, acquisitions, divestitures, refinancing, and foreign currency translation) that few if any managers choose to describe in their statements. Thus, you can enhance your GAAP financial statements by explaining these differences.

Supplemental Disclosures

Although our suggestions for producing enhanced GAAP compliance will help satisfy the unserved user demands for useful information, we think that more quality will be provided if managers go ahead and provide a new cash flow statement that doesn't implement the FASB's compromises. Specifically, the operating section would show the direct method without pollution from the cash flows for financing activities (interest expense) and

FIGURE 17-1

A Supplemental Restructured Cash Flow Statement

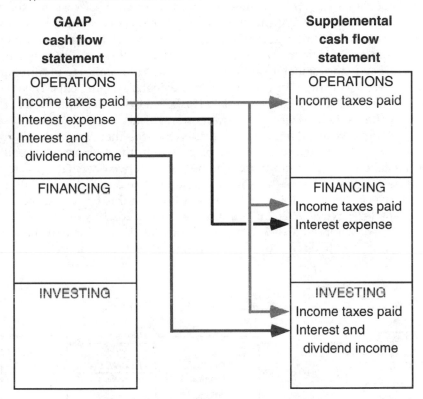

investing activities (interest and dividend income). It would also allocate the income tax payments among the cash flows for operating, financing, and investing activities according to the type of event that triggered the tax payments. Figure 17-1 describes our suggested restructuring.

You should also provide the inverted format indirect reconciliation because some people seem to demand this information. Its contents would be a bit more complex because you would need to explain the difference between the net cash flow and the market value–based net income instead of the GAAP net income.

PENSIONS AND OTHER BENEFITS

GAAP for pensions and other benefits are among the most arcane and difficult to understand of all authoritative accounting practices. There are several reasons things ended up this way. First, a defined benefit plan is economically irrational because management promises to pay an unknown amount to an unknown group of people for an unknown period of time. Thus, managers cannot know how much their promise has cost the stockholders or how much borrowing capacity they have consumed by going into debt to their employees. If the plans are irrational, there is no rational way to account for them. As if that wasn't enough, the accounting profession turned to the regulatory system (the FASB in particular) to produce an innovative way to describe these plans in the financial statements. Then the constituents came back later and asked the board to use the same system to resolve the issues involving postretirement medical plans.

In 1998, we heard Jim Leisenring, then the vice-chairman of the FASB, speculate out loud that the number of people in the country who really understand pension accounting has to be less than two dozen. It's possible that he exaggerated—we think it may be more like one dozen.[3] We don't think we can increase this number much through this book, but we can help you learn why GAAP for pensions aren't any good.

As shown in Figure 17-2, the fundamental situation is that the employer is in debt to its employees for compensation to be paid in the future

FIGURE 17-2

The Economics of Defined Benefit Pension Plans

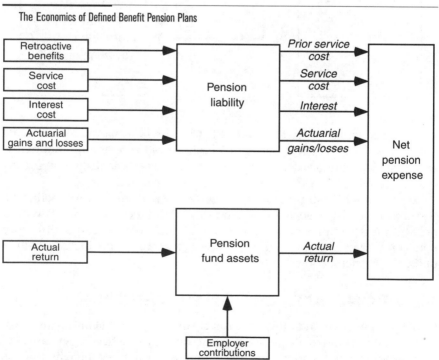

for work that has already been done; thus, the employer has a pension liability. As required by federal law, this liability is collateralized by a pension fund's assets, which can be used only to pay that debt. Thus, the employer has a de facto asset, even though legal title resides in a third-party trustee; in effect, the employer is the beneficiary of the trust because its holdings are committed solely to being used to retire the employer's pension debt.

The liability grows through two primary factors: (1) new deferred benefits earned by the employees (called *service cost*) and (2) increases in its market value as it nears maturity (usually called *interest*). The liability also changes size when the employer's managers decide retroactively to pay more benefits for prior service (including their own, to no one's surprise). Its estimated amount can also grow or decline as the actuaries modify their assumptions and predictions to reflect current conditions, including market discount rates for pension liabilities. Of course, the liability gets smaller when benefits are actually paid out.

The assets in the pension fund grow when new funds are contributed by the employer and as it earns a return. It gets smaller when benefits are paid and when the actual return is negative. The returns earned by the fund include not only interest and dividends received but also changes in the investments' market values.

Although the FASB proposed accounting for pensions to reflect these fundamental realities, the political process turned this sleek racehorse into a committee's clumsy camel. As shown in Figure 17-3, it turned out that the preparers responding to the board's proposals were deeply concerned about revealing the extensive real volatility in their financial statements. Never mind that they were borrowing long and investing short; never mind that they had exposed the stockholders to huge market risk (in both the asset and debt markets); they just didn't want to see their reported income bouncing all around. After all, some users might figure out that the company faced a lot of risk. Having a great deal of political power, and working with a board that was reeling from the conceptual framework failure, the preparers induced the FASB to make one compromise after the other. As a result, the employer's balance sheet doesn't show the asset or the liability. The income statement doesn't report what *did* happen but what the actuary *expected* to happen. In particular, the net pension expense is computed by deducting the expected return on the plan assets instead of the real return (just think what kind of results this compromise produced with the unexpected events in the stock market of 2000 and 2001).

With regard to those retroactively increased benefits for past services, SFAS 87 treats it like a kind of employee goodwill and requires managers to amortize it into pension expense, although its balance never appears on the balance sheet.[4] And, if the actuaries revalue the liability, that change doesn't

FIGURE 17-3

Accounting for Defined Benefit Pension Plans under SFAS 87 (Compromises Indicated by Shading)

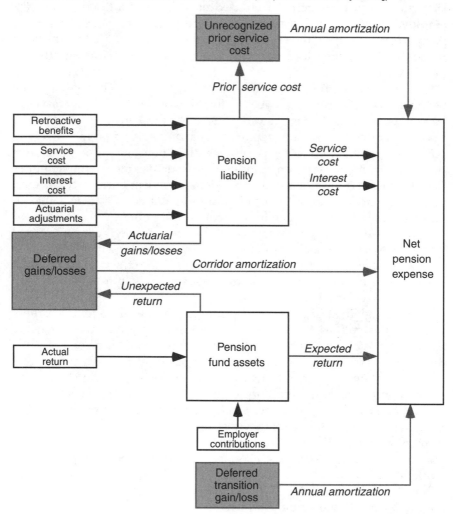

appear on the income statement either; it is deferred indefinitely and offset against those unexpected gains and losses on the pension fund assets. The board responded to worries that the total deferred gains and losses might grow too big by setting up the "corridor amortization" process to make it smaller again.[5] Keep in mind that all this truth is hidden *by design* in order to avoid telling the capital markets just exactly how much better or worse off real economic events have made the employer.

Not quite being out of the woods, the FASB came up with a smooth way to deal with the transition to SFAS 87 from its predecessor. In particular, the preparer constituency didn't think there was any point in telling anyone that most of the plans were terribly underfunded when the standard was being developed. That information was confined to the footnotes and the employers bled an extra charge into pension expense in each of the next 15 to 20 years. As we like to say, the bad news was "deferred and spread like jam on bread."

At the very least, this description of the high points of SFAS 87 should help you see why so few people really understand pension accounting.

As if accounting for pensions wasn't bad enough, the FASB imposed the same sort of convoluted treatment on postemployment medical benefits, with a few more compromises. We don't see any point in straining your brain by going any further into the details in this context. It is enough for you to know that the results are just as convoluted, bizarre, and useless as the pension numbers.

Traditional GAAP

To comply with GAAP, you should just produce the off-the-books schedules that you need, throw the arcanely calculated numbers into the financial statements and the footnotes, and hope that no one questions them. In fact, while you're at it, you might as well make the footnotes really hard to understand. Although that will increase the users' frustration, their esteem for and confidence in your managerial ability will be boosted and your stock price will head up. And if you believe this strategy will work that way, we have some shares of Enron stock we'd like to sell you.

Enhanced GAAP

The various calculations related to pensions and other benefits are set by the reporting standards, so there is very little flexibility in computing the amounts. However, there are plenty of degrees of freedom in composing the footnotes, so there is no excuse for leaving the markets uninformed or misinformed about your real situation. Some pro forma results could be really helpful, we think, especially in showing what the real expense is instead of the deferred, spread, and smoothed amount reported on the income statement.

Without going into a lot of detail, you might try formatting your footnote something like this:

Expense Item	SFAS 87	Real Events
Service cost.	$750,000	$750,000
Interest on the pension liability	240,000	240,000
Actual return on the pension assets . . . . —		(100,000)
Expected return on the pension assets	(300,000)	—
Actuarial adjustment to the liability . . . . —		325,000
New prior service cost. . . . . —		250,000
Prior service cost amortization	80,000	—
SFAS 87 transition amortization	50,000	—
Corridor amortization.	(15,000)	—
Total pension expense.	$805,000	$1,465,000

Any analysts worth their salt will be delighted to see these enhanced numbers because (1) now they don't have to look all over for them and guess when they can't find them, and (2) they can be confident that you are smart enough to know that the compromises of SFAS 87 produce totally artificial results that have virtually no connection with economic truth. They will love you for it.

Supplemental Disclosures

To go beyond GAAP, we think QFR-seeking managers will try to provide as much information about their pension and other benefit plans as they can to ensure that the markets get a handle on the real risk exposure instead of the apparent one. Sensitivity analysis will be especially helpful here.

STOCK OPTIONS

In light of all of our whining in previous chapters about the FASB's compromised standard on reporting compensatory stock options, you had to know that we would come back to it in this section.

It's clear to everyone except those in deepest denial that stock options are an expense that belongs on the income statement if it is going to provide a complete description of the company's results of operations. Despite the FASB's failure in SFAS 123, we believe that rationality will eventually prevail and lead managers to reveal this amount out in the open. We and a great many others are actually looking to the International Accounting Standards Board to provide the leadership that the FASB could not deliver in 1995.

However, we want to be sure that no one is left with the impression that everything would be fine if only managers would move the footnote information on options expense onto the income statement. In fact, we find that the measurement principles in SFAS 123 are much too simplistic to capture the full impact of issuing options as compensation. According to the standard, the employer estimates the value of the options granted in the year. Then this number is actuarially reduced to anticipate departures of employees during the vesting period. The net cost is then allocated roughly on a straight-line basis over that vesting period, with modifications for changes in the actuarial projections. Importantly, nothing is done to change the expense for subsequent changes in the value of the options while they are outstanding.

Suppose, for example, that it is estimated that the granted options have an initial market value of $10 million with a four-year vesting period. Assuming no actuarial adjustments, the expense will be reported at $2.5 million per year for each of those four years. But, if the value of the options were to subsequently increase to $50 million during the vesting period, the employer would keep putting only $2.5 million into expense each year. Or, if the value of the options declined to $1 million, the employer would continue to report $2.5 million of expense each year.

We believe that more useful information would follow from immediately recognizing an expense and a liability when the options are granted. As time passes, the liability would be marked to its market value at every financial statement date. If the value of the options increased, so would the size of the liability, and an additional expense would be reported. If the value of the options went down, the liability would shrink, and the income statement would report a negative expense to represent the fact that the eventual future sacrifice is now smaller.

Yet another flaw in SFAS 123 is its treatment of the employer's tax savings from being able to deduct the options' value at the time they're exercised. For example, suppose that employees exercise their options by paying the employer $5 million to get stock worth $25 million on the exercise date. According to tax law, the employees have to report $20 million of personal taxable income; in turn, the employer takes a $20 million deduction on its own tax return, although this compensation expense never appears on the GAAP income statement, even under the recommended FASB approach.[6] If the tax rate is 40 percent, the company saves $8 million in tax. According to the FASB's recommended treatment (and APBO 25), the employer's income statement reports tax expense (and net income) as if that $8 million savings never happened.[7] The result is significant incompleteness because the employer's reported net income never reflects its actual cash flows for taxes.

A final defect in SFAS 123 is again due to the board's willingness to elevate suppliers' convenience above users' demands for useful information. In particular, they set up a transition method that requires management to report only the expenses arising from new options issued after the standard's effective date of December 15, 1995. The employer is not required to acknowledge even a pro forma expense from the preexisting options. If, for example, some options were issued on December 15, 1995, with a 10-year life, none of that expense would ever be reported over those 10 years on the income statement or in the footnote. This compromise has the potential to grossly understate the options expense for all companies in any year during what can turn out to be a very prolonged transition period.

Traditional GAAP

If all you want to do is sneak your financial statements under the GAAP door without any extra effort, or without any concern for conveying full and complete information, or if you have no desire to establish a reputation for trustworthiness, go ahead and just do what everybody has already done (including you, in all probability) and merely put together a minimum pro forma footnote.

According to some research performed by Professors Christine Botosan and Marlene Plumlee of the University of Utah, practice in this area is even worse than they (and we) thought. Specifically, they found that the managers of over one-half of the 100 companies in their sample failed to comply in material ways with the additional disclosure requirements established in SFAS 123. The problem is compounded, of course, by the auditors' complacency in the face of this flaunting of authoritative GAAP.[8]

Enhanced GAAP

Given the obvious compromises in SFAS 123, it doesn't take the sharpest knife in the drawer to come up with ways to enhance GAAP financial statements to make them more useful for analysts and other users The obvious way is to start by putting the expense prominently in the income statement instead of hoping (futilely) that no one will notice the information in the footnote. Also, instead of grudgingly revealing the barest minimum of relevant information in the footnote, you should consider telling all that is necessary to explain the calculation and its effect on income. If you want to really go far, try providing a pro forma measure of the expense at the amount it would have if you retroactively expensed all the other options that you issued before the effective date of SFAS 123. Users will also appreciate any information you provide about the current market values of all previously issued and outstanding options.

Finally, we cannot imagine why managers choose to hide the actual tax savings they experience when options are exercised. Our own research found that the managers of less than one-third of our sample companies provided any disclosure of this amount, and many of those did not provide a clear description. Since the consequence of the tax benefit is a reduced cash outflow, and complying with SFAS 123 potentially produces a significantly smaller measure of reported or pro forma net income, we would think that even non-QFR managers would jump on this one in order to look better.

Supplemental Disclosures

As you might expect from our discussion, we think there is a huge amount of supplemental information that management could disclose. Not only are options complicated instruments with great variability among plans, their very existence is sensitive. In practical terms, managers award options to themselves, and stockholders have little if any practical way to control that process or to seek redress if it gets out of control.[9]

Of course, we suggest that the options liability should appear on the market value balance sheet and that the change in that liability should appear on the market value income statement. The effect of the income tax savings from exercised options would be usefully reported as a reduction in the tax expense for the year. The possibilities go on and on, if the goal is to fully inform the capital markets and allow them to include the effect of options in their assessment of the attractiveness of investing in the company's stock.

In case you're still undecided, you could always just emulate Warren Buffett and never issue any options to anyone for any reason at all.

EARNINGS PER SHARE

Way back in the 1960s, the U.S. stock market was going through a huge growth boom, fueled, many thought, by something called "go-go" accounting. A lot of managers were apparently conjuring trends in earnings per share (EPS) that made them look very attractive. A closer look by regulators revealed that they were, shall we say, taking some liberties in computing the earnings per share numbers that they trumpeted in press releases and occasionally on income statements. The controversy was thrown in the direction of the Accounting Principles Board, which, true to form, approached the problem by refining the way information was being supplied without considering the demand from the market.

The consequence was APBO 15 (and a lengthy interpretation) that put together all sorts of arbitrary rules and calculations. The dominant theme of the opinion is that EPS is a technical problem worthy of a technical solution. Of course, it is much more than that—EPS is a behavioral variable that managers try desperately to control in order to present a positive appearance. They also mistakenly think that it is the driver of stock prices, regardless of how it is computed. This view is a crass oversimplification because the numerator (reported net income less preferred stock dividends) is by no means uniquely determined but is subject to unlimited machinations and manipulations. Just think of the incomplete measures of expenses for cost of goods sold, depreciation, amortization, research and development, pension, and compensatory options whenever you start to believe that GAAP net income is a precisely measured statistic.

Thus, for games-playing managers, flexibility in determining EPS is a golden opportunity to look good—even really, really good—by changing the calculation without changing the underlying economic behavior that it is supposed to describe.[10]

To its credit, the FASB joined with the International Accounting Standards Committee to replace APBO 15 with SFAS 128 in 1997. However, the main goal was to simplify the calculations, not produce a more useful number. Once again, supply-based thinking overpowered demand-driven considerations.

To give you an idea of the futility of attributing any precision or credibility to the calculation, the denominator (roughly the weighted average number of outstanding shares) is modified if the company has issued stock options. If the options' exercise price is less than the stock's market value, the accountants pretend that the options were exercised, which means that they have to pretend that the company now has more outstanding shares and a lot of cash on hand. Then, they pretend that they use the make-believe cash to buy back as many of the make-believe shares as they can (at the average share price for the year). The impact on the denominator is to add the incremental make-believe shares to produce a hypothetical (and worthless) number. Other sorts of things happen with convertible preferred stock and convertible bonds as well as contingent issuance agreements.

Do we have a conclusion? As a matter of fact, we have two. When push comes to shove, we would just prefer that managers provide the raw information and let financial analysts do their own calculations. Second, we cannot imagine that there is any wisdom in having reported EPS as a factor in a management incentive plan. The consequence would be some really intense and bizarre game playing that could produce bonuses while driving stock prices down.

Traditional GAAP

To do what everyone does, you can start by messing with the net income calculation and then manipulate the number of shares to get the result you want. The game gets more complex when the target is set by someone else, such as manipulative financial analysts who are trying to get an advantage over others. You can play this game, and you can get your auditors to go along, but don't make the mistake of believing that the result means anything. For sure, don't believe it for yourself. Keep in mind that the capital markets are not easily fooled and do not easily forget.

Enhanced GAAP

Because SFAS 128 requires EPS to be reported, you don't have the option of just leaving the calculation up to the market. However, you can be sure to provide enough information to let the markets see what went into your numbers. That includes facts about the policies you applied to produce the reported net income result as well as the details of your denominator calculation.

Some sensitivity analysis will also prove to be helpful to the markets, and to yourself for that matter. One of the benefits will be that you can gain your own personal insight that this performance indicator can never be as precise as it is portrayed in the business press. Only uneducated novices would ever believe that this number could be computed to the nearest penny with any confidence or usefulness.

Supplemental Disclosures

As we suggested, we don't think we would compute an EPS result for the net income reported on our market value income statement. We would be sure to give enough information to allow the financial statement users to make their own calculation if they wanted. Other than that, we don't have anything to recommend.

REPORTING FREQUENCY

Back in 1934, the Securities and Exchange Act emerged from Congress in followup to the Securities Act of 1933. The earlier law had created a requirement for filing financial and other information with the government (the Federal Trade Commission, to be exact) before management could issue securities to the public. The 1934 Act expanded the requirements to call for quarterly and annual reports to be filed by managers of each public company. It also authorized the creation of the SEC as an independent federal agency, separate from the legislative, executive, and judicial branches.

In any case, there must have been something magical about the decision to require reporting once each quarter, because that time interval has remained in place over the ensuing years. As we stated in Chapter 14, it's time to change. Since it doesn't appear that the SEC has any inclination to do anything to increase the frequency, the initiative has to be seized in the private sector by managers who are eager to build a bridge to the capital markets through QFR.

Traditional GAAP

If you want to do the minimum, just keep on complying with the quarterly and annual reporting requirements. Furthermore, don't get your auditors involved in reviewing the quarterly information. After all, that will cost you some money and they won't do anything but make you change what you want to say. You can just wait until the fourth quarter and straighten out everything when they come in and raise their issues. Of course, there is no sense getting the reports to Washington a day early. Take your time and just get them turned in when you have to.[11]

Enhanced GAAP

One way to step up the quality level is to get your auditors involved in the quarterlies. If they are doing their job, and if you let the markets know about it, their review will help reduce uncertainty about the numbers and thus reduce the risk perceived by investors. It also seems smart to get the reports put together before the last moment. There's something about appearing to be more organized that the markets are likely to appreciate. In fact, in *Financial Reporting in the 1990s and Beyond*, the AIMR committee says on this point:

> Financial reports also should provide assurance that the organization is under control. At one extreme, this means that it conducts its affairs at least lawfully and conforms to the ethical norms of the jurisdictions and cultures in which it operates. In another sense, we seek assurance that the company is being operated in the interests of its shareholders and creditors for its stated purposes and with the goal of maximizing wealth in a responsible manner. (p. 21)

These thoughts should help dispel the myth that the only thing capital market participants care about is the numbers, especially the latest quarterly earnings. Their interest runs much deeper and includes nonfinancial characteristics.

Supplemental Disclosures

We think it would make a lot more sense to accelerate reporting of all that can be accelerated, to the point of providing monthly, weekly, or even daily information that will dispel the deep uncertainty that accumulates as nothing is heard from management for another 90 days. We are not suggesting that a full income statement be provided every month, week, or day. However, there are some statistics that can be provided with that frequency, such as sales, orders received, backlog, units produced and shipped, inventory levels, payroll and head count, and still other things that we haven't thought of. You know your company and your industry better than anyone, so you're in a better position to identify the performance indicators that best predict future conditions and events.[12]

It goes almost without saying that it would behoove you to accompany these unofficial information releases with clear disclaimers that indicate that they are tentative and subject to change. It will also be imperative that any corrections be announced quickly and fully explained. The extra reporting effort will not accomplish anything positive if the markets cannot have confidence that the information is reliable.

There is one more point that we also made earlier: use the Internet to distribute the information quickly to as many people as possible. You may still need to send printed quarterlies to those who want them, but you will chip points off your risk rating if you disseminate the information to everyone at the same time.

OTHER POINTS

No list can really be considered complete unless it has a "miscellaneous" category at the end. Our goal is to ensure that we have made it clear that it is a huge mistake to think that financial reports, even with enhanced GAAP compliance and supplemental disclosures, will be enough to keep the markets fully informed about what you're doing and what the future holds. You need a fully developed and dynamic information strategy to ensure that you have done what you can to reduce the uncertainty so that users face less risk, you have lower capital costs, and the market produces higher stock prices. It's nothing short of foolish to rely on the FASB and the SEC to fully define this strategy for you.

Traditional GAAP

Speaking of foolish, your reporting strategy can be to comply with the absolute minimum required by GAAP and SEC regulations, if your company is public. Your motto would be, "If it isn't required, we aren't doing it." A second motto would be, "If it isn't forbidden, we're going to do it." Don't count on a positive response from the markets, though.

Enhanced GAAP

You can step up to the next level by following the motto, "If it has been recommended, we're going to do it." This strategy will send a positive signal that's totally lacking under the minimum compliance route.

Supplemental Disclosures

On the other hand, you can go several levels higher if you voluntarily determine what people want and need to know about your company and then give it to them, even if there is nothing vaguely like it in the FASB's standards or the SEC's rules. We encourage you, as we have countless times before, to experiment with new ideas that are not included in standard reporting packages. The sky is your limit, although we encourage you to be constrained by truth telling if you really want to adopt QFR.

We make that last point in two ways. First, telling the truth is a positive ethical value that makes society function much more smoothly. Second, earning a reputation for telling the truth will reduce uncertainty for the capital markets, and by now you know where that is going to take you and your cost of capital.

IN CLOSING

What we just cannot leave unsaid, one more time, is that we do not want you to read these suggestions and believe them because they're written down. We don't care if you have developed great confidence in us and our point of view, we want you to do only that which you are firmly convinced makes sense for you in your situation. To do otherwise would be totally contrary to the way of life that we have christened Quality Financial Reporting.

NOTES

1. As a friend confessed to us about his auditing experience, he never got to the cash flow statement until his budget was almost used up. Thus, his only objective was to be able to reconcile the net cash flow to the change in the cash balance so that he could close off the job. He said that it never crossed his mind to ask whether the statement meant anything. He has since begun the process of becoming one of the first CFOs to accept QFR.

2. Paul Bahnson, Paul Miller, and Bruce Budge, "Nonarticulation in Cash Flow Statements and Implications for Education, Research, and Practice," *Accounting Horizons,* December 1996.

3. We do know through Paul Miller's personal experience that the SEC chief accountant and virtually all other accountants on the commission's staff did not fully understand SFAS 87 when it became effective.

4. The standard calls this off-the-books debit balance "unrecognized prior service cost."

5. If we explained how this process works, we would have to shoot you.

6. Under the liability method we described, this $20 million would indeed have appeared as an expense as the liability climbed from its initial balance up to its final balance on the day the options were exercised.

7. To make the debits and credits balance, the employer would record $8 million of additional paid-in capital with a credit while reducing its actual tax liability with an equal debit. The income tax expense would be unchanged.

8. Botosan's and Plumlee's work was published in the December 2001 issue of *Accounting Horizons* under the title "Stock Option Expense: The Sword of Damocles Revealed." We also wrote about this research and its implications in a column entitled "The Case of the Missing Disclosures—Did the Dog Eat Them?" that appeared in the September 24/October 7, 2001 issue of *Accounting Today*.

9. The June 25, 2001 issue of *Fortune* included several articles plunging into these issues concerning top management compensation. Among other things, the writers characterize GAAP after SFAS 123 as "insane," "awful," "nuts," "enabling," "a big stinking lie," and a "scandal." It isn't just the two of us who feel this way.

10. In considering this situation, we're reminded of a campus discipline problem one of us encountered when a student in the university was given access to the grades database as part of his on-campus job helping the registrar's office. The student soon discovered that he could get into his own file and change his grades. He started by fixing up his existing grades, but then grew so confident that he began signing up for courses and not doing any of the assignments or taking any tests. He would just go into the system after the grades were submitted, change his F to an A, and be done with it. He didn't realize two things. First, even though no alarms went off, every change was recorded in a security file that identified him by his password. Second, one of his professors remembered failing him in a required course and started an inquiry when he saw the student's name on the graduation list. In the same way, some managers think they have successfully managed EPS with impunity because they haven't gotten caught. However, the capital markets have long memories and keep "security files" with managers' names on them. This earnings management game is worse than futile, no matter how many other people are playing it.

11. One of Paul Miller's humorous memories from his time on the SEC staff was the block-long lines of Federal Express trucks pulling up to headquarters on March 30 and 31 to dump their cargoes of box upon box of 10-Ks being filed at the last possible minute.

12. This is the direction established by the PricewaterhouseCoopers effort to start its ValueReporting revolution. We again recommend that effort to you.

Finishing Up

At this stage, our main points are made as well as we think we can make them through the written word and with the limited space available to us. The most fundamental one is that the perennial focus on the problems of supplying financial reporting information has produced a culture accustomed to not worrying about the demand. This condition is clearly the result of a regulatory system that has granted accountants in general, and Certified Public Accountants in particular, a monopoly over the production of financial reporting and auditing standards. Through a long evolution, the standard-setting process has been thoroughly politicized to advance the interests of auditors and managers (at least as they perceive their interests), while the needs of users, the capital markets, and the economy have suffered because the monopoly has produced inadequate efficiency.

Chapter 18 is clearly a "what if . . ." discussion that considers what standard setting would be like if Quality Financial Reporting actually took hold. We feel confident in arguing that this rule-making activity would not just disappear from the scene. However, it would take on a different form and its business would be conducted differently. We also think it could produce a new type of standard to encourage QFR, and another kind of agency to accredit companies and audit firms.

Chapter 19 describes an example of what happens when QFR is not practiced. It digs into the collapse of Enron in 2001, which was due in large part to the management's attempts to trick the capital markets and all the company's stakeholders by using its financial statements to hide facts and otherwise create false appearances. In effect, this case describes how *not* to apply Quality Financial Reporting.

CHAPTER 18

QFR and Standard Setting

In light of our claims that GAAP are limited in their ability to produce complete information and that the standard-setting process is hopelessly political and non-innovative, we will excuse you if you might think that we would not find much of a role for a standard-setting agency in the Quality Financial Reporting world that we envision. In fact, we think that there are important roles for this kind of an agency, even the existing FASB. This chapter describes our thinking in this area.

OIL AND WATER?

It is obvious to us that the standard-setting process has not worked in such a way as to successfully persuade managers to put enough quality into their financial statements. Somewhat inelegantly phrased, we have asserted that GAAP aren't good enough to meet the needs of the capital markets for useful information, and we have demonstrated that claim over and over again. At the same time, we have said that QFR-minded managers need to exercise their own initiative in finding ways to provide new kinds of information that the markets aren't getting through GAAP financial statements.

Our continuous criticism and calls for individual innovation might be interpreted as a suggestion that we would be just as happy if there were no standard-setting process, or even no standards, for that matter. However, that assertion is far from our point of view. In fact, we quote ourselves on that point from pages 95 to 96 in Chapter 6:

> Therefore, just in case anyone thinks so, we state unequivocally that our advocacy for QFR is *not* a call for deregulation. Instead, it is a call for a

more intelligent response to regulation by managers so that they will not terminate their reporting efforts as soon as they meet the regulatory minimums. Those minimums do serve the important purposes of creating confidence in the markets and providing for justice to be done. We do not think those advantages should be sacrificed by deregulating the practice of financial reporting.

In fact, we think that a widespread adoption of QFR would result in more calls for tougher regulation against those who try to deceive. Perhaps no one would benefit as much from more effective regulation as those managers who choose to provide high-quality information because the tougher regulations would be likely to expose the fact that some of those managers competing in the markets are playing fast and loose with the truth while trying to look like they're producing sound financial reports. The consequence would have to be a lower level of perceived overall risk and a lower market-level cost of capital.

An old expression says that "a rising tide raises all ships," usually meaning that an economic boom will make everyone better off, even the low performers. We think it can also be used to describe the quality of information flowing to the capital markets. If the minimum level of quality is increased by regulation, then the cost of capital for all companies in that economy is reduced because of the more informative reports flowing to the markets.

Therefore, the same logic that leads us to encourage the managers of individual companies to improve their financial reporting quality also compels us to encourage standard-setting agencies (primarily the FASB, the SEC, and the IASB, but others as well) to take steps to improve the minimum level of financial reporting quality in their economies through better standards. By better standards, we mean standards that respond to unmet demands from financial statement users for information about events that have occurred and the conditions that exist for individual companies.

Three Purposes for Standard Setting

Our thinking boils down to three purposes for standard setting in a QFR world. First, we think standard setting will and should continue to set the minimum standards for all managers to follow in meeting the markets' needs for useful information. Without these minimums, capital costs would be higher because of the increased uncertainty and risk.

Second, we believe that standard setting can contribute to the economy by continually raising the bar through new standards that increase the minimums. In other words, we think standard-setting agencies can keep doing what they do. However, as we explain momentarily, they should find it easier to do in a QFR world.

Third, we envision that standard setters can demonstrate leadership through activities that will help instill the QFR attitude in managers. They can show this leadership (1) by not folding their tents when a proposed standard is disputed and (2) by writing a new kind of standard that will challenge managers to go beyond the minimum.

A Whole New World

As we see it, QFR will lead standard-setting agencies to create a "whole new world" in which we can see:

- A whole new motivation for standard setters
- A whole new search
- A whole new political system
- A whole new kind of output
- A whole new kind of agency

The following pages explain these thoughts.

A WHOLE NEW MOTIVATION FOR STANDARD SETTERS

In the current standard-setting world, the motivation for new standards is to coerce managers into revealing more about their companies that they already know but are not willing to report. In effect, the FASB exists in today's world to make managers do what they don't want to do. As a result, it is in continuous conflict with this constituency and having to fight off its attacks, both during comment periods and between them. It takes a special sort of person to merely survive, much less thrive, in this sort of environment, and we're not convinced that it rewards the kind of vision and innovation that QFR should produce.

In contrast, in a financial reporting world in which managers are indeed striving on their own for lower capital costs by finding creative ways to reveal more of the truth about themselves, standard-setting agencies would have a different task. Instead of coercing managers to do a little bit more than they're willing to do, they would be working with the managers to help them do what they want to do even better than they're doing it. No longer bashing recalcitrant managers over the head, the standard setters would be walking alongside them, showing them how to discover new demands for new kinds of information and helping them figure out new ways to meet those demands.

Are we daydreaming? Perhaps, but we don't mind sharing our vision with you. As much as or more than most, and a tad less than a few, we know firsthand about the political pressures that the FASB and SEC feel whenever they try to institute change in today's world. It's an uphill battle because the managers are holding tight to their old misbegotten paradigm that the capital markets reward them for spinning tales and don't penalize them for fudging the figures, even while they comply with GAAP. We are confident that QFR will change this world and create a whole new reason for standard setters to come to work on Mondays that is quite different from the one that gets them into the office now.

A WHOLE NEW SEARCH

Under the current paradigm, the FASB in particular, and other standard setters as well, search for new ways to force managers to supply new kinds of information. They are constantly dealing with the question of how new information can be produced. As we just said, their task is to force people to do what they don't want to do, and accomplishing that feat requires them to have significant authority. If the FASB were to lose its endorsement by the SEC, it would not be nearly as active or effective as it is. It simply needs that political power to force managers to supply the information they don't want to provide.

In the QFR world that we envision, the FASB will also serve the role of getting out into the capital markets to identify new kinds of information that investors and financial analysts demand instead of focusing so intently on supply issues. In effect, the FASB can serve as a type of mutually supported market research agency (a sort of think tank) that will be hired by a consortium of companies to assess consumer attitudes and behaviors. The board will be bringing new ideas to the table with the attitude that says, "Look, we've found this new opportunity, now what do you want to do with it and how can we help you?"

For example, suppose managers are really sensitive about their own compensation and think that they can hold onto it only if they don't tell their stockholders and potential stockholders how much it's worth. Now, the FASB comes on the scene with clanking spurs, a tough glint in its eye, and a sidearm strapped to its hip, and says, "We're ready to force you to provide new information about options that you have been issuing to yourselves. We don't care what you think because our conceptual framework tells us there is an expense. So, we're going to use our political power to get you to do what we want even if you don't want to do it." The opposition to the proposal is certain to be tough and determined, and rooted in resistance to the FASB's perceived attitude as much as its proposed action.

In contrast, imagine a world in which managers are conscious of their need to provide really useful information to the capital markets so that their stock prices increase. Along comes the FASB with no spurs, glint, or sidearm, and says, "We've have been out there talking to investors and looking at new trends in financial analysis, and we've discovered that the markets are demanding more information about stock options than we have been requiring you to report. They really want to know what the options are worth and they would like to know how much expense can be attributed to each year. What sorts of things do you think you might try that would allow them to receive that information, and what can we do to help you meet that demand?"

Then, suppose that the managers realize that they need to respond by providing measures of the value of the options issued but they don't really know how to produce those numbers. They could then commission the FASB to use its expertise to find a useful measurement method that the managers could go on to apply to their own situations. If managers use this standard method instead of ones that they have each cobbled together on their own, their measures will have more credibility with the markets. That credibility wouldn't come from forced (and compromised) uniformity but from a conscious and deliberate decision to promote quality disclosures by applying the industry's best practice.

What a completely different attitude that would be! We think it would produce an entirely different standard-setting agency than the one we now have, and one that would make an entirely different contribution to the economy and society in general. It would be searching for new ways to bring useful information to the capital markets instead of new ways of forcing managers to do something against their will.

A WHOLE NEW POLITICAL SYSTEM

We hope our previous discussions of the political nature of the standard-setting process have made it clear that the FASB has been forced to issue minimum standards because of political pressures that have been continuously brought to bear on the members. In particular, our discussion in Chapter 5 described how the board compromised in response to various kinds of threats in its high-profile projects, including but not limited to foreign currency, changing prices, pensions and other postemployment benefits, income taxes, stock options, and investments. The list could go on to include a great many others. It is almost as if the board and staff are asking the question, "What can we get the preparers to agree to?" instead of "What information would reduce users' uncertainty the most?"

Perhaps the high water mark for pressure was the options project, in which the five-member majority of the board voted to recommend pro forma disclosure instead of recognition on the income statement. Chapter 5 quoted these excerpts from SFAS 123 in the FASB's explanation of this decision:

The debate on accounting for stock-based compensation unfortunately became so divisive that it threatened the Board's future working relationship with some of its constituents. Eventually, the nature of the debate threatened the future of accounting standards setting in the private sector. (par. 60)

The Board chose a disclosure-based solution for stock-based employee compensation to bring closure to the divisive debate on this issue—not because it believes that solution is the best way to improve financial accounting and reporting. (par. 62)

The board members did not even try to make a pretense that disclosure was a good answer in theory or in practice, only that it allowed them to live and fight another day.

When we transport ourselves to a QFR world, we don't see these kinds of clashes happening anymore. Rather, when differences arise, the parties will be focused on the same issue—"How do we meet this identified need for information?"

We think that most preparers in this future will be interested in cooperating with the board to test out new ideas to reduce uncertainty. We also think auditors will be eager to help out with the discussions in various ways because they will see new methods for adding value to their clients' financial reports. Of course, some slow-moving managers will continue to insist that less information is better than more, but we think that their numbers will dwindle in the face of the good results achieved by those who are pushing the envelope. Some auditors will hold back out of innate and reinforced aversion toward change and risk. We think that they, too, will soon learn that QFR creates new and almost limitless opportunities.

Surely the biggest change of all will be a higher profile in the standard-setting process for financial analysts and other financial statement users. When the FASB was created, it did not have any users among its members. Instead, the members were all auditors, corporate accountants, or government accountants. That continued until around 1980, when Frank Block was appointed; however, he held firmly entrenched ideas that the status quo was worth keeping intact and was one of the staunchest opponents to reporting market values. When his term expired, he was not replaced by another person from the analyst community until 1993, when the Financial Accounting Foundation trustees appointed Tony Cope (now a member of the IASB). This situation prompted these plaintive words in the 1993 AIMR committee report:

With the exception of the two full-time FASB members [Block and Cope], . . . individual analysts . . . serve as volunteers and render their services to the standard setting process *in addition to,* not as part of, their regular work as analysts, money managers, research directors, academics, etc. Their dedication is commendable. Furthermore, they have the task of representing, with both time and funding in meager supply, the majority of professional users of financial statements. Their views deserve to be heard, even though they are outnumbered and outspent by the legions of business firms, industry and business policy associations, large auditing firms, and professional associations of accountants, many of which have full-time, paid staffs to research and advocate their views on financial reporting matters. (p. 74)

Because the essence of QFR is elevating users' demands to the forefront, it only makes sense that the FASB and any other standard-setting agency would ensure that users' views and needs are front and center and that their arguments are not drowned out by loud noises and complaints generated by other better-funded constituents, especially those trying to hold onto an obsolete and unresponsive supply-based paradigm. Thus, the Financial Accounting Foundation trustees made a good move when they appointed professional financial statement user Gary Schieneman (both a CPA and a member of the AIMR) as Cope's successor in 2001.

We think this arrangement can evolve as thought patterns change to understand that the objective for financial reporting is reducing uncertainty, not painting pretty pictures that bear no semblance to the truth. It is inevitable that the outcome will be much more useful financial reporting standards and financial reports. There is a long way to go until the world arrives at this condition, however, and no one knows that more than us.

A WHOLE NEW KIND OF OUTPUT

With new motivation, new searches, and new political surroundings, we think that standard-setting agencies will also find themselves producing new kinds of documents. Right now, the FASB tends to produce a great many more standards than research reports. We think that ratio will reverse as the board is inspired by its search for quality-enhancing reporting methods while understanding that its standards are issued only for the purpose of setting minimum performance levels. The premium will be on new ideas that deal with users' demands, not with finding ways to coerce managers to do what they are unwilling to do, even though it might be better for them.

It is here that we have experienced our own personal epiphanies. In particular, we used to disparage three of the board's standards: SFAS 89, 95, and 123. (As reminders for those who have trouble playing the FASB numbers game, SFAS 89 eliminated mandatory disclosures of market value information while encouraging that it be reported voluntarily; SFAS 95 recommended using the direct method of reporting operating cash flows while permitting the indirect method to be used; and SFAS 123 encouraged managers to report options expense on the income statement while allowing it to be reported in a pro forma footnote.) We criticized each of these standards in the past because they embraced compromises between doing what the board actually considered to be useful and an inferior practice that the preparer community was willing to implement. We know that the board knew the right answers but just didn't have the political will to make managers put them into effect.

Ironically, however, we see in these compromises a prototype for future standards, with one simple but profound change. First, we would like to see the standard setters perform a great deal of research to uncover demands for information and develop methods for supplying it to the capital markets. We think that these efforts will reveal a best practice, as well as alternatives that offer some advantages and disadvantages. Second, in a noncoercive but nonetheless challenging way, the standards will strongly recommend the preferable method while allowing managers to choose to use one of the lesser alternatives. But, we would go to a third step that differs from the three examples. Specifically, we would have the FASB and the SEC establish a requirement that would force managers who do not choose the preferred method to provide credible discussions explaining why they have chosen to provide less than fully forthcoming information to the owners in particular and the capital markets in general. For example, if they decided to go with footnote disclosure of options-based compensation expense, they would have to explain why that approach produced more useful information than complying with the recommended approach of reporting an expense on the income statement. The managers would be required to address issues of uncertainty and capital costs as well as preparation and processing costs in order to justify the omission of useful facts and the imposition of additional efforts and risk on the users. This disclosure requirement would encourage managers to think through their accounting policy decisions much more carefully and critically. It would also make them articulate their paradigms so that the markets could assess the value of the reported information with greater confidence.

Under today's practices in these example areas, we are not aware of any substantive discussions by managers that explain why they are not reporting supplemental market value information, why they are not describing gross operating cash inflows and outflows, or why they are putting the options expense in a footnote. Instead, they seem to think they can figuratively cower behind the flimsy parapets of GAAP and escape the market's retribution. We believe that they would find themselves in a bit of bind if they really had to come up with a rational-sounding reason for deciding against responding to well-articulated and thoroughly researched demands for the preferred methods.

If you are a manager, we encourage you to take a moment to test yourself by composing a four- or five-sentence footnote that clearly explains your refusal to adopt financial reporting methods that the top experts and authorities have determined are the best. We don't think you can do it. If you can't, think about what that means to the capital markets. Are they willing to accept your decision to leave them uninformed without some sort of penalty? We don't think so.

A WHOLE NEW KIND OF AGENCY

Our presentations and discussions with others have often produced a question of whether some new kind of quality-monitoring agency might be inspired by a wholesale embracing of QFR by managers. Specifically, many have asked whether it would be possible to create an interdisciplinary body that would examine the financial reporting practices of various companies in order to designate them as compliant or noncompliant with QFR standards. The comments invariably connect with the efforts in operations management circles that produced the ISO 9000 designation for very high quality production systems.

In the QFR context, this agency would consist of representatives from all constituencies (users, preparers, auditors, regulators, and academics) who would first determine what sorts of activities and outputs constituted Quality Financial Reporting. While they might start with GAAP and SEC reporting requirements, they would certainly not stop there, but would go on to consider what management might do to provide greater quantities of higher-quality information. Once these standards were in place, company management teams could apply as candidates for accreditation. Their financial statements and other disclosures would all be scrutinized for compliance with these standards. In addition, their report-generating systems would be examined for quality control. Perhaps more important than anything would be an assessment of the management's commitment to the QFR attitude, starting at the top and filtering all the way through the organization.[1]

A similar process could very well be developed for accrediting auditing firms. The candidates would have to show the accrediting agency that they have various quality standards in place concerning such things as independence, fee structures, client acquisition practices, opinion shopping, triggers for additional testing, and negotiating adjustments with management. The outcome would be a designation (or nondesignation) of the auditors as suitable (or unsuitable) for managers who want to achieve Quality Financial Reporting.

There are plenty of models for accreditation and accrediting agencies for other activities outside accounting. We think that the accounting profession has somehow excused itself from any external validation processes because of the virtual monopoly that has been given to CPAs to perform audits for public companies and other entities. The presumption seems to have been that all auditors and audits are the same, with no real distinctions among them to allow them room to compete. The availability of this special accreditation would be a powerful force for improvement.

CONCLUSION

Despite our criticisms of the current state of accounting practice, we do not envision that QFR is the end of standard setting. While it might be the end of standard setting as it now exists, QFR has the potential to make it into a much more viable and valuable public service. We do not see Quality Financial Reporting as reducing the significance of the FASB, SEC, or IASB, but as liberating the members of these agencies to think more broadly and innovatively. In particular, we think they will be freed from many of the pressures they now feel to produce a standard that satisfies the suppliers of financial information without really addressing the needs of those who demand that information.

We are clearly in a time that calls for leaders who can envision a new future that is far different from the present. We believe those leaders are out there in the ranks of management, finance, and accounting; it's just that they have not been operating within a system that values their vision and their abilities. In fact, just the opposite has been true, as advancements have gone to those who are skilled in managing earnings to serve some top managers' dysfunctional attitudes toward the markets. This power has resided in those who see the capital markets as capable of being fooled, misled, and otherwise kept in the dark for someone else's advantage. We don't think this attitude has ever been worthwhile, and we are confident that it can and will be replaced—perhaps by someone reading this page right now.

N O T E S

1. We think the AIMR quality rankings described in Chapter 9 offer a glimpse of the sort of service and ranking we're proposing.

CHAPTER 19

How Not to Do QFR—
The Enron Case Study

After this book went into production, the story of the spectacular collapse of Enron began to break. Like everyone else, we were stunned by the flood of revelations about what the management and the auditors had been doing with the financial reporting activities. We were also disappointed to learn about the apparently compromised relationship between the company and its auditors. In response, we decided that we had to add more material to our original manuscript to present Enron as the nearly perfect case study in how *not* to practice Quality Financial Reporting. Up to this point, you will have noticed a few Enron-related references in earlier chapters. We also decided to include this entire chapter to focus on what we believe to be the mistakes that Enron's managers made, along with the financial reporting errors and failed judgments committed by the auditors from the Andersen firm. Although we don't know the whole story (and perhaps no one ever will, in light of the far-reaching scope of the fraud and the shredded documents), we have learned enough to comment credibly on the situation. We want to make it clear that we believe the pattern of undeniably deliberate deception through false reporting amounts to unethical and illegal behavior. As such, it cannot be mistaken for a simple case of not applying QFR. However, we are totally confident that managers who choose to practice Quality Financial Reporting are not going to cause their companies to be other Enrons. Furthermore, their stakeholders will have a higher level of assurance that what happened to Enron's owners, creditors, and employees won't happen to them.

The story of Enron came crashing into the news in the late fall and early winter of 2001. There are hundreds if not thousands of different articles in the popular and business press on what happened, and hours upon hours of coverage on the news networks and talk shows. We cannot claim to comprehend the full motivations of the actors, and we certainly cannot anticipate all that will come out of this episode. Nonetheless, the case provides lessons for a great many people, and we think that most of them will reinforce what we have already written about Quality Financial Reporting. This chapter first gives a thumbnail sketch of the facts about the Enron situation, and then shows that the management and the auditors committed all seven of the deadly sins of financial reporting that we described in Chapter 2. We then speculate briefly about the answers Enron managers might have provided on the questionnaires presented in Chapters 11, 12, and 13, if they had been given the opportunity to respond to them. Finally, we provide our own summary comments.

WHAT HAPPENED AT ENRON?

Enron was created in 1985 through the merger of two stodgy, even boring, utilities in the natural gas business. It started out operating some pipelines, making its money by providing a service to its customers, and perhaps enjoying the benefits of occasional price imbalances in markets that allowed the company to buy gas at one price and then sell it at another for a profit. At some point, the management conceived a new business model that would widen the scope of the company's operations tremendously. The model was designed to take advantage of three developments: (1) the completion of more fully integrated pipelines that allowed natural gas to be produced in one part of the country and sent to another, (2) deregulation of natural gas prices, and (3) burgeoning forms of rapid communication. The strategy that emerged called for Enron to become a central marketplace for natural gas, much as the New York Stock Exchange is the marketplace for large public companies' stocks. Success spawned another similar business plan based on electrical power. The same phenomena had occurred in the sense that the national power grid was in place and deregulation began to be more common, thus allowing many power companies to buy needed power or to sell excess power to other power companies. In effect, electric utilities with excess capacity came to Enron to offer power for sale to others that were short of capacity. This spot market allowed the sellers to compete for the highest price while allowing the buyers to compete for the lowest price. The economics were positive all the way around, and Enron became even more successful in providing its basic service of matching supply with demand. After experiencing these double successes, the management branched out into markets for other things, and the list eventually came to be quite long. The business boomed, and the company enjoyed extraordinary prosperity, eventually climbing to a position of seventh on the Fortune 500 list. Its management also became influential in Houston, and took the step of getting the company's name on Enron Field, the new major league baseball stadium built for the Astros.

In addition, the management, under the direction of CEO Kenneth Lay, began to cultivate high-level political connections, largely through personal contact but also through a huge quantity of campaign contributions. One fact that came out early in 2002 was that a majority of the members of the U.S. Senate and about half of the House had benefited from Enron's largesse. The managers were covering all sides, both eventual winners and losers, and Democrats and Republicans, presumably to be ready to deal with whoever ascended to power.[1]

In response to the managers' ambition to grow, they decided at some point that it wasn't enough to be making money through commissions on transactions. Specifically, they started to enter into a variety of derivative-based contracts involving the commodities that they were trading for others, thus exposing the company to a great deal more uncertainty. While this uncertainty could be mitigated through various financial techniques, the executives made the big mistake of thinking that its impact on the company's stock price could also be managed by keeping the extra risk under wraps through carefully selected and managed financial reporting techniques. This approach to providing limited information seemed to fit well with the aggressive and secretive business culture that the management team had developed.

Enron's stock climbed to exceed $80 per share in early 2001, and the total market capitalization was more than $60 billion. As shown in Figure 19-1, the stock price began to slip with some abruptness near the beginning of 2001, long before any information about problems was obviously available to the public. The company's financial reports continued to show positive reported earnings, but the statements and footnotes were notoriously difficult to understand. In addition, the company's managers had developed a reputation for not being forthcoming and transparent. So, when the price began to slip, the managers brushed aside questions and ostracized those analysts who dared to ask them.

In August 2001, Enron's CEO, Jeffrey Skilling, suddenly resigned after only six months in the position, citing personal reasons (including a statement to the effect that he had missed too many of his children's soccer games). By now the stock price had dwindled to about half its previous high. Skilling was replaced by Kenneth Lay, the prior CEO who had authored the evolution of Enron into its new form. After returning, Lay made statements to the employees and the public that the company was in great shape and that the stock price would soon rebound.

However, as soon as Lay arrived, he received an anonymous internal memo pleading for a housecleaning of management and the financial statements to rid the company of several schemes that had been concocted to produce misleading public reports. (In January 2002, the writer of the memo was publicly identified as Sherron Watkins, one of the company's vice presidents and a former Andersen employee.) Lay did not fully im-

FIGURE 19-1

The Rise and Fall of Enron's Market Capitalization (adapted from *Fortune,* December 24, 2001, p. 66)

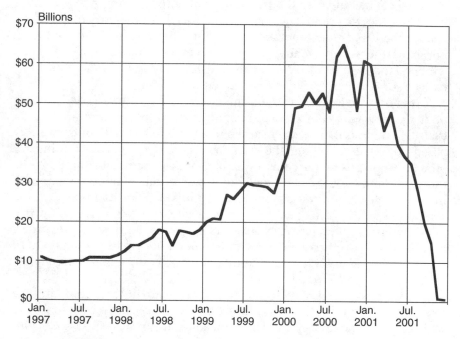

plement that advice and continued to press ahead with a public image that everything would turn around, even as the stock price continued to plummet. Then, a bombshell exploded in October 2001 when he announced that the company had booked a $568 million downward adjustment to prior years' reported earnings. The adjustment was described as correcting accounting errors in several prior income statements. In technical terms, "accounting errors" include both inadvertent mistakes and deliberate misapplications of GAAP. In this case, the adjustments were made for the latter reason.

With this announcement, the cat was out of the bag—the management had authorized fallacious entries that had raised the company's reported earnings when there were no corresponding increases in real earnings. At the same time the adjustment was announced, but with no substantive comment or explanation, the Enron management recorded a $1.2 billion decrease in stockholders' equity. What did not become clear right away was that the huge drop was triggered by the declining credit status of the company. Only later was it revealed that the source of the crunch was the collapse of some of the thousands of "special purpose entities" (SPEs) that management had created for the sole purpose of taking huge amounts of

Enron's liabilities off the published balance sheet so that the company's credit standing would appear much better than it really was.

On October 23, Lay expressed total confidence in the company's CFO, Andrew Fastow, despite these problems. But, on October 24, the company announced that Fastow had been placed on an indefinite leave of absence. It was eventually revealed that he had acted as the general partner of some of the largest SPEs, ostensibly acting as an individual, not as a company officer. This dual role had been explicitly approved by Enron's board of directors in 1999 as an exception to the company's ethics rules regarding transactions between Enron and its officers. By a narrow technical interpretation of GAAP, the situation permitted the entities to be treated as if they were not subsidiaries. Therefore, their assets and liabilities were not combined with Enron's assets and liabilities in the consolidated financial statements.[2] It turned out that the largest partnerships' names included the initials of Fastow's wife and children (LJM and LJM2) and another was named for his dog. Altogether, it was reported that he had personally gained more than $30 million from the ruse.

Ironically, Fastow was honored by *CFO* magazine with its Excellence Award for Capital Structure Management in 1999, with special praise for his innovative financial strategies. After the schemes were revealed, the editors of the magazine used these words in an article titled "Wrong Numbers," which appeared in the January 2002 issue, to explain how Fastow had misled them in describing Enron's convoluted financing activities:

> More than two years ago, as part of an interview with *CFO*, Fastow boasted that he had helped keep almost $1 billion in debt off Enron's balance sheet through the use of a complex and innovative arrangement.
>
> "It's not consolidated and it's nonrecourse," he told this magazine. Maybe it depends on how you define "nonrecourse." In fact, the 10-Q that Enron filed on November 19, 2001, states plainly that the debt ultimately was Enron's responsibility. According to the filing, the $915 million debt was backed by Enron's obligation to extinguish it, if necessary, with cash.
>
> That obligation, as reported in the 10-Q, would fall to Enron if the company experienced a downgrade below investment grade by any of the three major credit rating agencies. Sure enough, that downgrade took place shortly after the disclosure of the $915 million obligation, along with another $3 billion in similar off-balance-sheet liabilities. (p. 16)

With the public revelations of October, the rest of management's schemes came unraveled like a poorly knitted handmade sweater. Lay could do nothing to stop the continuing stock price decline, even after reportedly seeking an intervention through contacts with Cabinet-level federal officials. At one point, a freeze was put on Enron employees' individual retirement holdings in their 401(k) accounts that would not allow them to sell their Enron shares. They were told that the situation was caused by a changeover in plan administrators; in our estimation, management may have been trying to prevent panic selling and the resulting downward pressure on the stock price. It was also reported that many top managers were exercising large numbers of options that were still in the money and bailing out of their own stock holdings.

By December 2001, the stock price had fallen below $1 per share, and the market capitalization was essentially zero. With a huge effort, the company's attorneys filed a bankruptcy declaration early on December 2, a Sunday morning, trying to protect the last remaining bits of its assets. Within a few weeks, the New York Stock Exchange stopped trading the stock, and the destruction was complete.

Another piece of the story concerns the relationship between Enron and its audit firm, Andersen (formerly Arthur Andersen). According to the company's proxy statements, the firm received total fees of $52 million in the most recent fiscal year, of which $25 million was reportedly for audit services and the remainder for nonaudit services. It has also been reported that the $25 million of audit fees included unspecified amounts paid to Andersen to serve as the company's internal auditors.

When the October adjustments were reported, attention naturally focused on the public accountants to explain how the large errors and misstatements could have escaped their detection. Andersen's relatively new managing partner and CEO, Joseph Berardino, took the offensive in *The Wall Street Journal* and in testimony before the House Congressional Committee on Financial Services. On the one hand, he stated that his firm accepted responsibility, but on the other he blamed the financial reporting system and the client for having created the situation. (Berardino subsequently resigned from Andersen in the spring of 2002.)

The tone shifted dramatically in January 2002 when investigators discovered that Andersen employees had been ordered by David Duncan, the partner in charge of the Enron audit, to destroy vast numbers of documents and computer files related to the firm's activities. In the same month, Duncan was fired by Andersen while other partners working on the Enron engagement were placed on administrative leave. The big question to be resolved, of course, was whether anyone higher up had directed Duncan to give the shredding order to the employees. It was also reported that a large proportion of the accountants employed by Enron were Andersen alumni. In any case, it was readily apparent to us that Andersen was in a very difficult situation and had created a nearly perfect example of how to not handle a large client. As we were finishing the book production process, Andersen was found guilty on charges that it had obstructed justice through its activities in the fall.

There is, of course, much more that could be written, but this is enough for our purposes. Certainly, a great deal more will be discovered and disclosed about this case in the future. Regardless of what is revealed from this point on, we are convinced that Enron's managers and auditors were located nowhere in the neighborhood of Quality Financial Reporting.

ENRON AND THE SEVEN DEADLY SINS OF FINANCIAL REPORTING

Chapter 2 described the seven deadly sins of financial reporting that managers can and do commit. It looks to us like the Enron team went seven for seven, with a special twist on the seventh sin. The following pages describe why we feel this way.

Underestimating the Capital Markets

Even though they had a good business model, it appears that Enron managers decided they would not be satisfied with a mere solid return—they wanted much more than usual. But, they made the mistake of not trying to improve the model; instead, they set out to squeeze that return higher by playing the capital markets for patsies by managing the flow of information instead of managing the flow of cash into the company from its operations.

Back in Chapter 1 we presented the diagram in Figure 19-2 to represent the two things that a management can offer the capital markets: future cash flows and information about those cash flows. We think Enron's managers decided they could get that higher return by painting pretty pictures that made the prospective cash flows merely look better. In their view, it must have seemed easier to manage the numbers in the financial statements than to actually increase the success of the operations.

We're convinced Enron's managers completely blew their chance when they became obsessed with finding ways to produce false information. They were, it appears to us, so motivated to attain huge wealth and so convinced that the capital markets are composed of fools that they thoroughly cooked the books and piled one lie on top of another to keep that good-looking information flowing. It turned out that they were the fools, perhaps the biggest that the financial world has ever seen. Like King Canute of old England, they sat there at the shore and demanded that the tide of truth turn back.

(An ancient legend about a Viking king of England named Canute tells that he was surrounded by a fawning court that flattered him over and over again about his immense power. Because he was wise, Canute knew that their flattery was not deserved and he became thoroughly annoyed by it. At his command, his throne was placed on the beach at the low tide mark. He then took his seat, surrounded by his obsequious entourage, and issued an order to the tide to not come in. Of course, when

FIGURE 19-2

The Firm with Its Twin Offerings

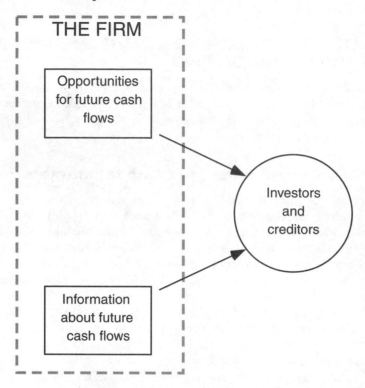

the water advanced, his throne and he were engulfed in it, as well as the various nobles. He then got up without a word and waded through the surf and back into the castle, confident that he had taught a lesson about the limits of mere mortals against overwhelming natural forces.)

Much the same as Canute's cocky courtiers, the Enron managers apparently thought they could stem the vast economic power inherent in the truth by keeping the real facts from getting to the capital markets. In our view, they compounded this hubris with extraordinary greed and disregard for the interests of all the company's stakeholders, including its employees, stockholders, creditors, and customers. Before much time passed, and before they could really enjoy their misbegotten riches, the truth overwhelmed them and exposed all the trickery they had tried to pull off.

Classically, they seem to have started off the fraud by making some relatively small moves to increase reported earnings, perhaps by marking their derivative investments to market values that were a shade too high. When confronted by the auditors, the management pushed back and convinced Andersen to consider the proposed adjustments to be immaterial and thus not worth making. We don't know, and might never know, but the existence of those huge fees may have helped the audit partner understand the issues from the client's point of view.

Not content with the initial success, Enron management's manipulations reportedly continued and grew in complexity and size. The goal came to be getting good results in the financial statements at all costs, without regard to what was really happening. Closer and closer management came to the edge of acceptable behavior, always thinking that the only thing that mattered was the financial image in the statements, not the truth. The managers may have worked with their favored financial analysts to promote the impression that earnings were solid and growing. If so, these analysts were either duped or duplicitous, hoping they could make the right noises and find bigger fools who would buy the stock at a higher amount. Yet, as revealed by the steady decline of the market value for GAAP stock that began early in 2001, some people had seen through the smokescreen and had begun to position themselves to avoid the calamity that was sure to come.

Even when the October earnings adjustments were announced, the Enron people thought they could persuade the markets to pay more for the stock. They restated the earnings but emphasized that a future turnaround was surely coming. They didn't even mention the $1.2 billion downward adjustment to equity caused by the collapse of the limited partnership scheme. To use another literary figure, think of the charlatan pretending to be the Wizard of Oz telling Dorothy and her friends to "pay no attention to that man behind the curtain" after Toto unveils the humbug that he was trying to perpetrate. Even at the end of the collapse, the Enron management did not seem to grasp that the markets are too smart, too persistent, and too cynical to be fooled for long, if ever.

Beyond any doubt in our minds, a decision to practice Quality Financial Reporting would have allowed the managers to avoid all of this trouble and heartbreak. If they had used QFR, they never would have started to deceive in the first place. They also never would have trod on the edges of GAAP or stepped out of bounds. They never would have considered engaging in off-balance-sheet financing, and they certainly would not have created limited partnerships with an officer as the general partner. They never would have told any of the cover-up stories they ended up telling, and they never would have committed the other sins we are about to describe. The bottom line is that if Enron's managers had truly respected the capital markets and understood the importance of telling the truth, the company would still be standing, employees would be working with intact 401(k) plans, and no one would be snickering about Minute Maid Park, the new name for the Astros' home stadium.

Obfuscating

A commitment to practicing QFR means more than just telling the truth. It means telling the *whole* truth and telling it clearly. Enron's managers appear to have committed to doing just the opposite. They claimed that they complied with GAAP, and that doing so was good enough. But their compliance involved doing as little as they could to look as good as possible, compounding their lying by publishing complex reports. As an example of their obfuscation, here is an excerpt taken from one of the footnotes in the 2000 annual report:

Footnote 10—Preferred stock
   In connection with the 1998 financial restructuring (yielding proceeds of approximately $1.2 billion) of Enron's investment in Azurix, Enron committed to cause the sale of Enron convertible preferred stock, if certain debt obligations of the related entity which acquired an interest in Azurix, are defaulted upon, or in certain events, including among other things, Enron's credit rating falls below specified levels.

This example is but one showing how the Enron management made a sincere, even total, effort to be as uncommunicative as possible.

   From what you have read in this book, obfuscation promotes uncertainty for investors. When they face uncertainty, they consider it to be risk and then demand a higher rate of return before they invest or lend. This pressure presented Enron with a higher cost of capital and lower stock prices.

   Frankly, we have to admit that we're puzzled the Enron charade worked for as long as it did. Some might suggest that this time lag proves the market is inefficient. Perhaps, but we don't think the evidence is persuasive. After all, the market did discover the flaws at Enron long before the press and the media did. The stock price began to plummet early in 2001, flying in the face of continuing buy recommendations from many analysts.

   The Enron penchant for obscurity and resistance was pretty well established, and according to common knowledge, the managers spoke to the public from a position of bold arrogance, in effect declaring, "We are who we are, and we have chosen to publish financial statements that are hard to read and maybe a little incomplete."

   A great insight is provided by a quotation from a November 5, 2001, *Wall Street Journal* article by Jonathan Weil entitled, "Andersen Faces Scrutiny on Clarity of Enron Disclosures." Weil quotes Karen Denne, the Enron spokesperson charged with the impossible task of representing management to the public, with these words reminiscent of Marie Antoinette's recommendation that the peasants eat cake: ". . . [I]nvestors who didn't understand the transactions didn't have to buy Enron stock." Bethany

McLean, in an article titled, "Why Enron Went Bust," in the December 24, 2001, issue of *Fortune*, offered a similar observation:

> Until recently Enron would kick and scream at the notion that its business or financial statements were complicated; its attitude, expressed with barely concealed disdain, was that anyone who couldn't understand its business just didn't "get it." (p. 60)

This stance makes no sense at all because it basically cuts a company off from intelligent market participants who suspect that the lack of transparency means that management is hiding something bad. If the company is in fact hiding something, it has to be a lot worse than anyone could imagine. Thus, in Enron's case, the stock price plummeted as the markets continued to discount it more and more.

When we read Denne's words, we were reminded of this comment from Warren Buffett that we quoted in Chapter 2 and again in Chapter 8:

> If I pick up an annual report and I can't understand a footnote, I probably won't—no, I *won't*—invest in that company because I *know* that they don't *want* me to understand it.

Our colleague Dr. Ron Mano of Weber State University has humorously described the real experience of a friend who called his uncle, an accounting employee of ConAgra, to ask for an explanation of a complex footnote in the company's annual report. The friend was rebuffed by his relative with the comment, "It's none of your damn business!"[3]

Denne's masters may have thought that they were being smart to brush off complaints, never understanding that doing so was a perfect strategy for reducing the stock's value. They thought turning aside inquiries about obscure reporting would somehow cause the markets to bid the value of their stock higher. How much more wrongheaded could they have been?

This fundamental economic relationship between uncertainty and risk is not rocket science, but its logic must have eluded the Enron managers, who were possibly too busy building their house of cards to look around and see that their scheme was stripped naked of its cover. Unfortunately for everyone, the auditors also decided against raising objections and thereby failed to meet their public trust, effectively putting Andersen into what looks to us to be its own death spiral. We think the deliberate management decision to obfuscate grew out of an unprecedented combination of stupidity, cupidity, pride, and guile that is unmatched, at least in recent business history.

Hyping and Spinning

Based on what we have seen, the name *Enron* has become a verb that connotes hype and spin, as in the phrase, "This company Enronned its reported earnings." Nothing that came out from Enron's management was easily believed by experienced company watchers. For example, who could have possibly believed Lay's explanation that he, like a kind understanding neighbor, had come out of retirement to stand in for Skilling so that he could start going to his kids' soccer games? The speciousness of the statement is staggering, especially in light of the fact that, two days after quitting, Skilling took a short position on a huge chunk of a rival company's stock, apparently in order to take advantage of the industry-wide plunge that he anticipated would surely follow when Enron's infected and now abscessed accounting practices were found and lanced. In addition, Lay was not above acting in the same way toward the employees who trusted him, especially with the reported incident of making it impossible for them to unload their own holdings of Enron stock.

The glaring evidence that this financial reporting sin was rampant was the great lengths the managers reportedly had gone to in hiding the debt. Simply put, there is no hype and spin as obvious as acting and speaking as if there is no debt because it isn't recognized on the GAAP balance sheet. The whole truth was that the company was deep in debt, regardless of what the management concealed. Additionally, the liabilities weren't on the balance sheet because of very expensive, intricate, and risky manipulations.

Spokesperson Denne defended Enron's accounting practices by saying that they were in compliance with GAAP. Joseph Berardino of Andersen took this defense to a higher level by implying that his firm had no choice but to allow its client to leave the debt off the balance sheet. His spin was that Andersen was a hapless victim just like everyone else.[4]

Regardless of what the parties said, are now saying, or will say in the future, the facts remain that $60 billion evaporated over the course of a year and a great many people lost their jobs. All the spin in the world won't cover up or make up for the damage that was done by committing this sin.

Smoothing

The smoothing sin involves taking steps to keep intact a steady upward trend in annual reported earnings by conjuring reported income when real income doesn't exist or by ignoring real income that does exist. For Enron, details of specific actions were still scarce when we produced this chapter, but we believe that management accomplished rampant smoothing by using fabricated market values for the company's derivative holdings and debts. (GAAP call for using market values in this context, and we applaud that requirement.) We are inclined to believe that the managers performed these manipulations to keep apparent earnings trends moving along. It has been claimed, for example, that at least half of the final year's reported earnings for Enron consisted of unrealized gains on these securities based on fabricated values. If so, we are not surprised, because this behavior reflects the same disregard for truth that characterized the company's managers in other areas.

As shown in Chapter 15, there are a great many sound reasons in favor of reporting market values in the financial statements (and outside them) in order to meet the demand from users for information that is useful for predicting future cash flows. Some might think that Enron's abuse is a crushing argument against using market values in financial reporting. In response, we say, "No, not at all." The management did not implement real market value accounting because all it did was make up phony numbers and call them market values. In any other circles, this practice would be called lying through your teeth, and would thoroughly discredit anyone who practiced it, whether it involved fake market values or fake costs. As a consequence, we are troubled, as others must be, that the Andersen firm seemingly failed to adequately fill its role as the first line of defense against reporting such fabrications in the financial statements. GAAP call for reporting *reliable* market values, not wild-eyed guesses that culpable managers merely call market values.

In conclusion, we are convinced that Enron's managers certainly committed the sin of smoothing. We are just as convinced that it did no one any good, even temporarily. That outcome is just as true for internal management reporting as for external financial reporting because hiding the truth allows managers to justify their continued failure to confront it. Doing anything to encourage that blind spot is a bad mistake.

Minimum Reporting

It's clear from one story after another that the managers at Enron did all they could to ensure that their financial reports contained nothing more than the minimum required information. John Emshwiller and Rebecca Smith wrote an article called, "Behind Enron's Fall, a Culture of Secrecy Which Cost the Firm Its Investors' Trust," that appeared in the December 5, 2001 issue of *The Wall Street Journal*, Among other things, they reported that

> [t]he company hired legions of lawyers and accountants to help it meet the letter of federal securities laws while trampling on the intent of those laws. It became adept at giving technically correct answers rather than simply honest ones.

If this analysis is correct, and we are inclined to believe that it is, the managers' goal was to report as little useful information as possible while remaining in technical compliance with the rules. They didn't seem to mind at all that the statements and disclosures didn't provide any useful descriptions, even though they were purported by management and Andersen to be reliable representations of the company's condition and results.

Despite our acceptance of the notion that the capital markets are efficient, we are not perplexed that the markets seem to have believed and trusted the financial statements for quite awhile. After all, the company had produced substantial cash flows in earlier years and Andersen was a reputable accounting firm. There was good reason to accept the numbers under these circumstances. We do have to admit, however, that we are a bit puzzled as to why the capital markets (both debt and equity) took so long to unravel the clues and decide that the statements were worthless. Our best explanation has two parts. First, the management pulled off a bodaciously effective deception. After all, as we mentioned earlier, Enron's Fastow was honored with *CFO* magazine's Excellence Award for 1999. The second part of the explanation is that management chose a period in the capital markets' history in which gullibility rose to unprecedented heights. In our view (and according to our hope), the Enron fraud may be the last gust of wind that will come from the collapse of the Internet bubble. We find evidence in support of capital market efficiency in the fact that the Enron market cap began to fall early in 2001, long before any widely distributed public information about the company's financial problems seems to have been available. (See Figure 19-1 on page 306 to observe the effects of this phenomenon.)

We cannot leave this discussion of minimum reporting without asserting that a fully committed effort to start and then stick with telling the full truth about Enron's activities may have prevented this collapse. We are not so optimistic as to think that an effort to come clean (and we mean really clean) about the misdeeds and the remaining prospects for future cash flows would have saved the company. However, it might have done so and eventually may have produced a new kind of honest prosperity for all its stakeholders instead of the embarrassing and devastating bankruptcy that was actually produced. We interpret the anonymous letter from Vice President Sherron Watkins to CEO Kenneth Lay as an earnest, even panicked, plea for him to deal forthrightly with the deception created by minimum reporting. Unfortunately for a great many people, it came too late, and the rest is history.

Minimum Auditing

As we have said before, it will take a long time before the full story of Andersen's role in the Enron collapse becomes known. In fact, it may never be known publicly if the firm is dissolved and the charges brought against it are never fully prosecuted.

Although Andersen's representatives have pledged full cooperation with all authorities, only time will tell whether that promise is full or empty. Certainly, doubts about the dependability of the pledge are created by the wholesale destruction of the auditors' paper and electronic files that began prior to public knowledge of the lies and distortions.

Even if the whole story isn't told, we do feel we know enough to conclude that the only thing Enron's managers wanted was an Andersen opinion stating that the financial statements complied with GAAP. Thus, they wanted only minimum auditing to cover their minimum reports. In pursuing this strategy, they didn't ask the questions that we recommended in Chapter 2 be asked at the end of an audit:

- Are these financial statements useful for decision making?
- What can we do to make them more useful?

To us, these questions are far better than the usual question of whether the statements comply with GAAP.

As we have read about this situation, we have speculated that Enron's managers may have indeed asked whether the statements contained useful information, but only out of a fear that the reports might actually help users penetrate the massive fraud. Then they must have followed up with their own question: "What can we do to destroy that usefulness?"

According to our interpretation of the reported facts, two things stand out about Enron and the auditors.

First, Andersen had early on recommended adjustments to bring the company's financial statements into compliance with GAAP. If so, those statements must have originally contained significant departures. The ensuing events show, however, that management stonewalled at the beginning and that Andersen backed off and rationalized its acquiescence in the name of materiality. In a sense, the auditors simply said, "Aw, forget it. These adjustments don't matter much anyway." Materiality can be a handy accounting tool because it allows small inadvertent errors and expedient departures from GAAP to be tolerated. However, Andersen's people seem to have rejected the concept that materiality judgments cannot justify deliberate lies or other efforts to mislead.[5] The principle is clear—there is no such thing as an immaterial lie, because the existence of the lie is relevant regardless of its magnitude. Only minimum auditing would tolerate immaterial but deliberately untruthful and misleading representations. Furthermore, Andersen's earlier acquiescence would have made it more difficult for the auditors to take a meaningful stand in later years. After all, they had given in once; why would they balk at doing so again? Each year would increase the pressure to go along while magnifying the penalty associated with backing off and having the previous questionable compromises exposed. We think that Enron's managers had set the trap, and Andersen stepped right into it.

We believe that a second point needs to be addressed. Specifically, minimum auditing also occurs when managers engage auditors and then compromise and otherwise diminish their independence. If the auditors are not really objective, they will tend to go along, but they can still sign the opinion if they maintain a technical independence without regard to their true or apparent independence. Specifically, the ethics rules of the profession allow audit firms to accept virtually unlimited amounts of fees for nonaudit services to their audit clients and still claim that they are independent.[6] Ordinary common sense draws a line that allows a small amount of nonaudit fees for incidental services. Holders of that same common sense surely have to balk at $27 million in fees in a year (plus the unspecified amount reportedly paid to Andersen for its outsourced internal auditing services). Thus, we think the Enron management deliberately put into place the pressures they felt they needed or could use to persuade the auditors to go along to get along. We wish our hypothesis were wrong, but we have to confess that we fear it is right.

Beyond reasonable doubt, a commitment to Quality Financial Reporting would have caused both Enron's managers and the Andersen auditors to make more intelligent decisions because they would have focused on reducing uncertainty both inside and outside the company. Maximum auditing would have done a much better job of improving the actual and perceived usefulness of the financial statements' contents. We have no doubt that a great many people at both the company and the audit firm are wishing that their managers had taken a completely different tack from the one they chose to pursue. As it was, the managers of both organizations must not have had the brains, heart, or courage to stand up and blow the whistle on what was happening. If only it had been otherwise.

Preparation Cost Myopia

When we described the sin of preparation cost myopia in Chapter 2, we focused our criticism on the conventional perspective held by most managers. That is, they look at preparation costs as unavoidable expenses to be minimized without regard to the consequences for the quality of the information contained in the financial reports. Part of the reason is that the CFO's financial reporting activities are probably operated as a cost center, with no consideration given to the value obtained from providing useful information in the financial statements. We call this myopia a sin because it causes uncertainty to rise, along with the cost of capital.

The Enron case also demonstrates the other form of deviant behavior with regard to preparation costs that we described in Chapter 2. Specifically, it appears to us that the Enron managers were willing to incur just about any and all preparation costs to produce deceptive financial statements that continued to support the fiction that they had previously created. In this case, they apparently spent huge amounts to keep outsiders (and probably some insiders) from learning just how rotten things were.

Unfortunately for a great many stakeholders, this effort to sustain the deception would have handcuffed any managers who wanted to deal with it by creating the false sense that nothing needed to be done.

In arriving at this conclusion, we were again guided by the words of Warren Buffett that we quoted in Chapters 8 and 10:

> We also believe candor benefits us as managers: The CEO who misleads others in public may eventually mislead himself in private.[7]

There also echoes in our mind the observation of Sir Walter Scott: "O what a tangled web we weave, when first we practise to deceive!"

Even though the Enron case took the myopia in this different direction, we are convinced that it is a financial reporting sin, especially in this case where it was reported that the management's dysfunctional behavior was aided and abetted by "legions of lawyers and accountants" hired to determine the least amount of reporting that the company had to do.

We cannot leave this last point without also condemning these legionnaires for their own deep character flaws evidenced by their help in accomplishing the deception. There cannot have been any doubt in their minds as to the purpose their labors were going to be used for. If they were to excuse themselves for simply applying their skill and knowledge to a task that a client demanded and paid for, they would be pleading the timeworn, inane, and ineffective Nuremberg Defense that they were only following orders. If they didn't stop to think that they were helping Enron's managers sustain a huge fraud, they are just as much without excuse as if they knew exactly what was going on. We hope that their role in creating the huge losses will somehow sober them up from their fog of self-interest so that similar events don't ever happen again for another company. Somehow, though, we don't expect that hope to be fulfilled. To these legions of co-conspirators, we plead, "Surprise us!"

Summary

Because they clearly committed all of the seven deadly financial reporting sins, we have no problem concluding that Enron's management created a perfect example of how not to do Quality Financial Reporting. The managers also created a perfect example of the extent of the disaster that can be created when management follows today's generally accepted financial reporting paradigm to its logical end. If the foundation of current practice is that the real purpose of providing financial statements is to trick investors and creditors into paying too much for securities, then why not try to fool them completely? The answer is that it won't work. For anyone.

Let's turn now to a brief consideration of the questions that we asked in earlier chapters.

THE QUESTIONNAIRES

In Chapters 11, 12, and 13, we presented three brief questionnaires intended to lead readers to determine whether they are close to practicing QFR. In light of what happened, we think it will be instructive to see what sort of answers would have been provided if the Enron management had been presented with those questions before the company imploded. Of course, our answers are somewhat speculative, but we have some confidence that our guesses are reasonable.

Attitude Check

In Chapter 11, we asked 10 questions designed to lead respondents to assess their current attitude toward the tenets of QFR. We think that at least the following five questions out of that list would have been answered affirmatively by the Enron gang, with the consequence they were not about to embrace the economic incentives for telling the truth:

	Yes	No
1. Do you think the capital markets react automatically to increases and decreases in reported earnings without carefully considering how those results were achieved?	✔	
2. Have you ever tried to keep the price of your company's stock high by inhibiting the flow of information about it to the capital markets?	✔	
3. Have you ever delayed reporting bad financial news until the last possible minute?	✔	
4. Have you ever chosen an accounting policy with the objective of helping your company meet an expected earnings result?	✔	
7. Has anyone ever left your financial reporting shop because of unresolved ethical misgivings over accounting policies and implementations?	✔	

Checking Choices

The overriding purpose of the questions presented in Chapter 12 is to get the respondents to assess whether they have actually implemented policies and other decisions that constitute Quality Financial Reporting or merely applied the old paradigm of trying to look good in the financial statements. We think the following six questions would have been answered affirmatively (others might have been, but we have no way of knowing), thus suggesting that the Enron executives would have had little affinity for QFR:

	Yes	No
11. Have you ever timed or structured your company's transactions simply to produce positive impacts on the financial statements or to avoid negative impacts on the financial statements?	✔	
12. Have you ever turned down an economically sound deal for your company simply because of how it would be reported on the financial statements?	✔	
13. Do you select accounting policies that reduce reported volatility without affecting the underlying causes of the fluctuations?	✔	
14. Does your statement of cash flows use the indirect method of reporting cash provided by operations?	✔	
15. Do you report compensation expense paid with stock options in a footnote?	✔	
17. Have you ever entered into lease arrangements specifically because they produced off-balance-sheet liabilities?	✔	

Checking Your Audit Relationship

The questionnaire in Chapter 13 was intended to lead respondents to evaluate their relationship with their auditors to determine whether they were in a position to reap the greatest real financial reporting benefit from their audit. It would also show whether they were compromising the audit's ability to increase the value of the financial statements by reducing uncertainty about their dependability. We think Enron's managers would have answered at least the following six questions affirmatively and thus revealed that they had no desire to use the audit to actually increase the credibility and usefulness of their financial statements:

	Yes	No
24. Do the nonaudit fees you pay to your auditing firm exceed 25 percent of the audit fee?	✔	
25. Have you ever stonewalled against your auditors' proposed adjustments?	✔	
27. Have your auditors ever recommended an accounting policy simply because it would make your financial statements present a more attractive image?	✔	
28. Do you still have the same auditors after many years?	✔	
29. Is your accounting department staffed with a large number of alumni from your auditing firm?	✔	
30. Do you view the audit as a perfunctory process required by the law?	✔	

When they're officially known, some of the facts may contradict these answers, but we are comfortable asserting that they are accurate representations of conditions at Enron before the fall.

Observations

In Chapters 11, 12, and 13 we indicated that even one "yes" answer out of the 30 questions would reveal room for improvement in the respondent's financial reporting practice. We have tabulated 17 positive answers for Enron. We are again led to conclude that the managers created a very complete case study of how financial reporting should not be practiced. They were clearly not engaging in QFR. If they had been, the picture would be quite different.

SOME CLOSING THOUGHTS

In observing, teaching about, participating in, and writing on financial reporting for a combined 50-plus years between the two of us, we have encountered a great deal of misbehavior by managers and auditors. As a way of coping, we want to believe that the frequency of our negative experiences has been biased upward by the fact that it is human nature to focus on sensational failures and misdeeds instead of the mundane, even dull events that occur every day when ordinary people merely do what they are supposed to do. In writing this book, we have tried to apply an optimistic perspective that reflects our deep-down belief that the great majority of managers, accountants, and financial statement users actually will come to voluntarily embrace the concepts behind Quality Financial Reporting simply because doing so makes sense economically. By reducing uncertainty, they should be able to avoid both high capital costs and the dreadful kinds of consequences that will be forever linked with the name of Enron.

We also think adopting QFR makes sense ethically because telling the truth produces trustworthiness, which brings its own rewards in self-respect and self-satisfaction as well the perception of integrity and the lasting respect of others. On the other hand, not telling the truth inevitably leads first to confusion and eventually conflict. These results can happen internally as individuals struggle against their consciences and other definitions of what is right and just. And, as the Enron case reveals, confusion and conflict can also occur between individuals when the deceived parties finally discover the deceptive acts of the miscreants. Enron will go down in business annals, and ethical annals as well, as the world record holder of its day. We imagine that most everyone hopes that nothing like it will ever happen again.

We certainly find it understandable that those people who have no ethical scruples can be sufficiently unbalanced psychologically to truly believe that deception is suitable or even desirable behavior, regardless of its consequences, as long as it can be hidden for awhile. We are prepared to admit that QFR will not make sense to these people because they are pathologically incapable of comprehending the fundamental power created by truth telling in personal and economic relationships. Because of their limitations, they simply are unable to engage in that kind of behavior, even if doing so will promote their own good. QFR is literally beyond their reach.

Thus, it is possible that one of the lessons of the Enron case is that QFR is not going to be accepted or practiced by everyone. As much as we might want to really believe it, we cannot now fathom that Skilling, Lay, and Fastow would have been turned from their path of destruction if they had been able to read this book 10 years ago. It may very well be true that they have psyches that are so deeply engrained to tolerate and promote deception that they could not be reformed by such a simple thing as thinking through their behavior from a new paradigm. On the other hand, we want to hold onto the possibility that the thoughts in this book on QFR would have emboldened other Enron employees to make more effective internal protests against the deceptive policies that were being used, or to have gone public with what was happening. As it was, only one spoke up anonymously, and then apparently retreated, and that's too bad. Nothing will dissuade us, however, from our solid belief that the widespread adoption of QFR principles will greatly reduce the possibility of something like this disaster ever happening again.

Before we close this chapter, we have to admit that, as much as we condemn Enron's management, we are even more deeply troubled by the apparent motives behind the actions of Andersen's people. The two of us have trained a great many auditors-to-be throughout our careers. Not once have we ever expressed tolerance for this kind of behavior, much less encouraged our students to act as they did. We cannot imagine that these auditors were trained by other accounting faculty at reputable schools to look the other way or to fail to ponder the implications of deception as a corporate financial reporting policy. We lament their personal decisions and wish that that they had not rejected their training and completely shattered the last shred of their professional and personal integrity. We also express our condolences to those of our academic colleagues who mentored them. They must be stunned by the magnitude of the character flaws revealed in their former students.

This apparently massive fraud (no other word sums it up quite as well), while discouraging and disappointing, does not dissuade us from our fundamental and strong belief that the spreading of the QFR philosophy will significantly change the financial and economic worlds. In our boldest moments, we actually think that coming to grips with Enron will lead thoughtful managers and accountants to more closely embrace the totally practical idea that truth telling is the most beneficial way to behave in every circumstance. If anything, Enron demonstrates the awfulness of pursuing the alternate practice of artful and purposeful deception to the extreme.

When we get down to it, this is our point in writing this book, and we choose to stick with it. We hope that everyone reading these words will agree with us, but, although we're naive, we're not sufficiently optimistic to think that unanimity will ensue. At the same time, we're also not so half-hearted in our own conviction that QFR is the answer that we're ready to give up because of this unbelievably costly failure on the part of a large number of people to understand what we have come to comprehend only lately in our own lives, and only after having the opportunity to do a great deal of unconventional thinking.

We have absolutely no doubt that the future of financial reporting can be much better than this wretched piece of accounting and business history.

NOTES

1. It was also reported that Enron money had been received by 212 of the 240 members of the House and Senate serving on committees expected to investigate one part or another of Enron.

2. This suboptimal, even blind, reliance on strict legal form in preference to real economic substance is a perennial failing of financial reporting that the FASB and its predecessors have struggled unsuccessfully to eliminate, thus proving again that GAAP aren't good enough.

3. This anecdote is described in Ron Mano, Matthew Mouritsen, and David Durkee, "A Lesson Not Learned Is a Mistake Repeated," *Accounting Today*, January 28, 2002.

4. A seldom invoked provision in codes of ethics for CPAs actually allows accountants to produce or opine favorably on financial statements that don't comply with GAAP if compliance produces misleading information. In this case, it seems abundantly clear to us that, with some measure of courage, Andersen could have acted under this so-called Rule 203 exception and stopped Enron's managers from committing this sin (or at least absolved themselves of some of the guilt). Instead, they apparently stood back and claimed that they had no ability to intervene as long as GAAP requirements were met. In addition, there is much food for thought in the decision in the Continental Vending case [(U.S. v. Simon et al, 425 F. 2d 796 (2d Cir. 1969)]. The doctrine established in that ruling is that strict compliance with GAAP is

not enough to discharge a company's obligation to provide full and fair disclosure of its activities and condition. Legal technicalities aside, auditors definitely have a social and professional responsibility to ensure that their clients' financial statements are not misleading.

5. The same sort of error occurred in the early 1990s when the Price Waterhouse audit firm failed to press adjustments for the statements issued by W. R. Grace to correct deliberate but initially immaterial misleading income measures for its health care group. Once the auditors stepped onto this slippery slope, they were cooked. The deception continued for five years and then exploded in everyone's face. The SEC initiated litigation that led eventually to a settlement and public humiliation for all involved.

6. In fact, SEC chairman Arthur Levitt attempted to eliminate this freedom with a rule-making effort in 2000 during the last six months of his term. His effort raised a huge controversy and brought out a great many criticisms and strong objections. Among those who testified against the proposed rule was Joseph Berardino, who would soon become the Andersen CEO. His testimony claimed that nonaudit services actually improve the quality of audits and do not compromise independence. We didn't believe him then, and we certainly don't believe him now.

7. "An Owner's Manual," www.berkshirehathaway.com.

Now that you've finished the book, take the time to complete the following questionnaires to see whether you learned anything, and if so, what. Answer each of the following 10 questions about financial reporting strategies and practices as if you are the top manager of a large company that must distribute its financial statements to its thousands of public stockholders.

Question	Answer
1. Would you prefer the company's annual reported earnings to be biased upward or to approximate the truth?	
2. Would you prefer all of the company's liabilities to be reported on the balance sheet, or would you like some to be left off the balance sheet to produce a lower debt-to-equity ratio?	
3. Would you prefer compensation expense from stock options to be reported on the income statement as a deduction from earnings or described in a footnote that presents pro forma earnings?	
4. Would you prefer that the company's independent auditors be easy to get along with or tough and thorough?	
5. Would you prefer that the company's independent auditing firm provide substantial amounts of nonaudit services or none at all?	
6. Would you prefer that the amounts paid to the auditors for audit and nonaudit services be disclosed plainly?	
7. Would you prefer the company's financial statements to be published more often or less often?	
8. Would you prefer the company's assets to be described in the financial statements at their depreciated historical cost or at their approximate market value?	
9. Would you prefer that the company's reported earnings be biased to be smooth or that they be designed to reflect real volatility?	
10. Would you prefer that the company's financial statements report its business combinations as poolings of interest or outright purchases?	

Now, answer each of the following 10 questions about financial reporting strategies and practices as if you are a financial analyst trying to assess the value of a large company's stock or one of its thousands of public stockholders trying to assess the top management's performance.

Question	Answer
1. Would you prefer the company's annual reported earnings to be biased upward or to approximate the truth?	
2. Would you prefer all of the company's liabilities to be reported on the balance sheet, or would you like some to be left off the balance sheet to produce a lower debt-to-equity ratio?	
3. Would you prefer compensation expense from stock options to be reported on the income statement as a deduction from earnings or described in a footnote that presents pro forma earnings?	
4. Would you prefer that the company's independent auditors be easy to get along with or tough and thorough?	
5. Would you prefer that the company's independent auditing firm provide substantial amounts of nonaudit services or none at all?	
6. Would you prefer that the amounts paid to the auditors for audit and nonaudit services be disclosed plainly?	
7. Would you prefer the company's financial statements to be published more often or less often?	
8. Would you prefer the company's assets to be described in the financial statements at their depreciated historical cost or at their approximate market value?	
9. Would you prefer that the company's reported earnings be biased to be smooth or that they be designed to reflect real volatility?	
10. Would you prefer that the company's financial statements report its business combinations as poolings of interest or outright purchases?	

As educators, we couldn't let this opportunity go by. We wanted you to complete this test again to see whether our thoughts have been effective in changing your attitude toward financial reporting.

At the beginning, we stated that we expected your answers as a CEO to be completely different from the answers you would give if you were a financial analyst or other financial statement user. Based on what you've read, you now understand that those initial differences were based on the fact that these two kinds of people look at the reporting function from two different points of view: CEOs see the issues from the perspective of the supplier, while users come at them as those who have a demand for the information.

In addition, you have read our arguments about the common flaw in thinking that the capital markets are so inept and inefficient that they are unable to penetrate the smokescreens thrown up by many managers to hide the truth, even while they're complying with GAAP. The biggest management mistake is in thinking that managing the reported earnings number actually works to establish a stock's price. Nothing could be further from the truth.

A second weak argument is the proposition that today's regular financial statements must be informative because they comply with GAAP. Those principles are simply too flexible, too political, and too old to provide the information today's capital markets demand. Managers need to go beyond these extremely low minimum reporting principles to get useful information to the markets.

The central theme running through the book involves these four axioms: incomplete information creates uncertainty, uncertainty leads to risk, risk increases investors' demand for a high rate of return, and a high rate of return produces a high cost of capital and low stock prices. Rather than fight against the inevitable, the attitude of Quality Financial Reporting leads managers to attack the problem of high capital costs and low stock prices by doing what they can to make the reported information more complete.

The practice of QFR is nearly nonexistent at present, and it certainly has received little play in the press. However, the economic forces behind it are very strong and compelling, and sooner or later they will catch up to and then overwhelm the existing paradigm that leads managers to want to starve the markets of information and then feed them GAAP statements that convey no useful information. Many managers also make the mistake of short-circuiting their audits by compromising their auditors' independence and otherwise diminishing their impartiality. Unfortunately, many auditors have misunderstood what has happened to their ability to reduce uncertainty and have played along with the managers.

We also showed that it wasn't just us saying all these things. To supplement our commonsense economic arguments, we brought in more than 50 comments from sophisticated financial analysts, described what other experts have discovered and said, and then reviewed a growing body of rigorous capital market research that confirms the axioms behind QFR. This evidence should not be ignored, especially if it contradicts everything you've believed about the markets and their reactions to financial statement information.

We are ready to have our ideas tried out in the real marketplace. We really hope that there were no differences between your answers on the two halves of the post-test because that will tell you that you are now ready to enter the ranks of the QFR-minded managers, or to go to work for one of them. If, on the other hand, your answers in the post-test are much the same as they were in the pre-test, all we can do is urge you to go back through the book another time. Surely you will benefit from thinking through the issues again.

What's next from us? Frankly, we're ready to sit back and see what you do with what we've said. We anticipate with confidence that new behaviors will begin to show up. We hope you will tell us what you think by showing us what you're going to do.

Before we sign off, we present you with this final quotation:

> Permanent improvement in accounting practices and in methods of corporate reporting cannot be brought about by legislation or by government regulation. The regulations laid down by a governmental bureau serve a good purpose but can never successfully take the place of individual initiative, intelligence, and courage. If any real progress is to be made towards continued improvement in corporate reporting, it must flow from the efforts of those charged with the direct responsibility of determining the policies of corporations. As professional accountants, we can contribute to this progress by emphasizing the advantages of adhering to sound business principles, by seeking to establish more firmly the standards for accounting practice, and by having the moral courage to cling to these standards.

The huge irony is that these words were spoken by the real Arthur Andersen at the annual meeting of the American Institute of Accountants on October 15, 1935, long before anyone ever conceived of financial reporting fraud on the scale practiced by Enron's management and not eliminated by auditors from the firm he founded. As we said, no one should accuse accountants of being glacial—after all, glaciers move.

We think QFR can change everything about financial reporting.

INDEX

PRONOUNCEMENT INDEX

ABOUT THE AUTHORS

Paul B. W. Miller, PhD, CPA, is professor of accounting at the University of Colorado at Colorado Springs. He was prepared to develop the Quality Financial Reporting concept by his unique background that started with degrees in economics and accounting from Rice University and a doctorate from the University of Texas at Austin. His career also includes forays into the highest levels of financial reporting regulation as a staff member of both the FASB and the SEC's Chief Accountant's Office. In addition, Miller investigated many alleged violations of professional ethics during three years on the AICPA's Technical Standards Subcommittee. His output includes more than a dozen books and over 30 journal articles. Among those books is the respected and often quoted *The FASB: the People, the Process, and the Politics,* coauthored with Rob Redding and Paul Bahnson and published by McGraw-Hill. In addition, Miller and Bahnson produce *The Spirit of Accounting,* a nationally circulated column that has appeared in every issue of the *Accounting Today* since January 1996. Through his writings and speeches, including testimony before the SEC, Miller has established an international reputation as a challenging, insightful, and optimistic critic of accounting practices, institutions, and leaders. He is also an award-winning educator and innovator. In fact, the ideas that led to QFR were conceived in 1996 while he and a colleague were developing a combined Accounting/Finance course for their university's groundbreaking and now highly successful Internet-delivered MBA program.

Miller and his wife Diana are the parents of David (a management consultant), Greg (an architect), and Angela (a middle school student). In the fall of 2002, Miller is expected to be named academic director of his school's PGA-accredited program in professional golf management.

Paul R. Bahnson, PhD, CPA, is associate professor of accounting at Boise State University. He holds a bachelor's degree in accounting and political science from Augustana College, an MBA from Indiana University, and a doctorate in accounting from the University of Utah, where he first met Paul Miller. Bahnson has taught at the University of Colorado at Boulder and the University of Montana and has received five teaching excellence awards during his career. Before becoming a professor, he worked as an auditor with a Big Five firm and served a one year postgraduate internship at the FASB. He is also a frequent speaker and leader of professional training seminars. Bahnson's research, which is dedicated to exposing limitations in corporate financial reporting practices, includes numerous published articles in professional and academic journals. A considerable portion of this work has been done in partnership with Paul Miller. Quality Financial Reporting, which lays out a new and better financial reporting strategy, is a logical extension and culmination of this research.

Bahnson and his wife, Kathie, have two teenage children, Sara and Andy.

The authors can be contacted at paulandpaul@qfr..biz.